P9-ECQ-196

ON THE POETRY OF PHILIP LEVINE

UNDER DISCUSSION

Donald Hall, General Editor

On the Poetry of Philip Levine

Stranger to Nothing

Edited by Christopher Buckley

Ann Arbor

THE UNIVERSITY OF MICHIGAN PRESS

Copyright © by the University of Michigan 1991
All rights reserved
Published in the United States of America by
The University of Michigan Press
Manufactured in the United States of America

1994   1993   1992   1991   4   3   2   1

Distributed in the United Kingdom and Europe by
Manchester University Press, Oxford Road,
Manchester M13 9PL, UK

Library of Congress Cataloging-in-Publication Data

On the poetry of Philip Levine : stranger to nothing / edited by
    Christopher Buckley.
        p.   cm. — (Under discussion)
    Includes bibliographical references.
    ISBN 0-472-09392-4 (cloth : alk. paper). — ISBN 0-472-06392-8
    (paper : alk. paper)
        1. Levine, Philip, 1928– —Criticism and interpretation.
    I. Levine, Philip, 1928– .   II. Buckley, Christopher, 1948– .
    III. Series.
    PS3562.E9Z8   1991
    811'.54—dc20   90-46210
                                                            CIP

British Library Cataloguing in Publication Data

On the poetry of Philip Levine : stranger to nothing —
    (Under discussion)
    1. Poetry in English. American writers, 1945–. Critical
    studies
    I. Buckley, Christopher   II. Series
    811.5409

ISBN 0-472-09392-4
        0-472-06392-8 pbk

Preface

For almost thirty years now, readers of contemporary poetry have known Philip Levine's work for its elegiac narrative, its forceful rhythms and rhetoric, and, to quote Levine quoting Whitman, its "vivas" praising the dignity of the human spirit as it survives the conditions of the world. Levine's awards include two Guggenheim fellowships, three National Endowment for the Arts grants, the Lenore Marshall Award, the American Book Award, the National Book Critics Circle Award, and the Ruth Lilly Poetry Prize.

As many have pointed out, Levine often speaks for the unfortunate in the world who do not have the opportunity to speak out for themselves. A poem from his first book, *On The Edge,* "The Horse," recounts the tale of mass hallucination after the bombing of Hiroshima and is representative of his early work. And while the poem works many images to poignant and inventive effects, Levine concludes with an image all the more powerful for its horrible reality:

> There had been no horse. I could
> tell from the way they walked
> testing the ground for some cold
> that the rage had gone out of
> their bones in one mad dance.

Levine's early period concludes with his fourth book, *They Feed They Lion,* with its well-known title poem decrying racism and political disenfranchisement.

The middle books, *1933, The Names of the Lost, Ashes,* and *7 Years from Somewhere,* show us a poet a little less defiant and furious with creation. They contain numerous elegies to his relatives and to the defeated heroes of the Spanish Civil War, as well

AUGUSTANA UNIVERSITY COLLEGE
LIBRARY

as to the pain and spare joys of growing up in working-class Detroit.

Levine's more recent books, *One for the Rose, Sweet Will, A Walk with Tom Jefferson,* show more concern for invented detail and situation than for the autobiographical subject. "On My Own," "I Was Born in Lucerne," and "The Fox" are examples of Levine poems at their most fictive. And often this newer work speculates directly about metaphysical subjects—life and the afterlife, our place on earth, a natural continuum. The poem "Belief" from *One for the Rose* concludes by inviting the reader to enter and share this vision:

> No one believes that tonight is the journey
> across dark water to the lost continent
> no one named, Do you hear the wind
> rising all around you? That comes
> only after this certain joy. Do you hear
> the waves breaking, even in the darkness,
> radiant and full? Close your eyes, close
> them and follow us toward the first light.

This volume, then, is intended to chronicle the progression of Levine's career. It is a selection from the many available reviews and essays. I have devoted these pages to comment that most directly addresses the structures and craft, the success and failure of the ideas and style, the vision and accomplishment of the poetry. I have also chosen with an eye toward the historical and have included early reviews and some shorter notices hoping to demonstrate the development of the response to Levine's work from the beginning. I think it is telling that not only is there much comment by critics, but also much by recognized poets who write about contemporary poetry.

The format of this volume is a simple one: a section of reviews followed by a section of essays. The reviews are grouped in chronological sequence. The essays are compiled in the hope of touching on aspects of Levine's career and poetic achievement that are not developed by reviews. The overviews by David St. John and Edward Hirsch are comprehensive and yet specific. Robert Hedin brings to light the anarchist undercurrent running through much of the poetry. Richard Jackson examines the structures and ideas of Levine's longer poems, a subject largely unexplored by reviewers to date. Glover Davis and Michael Peich review the fine press publishing of Levine's early poetry and speak to the design of printing and books as they complement Levine's style and themes. And Larry Levis offers a testament to Levine as poet and teacher that also bears witness to the power and importance of poetry in our lives. To be sure, not every essay or review is unqualified praise; divergent opinions are included because the purpose here is to offer a record of the response to the poetry, and some of the response has been negative.

Levine began commanding traditional forms. He was especially adept at syllabic poetry, at "the language of princes," as he put it in an essay for the landmark anthology of contemporary poetry, *Naked Poetry*. From there he developed the short, three-beat line and the anaphora that mark his voice. A close look at Levine's work, however, reveals experimentation and expansion as well; in later books especially, there are poems that work in longer lines, in couplets, and in short and long line configurations. And there are the long poems—"Letters for the Dead," "New Season," "Belief," "A Poem with No Ending," "A Walk with Tom Jefferson"—each with a different strategy, from imagistic, to narrative, to symphonic.

Although as some critics have pointed out, Detroit and a working-class life continue to surface in Levine's poems, this base of his work seems to have metamorphosed and been recast. If we consider later poems, such as "Sweet Will" and "28," and even newer poems from the *New Yorker,* such as "On the River," "Fear & Fame," "Coming Close," "M. Degas Teaches Art and Science at Durfee Intermediate School," we see the focus spiraling, directly and by implication, out beyond their situations and the transient facts of our lives. And although these poems still speak in a voice angry with political and economic causes of oppression, they also speak in a voice deeply aware of mortality, yet a voice that stands up to it. As his career progresses, a democratic compassion emerges in Levine's work, and this has given and continues to give readers poems that, to use Levine's own words, are a "stranger to nothing."

Contents

Part Two   Essays

Chronology

1928   Born January 10, 1928, in Detroit, Michigan, second of three children (first of identical twins) of Harry Levine and Esther Gertrude Priscol. Both parents born in Russia; they met and married in Detroit. Father fought with the British Army in World War I; mother came to the United States at age nine, her father having come ahead to find employment in Detroit. Twin brother Edward inherited the family business; he also works seriously as a painter and has a considerable reputation in Detroit. Older brother Eli retired in Santa Barbara after career in Chicago automotive parts trade.

1933   Death of father.

1928–55   Grows up in Detroit and is formally educated there.

1946–50   B.A., Wayne State University. Spends a good deal of time in the Miles Poetry Room at Wayne State. Meets with fellow poets Robert Huff, Paul Petrie, Florence Goodman, William Leach, Ruby Treague, and Bernard Strempeck. Discovers modern poetry and the beginnings of his own poems. Ulysses Wardlaw introduces him to the poetry of Whitman.

1951–53   First marriage, to Patty Kanterman.

1950–55   M.A., Wayne State University. Thesis on Keats's "Ode on Indolence." Before, during, and after college at Wayne State, works at various jobs. Leaves Detroit for good; completes degree by the mail.

1952   Because of financial difficulties, forced to reject original grant in fiction from Writers' Workshop, University of Iowa.

1953–54   Goes to Iowa to study with Robert Lowell. Lack of funds keeps him out of program, but takes a class with John Berryman. There meets many life-long friends—poets Henri Coulette, Donald Justice, Jane Cooper, Robert Dana. Remarkable class also includes W. D. Snodgrass, Melvin Walker La Follette, Donald Petersen, Fred Block, Shirley Eliason, William Dickey, and Paul Petrie.

1954   On twenty-sixth birthday, in Iowa, meets Frances J. Artley, actress and costumer, who is working on a teaching credential. In July they marry in Boone, North Carolina. Adopts her son, Mark, the following year.

1954–55	Frances teaches speech and drama at Florida State University while he writes and is first published in *Antioch Review, Beloit Poetry Journal, New Orleans Poetry Review, Poetry,* and *Western Review.*
1955	Ray B. West and Paul Engle help provide a job at Iowa teaching technical writing, Greeks, and the Bible. Son John born that December. Works two years at this job, during which time he meets Peter Everwine, Robert Mezey, and Ted Holmes and renews friendships with Coulette, Dana, and Petersen.
1957	Receives M.F.A. from Iowa.
1957–58	Attends Stanford on Jones Fellowship; studies with Yvor Winters, who introduces him to nineteenth- and twentieth-century French poetry.
1958	Turns down job at California State University, Los Angeles, and moves to Fresno, California. Son Theodore Henri born in October.
1963	*On the Edge* published by the Stone Wall Press in a fine print edition of 220.
1964	The Second Press prints *On the Edge* in a paperback trade edition of 1,000.
1965–66	Lives in Spain for a year with family—in Barcelona, Castelldefels.
1968	*Not This Pig* published by Wesleyan University Press. Receives Chaplebrook Award in the arts.
1968–69	Returns to Spain with family.
1970	*Five Detroits* published by Unicorn Press in a fine print limited edition. Chosen outstanding professor at Fresno State University.
1971	Chosen outstanding professor in the California State University System. *Pili's Wall* published by Unicorn Press in a fine print limited edition. *Red Dust* published by Kayak Books.
1972	*They Feed They Lion* published by Atheneum.
1973	First of three National Endowment for the Arts grants in poetry.
1974	*1933* published by Atheneum. Receives first of two Guggenheim fellowships in poetry. Receives Award of Merit from National Society of Arts and Letters. Receives the Frank O'Hara Memorial Prize.
1976	*The Names of the Lost* published by the Windhover Press (limited fine press edition) and Atheneum (trade edition). Receives Lenore Marshall Award for *The Names of the Lost. On the Edge and Over,* poems old, lost, and new, published by Cloud Marauder Press. Elliston Professor of Poetry at the University of Cincinnati.
1978	Visiting Writer for split position at Princeton and Columbia. Returns to Columbia for a semester in 1981 and again in 1984. Writer in Residence at the National University of Australia at Canberra, New

South Wales, during the summer. Receives the Harriet Monroe Prize given by the University of Chicago.

1979   *7 Years from Somewhere* and *Ashes* published by Atheneum. Both books together receive the National Book Critics Circle Award. (A limited fine press edition of *Ashes* published by Greywolf Press.) Receives a grant from the Columbia Translation Center to complete a selection of poems by Mexican poet Jaime Sabines. Twin Peaks Press publishes *Tarumba, Selected Poems of Jaime Sabines,* cotranslated with Ernesto Trejo. Visiting Writer at Vassar for February and March. Visiting Writer at the University of California, Berkeley.

1980   Receives the American Book Award for *Ashes.* Receives second Guggenheim Fellowship in poetry. Visiting Writer at the University of Alabama, Birmingham.

1981   Writer in Residence at University of Houston; teaches at Trinity College spring semester. Second National Endowment for the Arts grant in poetry. Receives the Levenson Memorial Award from *Poetry. One for the Rose* published by Atheneum. *Don't Ask,* a collection of interviews, published by the University of Michigan Press.

1981–87 Teaches the fall semester at Tufts University.

1984   Teaches at New York University. *Selected Poems* published by Atheneum in the United States and by Secker and Warburg in England. Visiting Writer at Brown University. Publishes *Off the Map,* poems of the contemporary Spanish poet Gloria Fuertes, cotranslated with Ada Long.

1984–85 Serves as Chairman of the Literature Board for the National Endowment for the Arts.

1985   *Sweet Will* published by Atheneum.

1987   Receives the Ruth Lilly Poetry Prize "for distinguished poetic achievements" from *Poetry* and the American Council for the Arts. Receives third National Endowment for the Arts grant for poetry. Edits *The Essential Keats* for Ecco Press.

1958–87 Along with Peter Everwine and C. G. Hanzlicek, works with student-poets Larry Levis, Lawson Inada, Glover Davis, Roberta Spear, Luis Omar Salinas, David St. John, Herbert Scott, Sherley Williams, Ernesto Trejo, James Baloian, B. H. Boston, Dennis Saleh, Dewayne Rail, Robert Jones, Greg Pape, Gary Soto, Jon Veinberg, Kathy Fagan, Dixie Lane, Jean Jansen, and Robert Vasquez among others, who are represented in the anthologies *Down at the Santa Fe Depot: 20 Fresno Poets* and *Piecework: 19 Fresno Poets.*

1988   *A Walk with Tom Jefferson* published by Knopf.

1989   *Blue,* a chapbook of new poems, published in a fine press limited edition by Aralia Press.

PART ONE *Reviews*

X. J. KENNEDY

From "Underestimations"

On the Edge, the long awaited first book by Philip Levine, is another with virtues hard to make too much of. I can't imagine that the ultimate anthology *Cold War American Poetry* (or whatever the glum title) will be able to do without three or more poems from it. After May Swenson and her roller-coaster, Levine is like a ride through the tunnel of horrors. Agony is a theme in "Passing Out" ("I hug my bruise like an old / Pooh Bear") and in "Gangrene" with its juicy details of torture; but I like much better the compassionate tribute "For Fran," and "Green Thumb," the ironic lament of a small-time Tristan turned autoerotic. At his slightest Levine is just plain grim, as in a piece about a pig hanged for eating a baby. A beautifully polished song, "Mad Day in March," dazzles but leaves doubt that it *is* mad; you suspect that, given more clues, you could make perfect sense of its dramatic situation. But Levine's unwillingness to paint obvious scenes is turned to good effect in "The Distant Winter," best poem in the book and, as far as I know, best narrative sequence since *Heart's Needle.* The diary of a Nazi army officer during the last days of World War II, it is all horribly clear, but fragmented. Not knowing at first who the speaker was, I was unsure, till the poem's fifth part, which side of the war he was on! There could have been swastikas and *liebfraumilch* all over the place, of course; but the poem gains by Levine's concentration on episodes and small details instead of on big scenes and stage properties. The focus is kept within the captain's mind, into which the outer world—the army—drops pieces of itself as it disintegrates. In the final section, as he awaits departure for the Russian front, the captain is being attended by his orderly:

"Underestimations" first appeared in *Poetry* (February, 1964), copyright 1964 by The Modern Poetry Association. Reprinted by permission of the Editor of *Poetry.*

But three more days and we'll be moving out.
The cupboard of the state is bare, no one,
Not God himself, can raise another recruit.
Drinking my hot tea, listening to the rain,

I sit while Stephan packs, grumbling a bit.
He breaks the china that my mother sent,
Her own first china, as a wedding gift.
"Now that your wife is dead, Captain, why can't

The two of us really make love together?"
I cannot answer. When I lift a plate
It seems I almost hear my long-dead mother
Saying, Watch out, the glass is underfoot.

Stephan is touching me. "Captain, why not?
Three days from now and this will all be gone.
It no longer is!" Son, you don't shout,
In the long run it doesn't help the pain.

I gather the brittle bits and cut my finger
On the chipped rim of my wife's favorite glass,
And cannot make the simple bleeding linger.
"Captain, Captain, there's no one watching us."

On the Edge has been painstakingly printed by hand press in an
edition of 220, which hardly seems enough to go around.

THOM GUNN

From "Modes of Control"

The only assumption shared by the poets who have emerged in the last ten or fifteen years is that they do not want to continue the revolution inaugurated by Pound and finally made respectable by the learned commentaries on the *Four Quartets*. Yet nobody has pretended that, once the revolution was abandoned, it was possible simply to take up where Hardy left off, as if the experiments of Pound and Eliot had never taken place. Clearly we must, without embodying the revolution, attempt to benefit from it, to understand its causes and to study its mistakes. . . .

Philip Levine is often too deeply involved in the shock of experience to do more than endure it. The attempt to control the experience is thus made more by will than by understanding.

He takes the situations of people "on the edge." There is the pain of the everyday malaise, for example, the malaise that has succeeded the ennui of Baudelaire, being milder, less easy to isolate, more commonplace, but none the less difficult to endure. "There is nothing," he says, with effective understatement,

> to think of except
> the insistent push
> of water, and the pipe's
> cry against the water.

And there is also the more obvious kind of pain: "Gangrene" is about the torture of Algerians. In this poem he decides to take the big risk, and present the subject directly: the consequence is that the poem splits into two separate kinds of discourse, first the description of the torture, and second a didactic address to the Reader. This is the most extreme example of overinvolvement in the subject-matter, but there are others: the dramatization of

Reprinted from *The Yale Review* 53 (March, 1964), copyright Yale University.

violence is Levine's peculiar temptation. Moreover, his tendency to dramatize often overcomes his purposes in dramatizing: the particular problems of the hypothetical life are insisted on with such urgency that they cease to have much meaning beyond that of the individual case. This is so, sometimes, even when he adopts the dramatic tone toward himself:

> I have endured, as Godless Nazarite,
> Life like a bone even a dog would slight.

This is not quite genuine, somehow: one senses the merging of the dramatic into falsification.

Such flaws are the more apparent because they contrast so decidedly with the understated quietness of the best poems in the book. In "Berenda Slough" he finds matter "as if the third day had not come." The concept of the state preceding order is placed exactly in experience.

> One sees only a surface
> pocked with rushes, the starved clumps
> pressed between water and space—
> rootless, perennial stumps
>
> fixed in position. . . .

Here and in "In a Vacant House" the contemplating mind of the writer is not shocked into rigidity, but is flexible, limber, able in the very act of describing to explore the thing being described.

"The Negatives" strikes me as the most successful of the longer poems. It consists of a series of carefully stated paradoxes, and ends in the last of the four monologues making up the poem with the paradox that encloses and contains those that have preceded it. The speaker, one of four deserters from the French Army of North Africa, thinks of the others asleep around him:

> Once merely to be strong,
> to live, was moral. Within
> these uniforms we accept
> the evil we were chosen
> to deliver, and no act

human or benign can free
us from ourselves. Wait, sleep, blind
soldiers of a blind will, and
listen for that old command
dreaming of authority.

The generalization of the first sentence is sufficiently wide to extend beyond the immediate dramatic situation, while at the same time applying to it very specifically. And again the intelligence is given enough freedom to explore the concept, as it moves from one point of the poem to the next.

Perhaps the best poem in the book is also the most modest, the poem one tends almost to pass over on a first reading. It is addressed to his wife, "For Fran," and its power emerges from the calm and consistent tenderness of the tone:

She packs the flower beds with leaves,
Rags, dampened papers, ties with twine
The lemon tree, but winter carves
Its features on the uprooted stem.

I see the true vein in her neck
And where the smaller ones have broken
Blueing the skin, and where the dark
Cold lines of weariness have eaten. . . .

Experience is once more carefully placed, and with an accuracy for which there needs no insistence in the poet's tone to tell us what is important and what isn't. The accuracy, the relation between spoken and unspoken, the deliberate underplaying of the feeling, combine to make a work of great strength.

ROBERT DANA

From "Recent Poetry and the Small Press"

Philip Levine's first book, *On the Edge* (originally published in a handset, hardcover edition by the Stone Wall Press) has just been reissued in paper by Stone Wall's subsidiary, the Second Press. Kim Merker has done his usual fine job of book design and printing, and Levine's poems are more than worth the purchase price.

Levine's stock in trade includes a beautiful economy and forth-rightness of language whether he writes in traditional meters or syllabics. There is no waste. There is none of the hysterical rhetoric of the "Beats"; nor the dry, axiomatic crimp of the academics (although one of Levine's "vices" is to become cere-bral, he is never dispassionately so). Furthermore, unlike many of our younger poets, his poems are full of poeple, events, and recognizable twentieth-century hardware. In a time when Beat poets are hipped on the grotesqueries of our consumer society, and when the academics seem obsessed with fountains, Hyde Park, and their ancestor aunts, it is refreshing to meet a poet who does not insist on a *parade* of the horribles (because there are enough horrors to go around without a parade), but who on the other hand does not fail to see the poetry of ordinary events: the sickness of a child, the aging of a wife, a young girl's hysteria in the face of pressure.

In part one of *On the Edge* the themes of courage, "the frail dignity" of man, and the knowledge that to live is to fail, run through nearly every poem. What Levine knows about these things is hard-won stuff:

North American Review 1 (1964). Reprinted with permission.

Those promises we heard
We heard in ignorance;
. . . .
And, in our innocence,
Assumed the beast was tamed.
On a bare limb, a bird,
Alone, arrived, with wings
Frozen, holds on, and sings.

Like his own "Sierra Kid" (the six poems which make up this saga of an old pioneer, an "aging son of Appleseed" are richly inventive), this poet knows that "All that we learn we learn too late, / And it's not much." Still, in part one, there is a determination to create something enduring and worthwhile in the face of meaninglessness and defeat. It gets its best statement in the eloquent lyric "For Fran": "Out of whatever we have been / We will make something for the dark."

Levine's determination to wrest something meaningful from life modulates sharply into an attack, in part two of *On the Edge*, on modern man's failure to develop his own humanity. In Levine's view, man is the victim of his own taste for terror, his "inner capitulation," and incredible callousness. This view, and the power with which Levine conveys it, is best seen in the four poems that make up "The Negatives," and in "Gangrene."

The material for these poems was provided by the Algerian Revolt, and "The Negatives" consists of four monologues, one each by four deserters from the French Colonial Army of North Africa. Indeed, the letter from Henri Bruette to his mistress might be taken as typical of Levine's own astringent anger with the failure of human society to cope with its own capacity for, and delight in, producing suffering:

. . . I have no pencil,
no paper, only the blunt
end of my anger . . .
if I had words how could I
report the imperfect failure
for which I began to die?

But it is in "Gangrene" where the attack on inhumanity and callousness is driven home. After careful rendering of the torture of Algerian rebels by French soldiers, comes this harshly candid direct address to the reader:

> Reader, does the heart demand
> that you bend to the live wound
>   as you would bend
>
> to the familiar body
> of your beloved, to kiss
>   the green flower
> which blooms always from the ground
> human and ripe with terror,
>
> to face with love what we have
> made of hatred? We must live
>   with what we are,
> you say, it is enough. I
> taste death. I am among you
>   and I accuse
> you where, secretly thrilled by
> the circus of excrement,
>
> you study my strophes or
> yawn into the evening air,
>   tired, not amused.
> Remember what you have said
> when from your pacific dream
>   you awaken
> at last, deafened by the scream
> of your own stench. You are dead.

Philip Levine's *On the Edge* is a remarkable first book. Its balance of toughness and sensitivity, its courage, its skill in handling a difficult range of subject matter, the clarity embodied in the language, the touches of humor that sting like alum, all make it a book that should be read by every nobody still interested seriously in poetry. Levine is a real comer.

ROBLEY WILSON, JR.

From "Five Poets at Hand"

The Philip Levine book [*Not This Pig*] has a striking—if ugly—
title, and the poem which contains the title as part of its last line
is as striking and ugly a poem as the book contains. In between
the two appearances of the phrase I found nothing to excite me
and a good bit to make me gloomy. I think both the themes and
the devices are pretty dull stuff. The business of sharing the
deprivations of one's fellow man, and then discovering in a
poem that one has thereby become the fellow man's brother—
this seems to me such a commonplace (even a hack like Yevtu-
shenko knows that game) that it can only be successfully reiter-
ated in some kind of prosodic *tour de force*. The necessity of
exploring the Jewish heritage and laying it both against one's life
as a person and a father, and against one's exposure to the coun-
try that built the death camps, I can certainly understand; yet it
leaves me sympathetic but cool. The indefatigable concern for
the squalor and pitiableness of the human condition—with a
mild sermon on the need for dignity despite all—seems to me
here to serve no other function than to display the poet's good
eye.

   And Levine does have a good eye; I don't mean to suggest this
is a bad book of poems. It is simply too flat to be long remem-
bered. Ten minutes after the event is described, the event has
vanished from the reader's mind; no image, no picture, no ca-
dence, no fancy survives. Most of the poems come visually alive
in the reading, then black out when the page is turned—partly, I
suppose, because of the relentless syllabics-in-sevens, partly be-
cause of the consciously negative quality of the poems' state-
ments, a sort of no-bird-sang effect done over and over in what
is apparently intended to be a dramatic effect but fails, for me, to

Carleton Miscellany 9 (1968). Reprinted with permission.

connect with the thrust of the poetry. And I respond in the same stolid way to the frequent occasions when the poem suddenly reaches outside itself to a vignette of Nature; I take it Levine wants to use the Natural as a correlative, but I have the strong feeling Nature could as often as not be excised without damaging the poems.

JUDSON JEROME

From "Uncommitted Voices"

Philip Levine's second volume, *Not This Pig,* shows him to be a poet of growing power and strangeness. ("Strange," I understand, is the "in" word at the writing workshops these days.) For example, "Baby Villon" depicts what seems to be an individual, and yet he cannot be, having suffered for being white in Bangkok, black in London, Jew in Barcelona, Arab in Paris. He is the symbol of the outcast, the criminal, the underdog, the fighter— "Stiff, 116 pounds, five feet two, / No bigger than a girl." A specific meeting, their first and last, seems to be described. As Baby Villon leaves,

> he holds my shoulders,
> Kisses my lips, his eyes still open,
> My imaginary brother, my cousin,
> Myself made otherwise by all his pain.

There is compelling specificity and realism, mingled with enough elements of contradiction to make it clear that the figure is less actual than archetypal.

Similarly, in most of his poems Levine sketches in an apparently concrete experience, but he blurs the edges so that the reader is propelled into the realms of mystery. He returns again and again to images of encroaching darkness—"the long / shadows deep as oil." Some of the tricks used to create this aura of strangeness are merely irritating:

> Later I will be in
> the parking lot looking
> for my car or I will remember
> I have no car and it

Saturday Review of Literature, June 1, 1968. Reprinted with permission.

```
        will be tomorrow or years
        from then.
                     It will be now.
        I will have been talking . . .
```

That seems a long and complicated way of saying time doesn't matter. From this point on in the poem we are apparently in a specific setting, talking to a specific (unidentified) person. The poet predicts:

```
              I will hear them
        moving at last and see them
        moving toward you in the light
        bringing their great sweetness.
```

It is the magnificence of lines such as these, or the closing lines of "Baby Villon," that convinces me of Levine's true depth as a poet. Often his mysteriousness seems mere vagueness, lack of focus; but in moments of precision his poems perform beautifully.

RALPH J. MILLS, JR.

From "Critic of the Month"

Philip Levine's second book, *Not This Pig,* shares certain qualities evident in Ignatow's poems—evident, in fact, in quite a lot of recent American poetry. These include directness of speech, sudden irruptions of the irrational, use of the ordinary details of contemporary life, and a colloquial intimacy which gives a reader the impression of being spoken to as a person by a person. Levine's poetry, at least in this collection, exhibits two prominent preoccupations which become theme and substance of his art: movement and travel—the poems reflect in oblique fashion the vastness of America, the loneliness of individuals—and finding a tongue for the speechless, for the poor, the outcast, the minorities: the "submerged population" to whose lives, Frank O'Connor once remarked, the short story lends a voice. Though Levine's presence can be felt everywhere in his poems—and indeed some pieces are about himself or events of a personal nature—he enters the life around him in America, in Spain, suffers it all in himself, and faces his own despair and inner disequilibrium:

> For a black man whose
> name I have forgotten who danced
> all night at Chevy
> Gear & Axle,
> for that great stunned Pole
> who laughed when he called me Jew
> Boy, for the ugly
> who had no chance,
>
> the beautiful in
> body, the used and the unused,

"Critic of the Month" first appeared in *Poetry* (January, 1969), copyright 1969 by The Modern Poetry Association. Reprinted by permission of the Editor of *Poetry.*

those who had courage
and those who quit—

. . . .

for these and myself
whom I loved and hated, I
had presumed to speak
in measure.
The great night is half
over, and the stage is dark;
all my energy,
all my care for

those I cannot touch
runs on my breath like a sigh;
surely I have failed.
My own wife
and my children reach
in their sleep for some sure sign,
but each has his life
private and sealed.

("Silent in America")

DICK ALLEN

From "Shifts"

Pili's Wall, by Philip Levine, is a ten-section poem about, well, a wall—illustrated with some small dull photographs of it. It is written "for the stone masons and plasterers, the wind, the sun, the rain & my Pili, the Spanish girlchild, all of you who made this wall & for Fran, who found it." The poem begins with "Why me?," describes hill, soil, cedars, a burrow, and asks, "What more?" In the second section the wall and the poet seem to be all things in the universe; and later the man asks, "What can a child know?" A hand reaches out, the poet is like a child:

> I am inside me
> squeezed tight, the
> bright tongue
>
> of the thistle
> at night

In section VII, "I stand and stand and stand into / this wall." Then comes "a simple dawn," the poet becomes Pili "waiting / for children / with particular names."

The object of the poem seems to have been to create a sense of oneness of all experience, leading to the wonder when one realizes how all can also be seen as distinct, without losing the mystical flood of the numinous. Or I may have completely misinterpreted it. In sum, this is a nice little chapbook of particular interest and perhaps meaning to the poet's friends. It seems too purposely vague, and personal, to be much more. I think Philip Levine is often a brilliant poet, but this work, at least outside a collection, strikes me as nothing really special from him.

Poetry (July, 1972).

RICHARD SCHRAMM

From "A Gathering of Poets"

When Philip Levine published *Not This Pig* in 1968 it was already apparent that he was a major contender for inclusion in the lists, randomly thrown out from time to time, of the handful of the very best poets writing in America. Now, three books later, his position is surer than ever. Along with W. S. Merwin and Galway Kinnell, Philip Levine is creating a poetry that is nearly relentless in excellence, that is grounded in a density of experience here and abroad which separates it explosively from the anemia of self-ness prevalent elsewhere, and that ranges from the crystaline evocativeness of Merwin at his most lucent to the blooded nightmares of Kinnell.

Open any Levine volume and the first thing you encounter is a concentrated, vibrant realness caught through a matrix of detail and precisely placed acts which open immediately on the event itself. There is no time in these poems for the ruminative opening, there are no tentative explorations before the main theme begins, and in his latest volume, *They Feed They Lion,* the force with which these openings secure the narrative is nothing less than dazzling. "Salami" begins this way:

> Stomach of goat, crushed
> sheep balls, soft full
> pearls of pig eyes,
> snout gristle, fresh earth,
> worn iron of trotter, slate
> of Zaragoza, dried cat heart,
> cock claws, ...

"A Gathering of Poets" first appeared in *Western Humanities Review* 26, no. 4 (Fall 1972).

And then the stanza proceeds to knead the ingredients together, deftly, with people and places, leading into a beautifully paired narrative, first of a stone cutter and his idiot daughter ("His puffed fingers / unbutton and point her; to the toilet . . .") and then of the speaker, wakened by the searing Tremontana, looking for his child as he staggers through his house full of premonitions of death. Like the stone cutter his blessing comes with a prayer, and each prayer breathes the pungence of the beginning:

> . . . In the last room
> where moonlight slanted
> through a broken shutter
> I found my smallest son
> asleep or dead, floating
> on a bed of colorless light.
> When I leaned closer
> I could smell the small breaths
> going and coming, and each
> bore its prayer for me,
> the true and earthy prayer
> of salami.

The setting for many of the poems in this volume, as well as *Red Dust* and *Pili's Wall,* is Spain and California—details from these countrysides, eucalyptus, olive, seas of burned yellow grass, shimmer through the pages until the places become as real as the man walking through them. Another setting often used by Levine is Detroit, and here, among factory workers, slums, human and industrial slag, his mixture of gentleness and nearly flamboyant toughness elsewhere held in check sometimes breaks apart. This happens for me occasionally in "The Angels of Detroit," a poem in seven parts where alternately a lyric warmth is lavished on frozen ground or a flat, dialectically reduced stanza clips out a broken life. But the sequence, and other poems in the same section, prepare for the title poem, and even if they did nothing else that would justify their extreme polarizations. "They Feed They Lion" has to be one of the most remarkable poems of recent times, a tour de force of paralleled rhetoric, Whitmanesque cataloging, and a repeatedly insistent ambiguity of syntax. On the page it is baffling and intriguing. When Levine reads it aloud it somehow breaks open miraculously, and the very things that made it seem murky and at loose ends with itself become justified, full, and resonant. The final stanza, which needs the rest of the poem to set up the parallelisms, goes like this:

> From my five arms and all my hands,
> From all my white sins forgiven, they feed,
> From my car passing under the stars,
> They Lion, from my children inherit,
> From the oak turned to a well, they Lion,
> From they sack and they belly opened
> And all that was hidden burning on the oil-stained earth
> They feed they Lion and he comes.

Less experimental than this and representative of the best of his writing are poems I can only mention by title here—"Angel Butcher," portions of the long sequence "Thistles," "To P. L., 1916–1937," and the last poem in the volume, "Breath." Something of their accomplishment is suggested in this shorter lyric, with its beautifully handled simplicity and its haunting sense of isolation, a theme characterizing much of the volume.

ALONE

> Sunset, and the olive grove flames
> on the far hill. We descend
> into the lunging shadows
> of goat grass, and the air
>
> deepens like smoke.
> You were behind me, but when I turned
> there was the wrangling of crows
> and the long grass rising in the wind
>
> and the swelling tips of grain
> turning to water under a black sky.
> All around me the thousand
> small denials of the day

rose like insects to the flaming
of an old truth, someone alone
following a broken trail of stones
toward the deep and starless river.

There are a lot of questions asked in *Pili's Wall,* a poem in ten
parts beautifully printed by Unicorn Press. "Why me?" the
poem begins, "Why am I here?" Later on the moon asks, "What
can a child know?" On the first reading I couldn't answer any of
these with much satisfaction, and I suspect that had the last
question been answered more clearly some of the sections in this
poem might have come off better. This is an unusually open
piece compared with the rest of Levine's work—open both in
syntax and dramatic frame—and though I admire the freshness
and newly hatched quality of many of the sections, the con-
stantly changing point of view gives the poem a rather muddled
sense. There are voices from nature, voices of children, voices
from the poet—more than one, since the plan is for the poet's
voice to merge with what he observes. Or for the wall to be
saying it all, and this is sometimes hard to accept. Many of the
sections come from the accompanying photographs of children's
drawings on the wall, and where these act as entrances into the
world behind the drawings (things, that is, from the poet's imagi-
nation that are more interesting than the drawings themselves)
they come off beautifully, as in the second section.

I am the one
you never drew . . .

. . . .

the shepherd
alone and herdless
who came one afternoon
sweat running
from his eyes

seven jackdaws
soundless, until the sky
darkened
and there was
no place

The eighth section, too, written from an omniscient point of view, is equally compelling. But it isn't until the last two sections that the range of voices is brought into coherent focus by the plainly identified speakers in each. Once this shape becomes clear the poem as a whole lifts up startlingly.

Red Dust, put out by Kayak with their usual exuberantly irrelevant drawings, has very much the same impact, and some of the same poems, as *They Feed They Lion.* Individual pieces in it— "Told," "In the New Sun," "Noon," and "Sisters," to mention only a few—are as accomplished and moving as any of the poems above. Still, the volume seems to have gotten stalled, if only slightly, in a way the Atheneum volume avoided, perhaps by its divisions, more likely by its selection. At times I found images, even statements, simply accumulating themselves like coins in a pocket waiting to be spent. Parts of "Where We Live Now" and "Angel of Suburbs" seem flattened to me in this way. More often, though, images are impelled by an immediately sensed rightness and dramatic movement, as at the end of "Holding On," a poem which embraces a sense of exile and belonging at the same time.

> If my spirit
> descended now, it would be
> a lost gull flaring against
> a deepening hillside, or an angel
> who cries too easily, or a single
> glass of seawater, no longer blue
> or mysterious, and still salty.

PAUL ZWEIG

From "1 + 1 + 1 + 1"

Philip Levine quietly has become one of the most interesting poets writing today in America. I say quietly, because Levine's poems do not contain many fashionable gestures. He never picked sides in the round robin of public quarrels which enlivened the poetry scene during the 1960s (New York Poets versus Black Mountain Poets, Deep Imagists versus Academic Poets, etc.). Instead, in his earlier books, *Not This Pig, Red Dust,* and *Pili's Wall,* he worked to develop a strong, precise language, expressing moments of illumination and compassion, expressing too the bass-tones of suffering and vulnerability which the emotionally open life must experience. In common with the best insight of many contemporary poets, Levine has learned to focus intensely on the "correspondences" which bind together different orders of experience. Stones and forests, the conflagrations of poverty, the Spanish landscape, the inhumanity of urban America, are yoked together into a structure of revelation which becomes the real subject matter of Levine's poetry. Not urban poverty alone, and not the mysteries of pastoral quietness, but the groundswell of understanding, the sharp, often dark energy which they share. The title poem of his most recent book, *They Feed They Lion,* is an example of the power which sweeps through the best of these poems:

> Out of burlap sacks, out of bearing butter,
> Out of black bean and wet slate bread,
> Out of the acids of rage, the candor of tar,
> Out of creosote, gasoline, drive shafts, wooden dollies,
> They Lion grow.
> > Out of the gray hills
> Of industrial barns, out of rain, out of bus ride,

Parnassus: Poetry in Review 1 (1972). Reprinted with permission.

West Virginia to Kiss My Ass, out of buried aunties,
Mothers hardening like pounded stumps, out of stumps,
Out of the bones' need to sharpen and the muscles' to stretch,
They Lion grow.
                      Earth is eating trees, fence posts,
Gutted cars, earth is calling in her little ones,
"Come home, Come home!" From pig balls,
From the ferocity of pig driven to holiness,
From the furred ear and the full jowl come
The repose of the hung belly, from the purpose
They Lion grow. . . .

. . . .
                      From my five arms and all my hands,
From all my white sins forgiven, they feed,
From my car passing under the stars,
They Lion, from my children inherit,
From the oak turned to a wall, they Lion,
From they sack and they belly opened
And all that was hidden burning on the oil-stained earth
They feed they Lion and he comes.

An energy of despair rises in the poem, ominous yet expan-
sive, deadly, yet almost joyful. The voice of the black poor
chants a language of apocalypse. "They Lion" feeds on suffering,
and grows; not only human suffering, but the suffering of grass
and stumps and gutted cars. The effect of Whitmanesque accu-
mulation building from image to image creates a fraternity of
darkness; the animate and inanimate worlds speak together in a
single chant. "They Lion," etched more deeply by Levine's dia-
lectal spelling, is a brother of Yeats's "rough beast" slouching
toward Bethlehem; it is a mockery of St. Mark's biblical lion.
When it comes, man and the earth will be devoured by one
hunger.

They Feed They Lion sustains throughout a mood of mature,
tough vision, in which the suffering of the earth, the suffering
of man, the anxiety of inward failure, mingle to create a
strangely literal Apocalypse, without chest-beating or the glam-
our of surreal imagery. Levine's phantasmagoria is real. These
are the Messianic pains, the upheavals of disaster preluding an-
other dispensation:

                    One brown child
        stares and stares into your frozen eyes
        until the lights change and you go
        forward to work. The charred faces, the eyes
        boarded up, the rubble of innards, the cry
        of wet smoke hanging in your throat,
        the twisted river stopped at the color of iron.
        We burn this city every day.
                                            ("Coming Home")

T. S. Eliot (quoting T. E. Hulme) once accused the romantic
poets of the nineteenth century of dealing in "spilt religion."
Philip Levine, like so many other poets of the past fifteen years,
has turned Eliot's disdain around. Not "spilt religion," but reli-
gion turned loose from the rituals of orthodoxy; religion freed
from the anti-worldly, anti-sensual prison of churches and institu-
tions. Rilke wrote, movingly, of his struggle to "build God," to
form the substance of revelation out of his labor to see, and to
create patterns of meaning. American poets too have begun to
create a new language of revelation. It is a syncretic language,
gleaned in Oriental cults, American Indian songs, the Kabbala,
the subversive, messianic strain of Christianity and Judaism.
However spurious it may seem in the hands of lesser poets, at its
heart, it is a deeply "pagan" language, which declares that all the
orders of experience, all the orders of perception, are one. Philip
Levine's work belongs to this new research of language and
feeling. His poems glory in "spilt religion," as in the haunting
series of "angel" poems in which a sequence of mythic "angel"
characters act out the energy of their despair ("Angels of De-
troit," "Angel Butcher," etc.). These poems express the turmoil
of desperate places, the way down which is also a way out:

                Don't matter what rare breath
                puddles in fire on
                the foundry floor. The toilets
                overflow, the rats dance, the maggots
                have it, the worms of money
                crack like whips, and
                among the angels
                we lie down.
                                    ("The Angels of Detroit")

29

Where *They Feed They Lion* fails, it is because Levine has a tendency to outrun his own vision. When he cranks up the intensity of his language, the sense of mystery becomes strained, and one feels a sort of exoticism in the imagery. A number of poems are simply too long, going through the motions of language when their actual strength has dwindled ("The Cutting Edge," "Saturday Sweeping," "Salami," etc.). But these are small blemishes. There remains so much good poetry in *They Feed They Lion* that it is without a doubt Philip Levine's best book, and one of the finest I have recently read.

MARIE BORROFF

From "Recent Poetry"

The poems of Philip Levine draw the reader into a world whose imagined solidity is all but palpable. It is no accident that the most conspicuously recurring feature of his dramatic scenery is stone: the stones at the bottom of rivers and streams, of dry stream-beds; the stones of beaches, the rocks at the tops of mountains, where can be heard "the long steady drone / of granite holding together." The silence, strength, and centeredness of stones are found values that symbolically extend themselves into

>   houses, trees, posts,
>   and cars, all
>   the closed presences of this world.

And stones are part of the hardness of the world against which man's strength is measured, which bruises and abrades his flesh. In "The Cutting Edge" the blade of a "green rock / covered with river lace" bites deep into a man's foot as he wades. The rendering of this everyday accident as myth is reminiscent of Dickey, but there is an instructive contrast between the characteristic outward-spiraling grandiosity of Dickey's narratives and the centripetal movement of Levine's poem, gathering inward, compressing to a regained clarity.

>   I sat down in the water,
>   up to my waist in water,
>   my pockets filling with it.
>   I squeezed the green rock,
>   pressed it to my cheeks,
>   to my eyelids. I did not
>   want to be sick or faint

Reprinted from *The Yale Review* 62 (October, 1972), copyright Yale University.

with children looking on,
so I held to the edge of the stone
until I came back.

Side by side with the powerfully realized natural landscapes of many of the poems in this collection rises an urban landscape realized with equal power. Levine is in touch; he knows the "23 yr / old draft dodger" on a mountain lake who has sent his girl away and watched his books burn; he remembers how

> in middle age we came
> to the nine years war, the stars raged
> in our horoscopes and the land
> turned inwards biting for its heart.

("Later Still")

The title poem is a litany celebrating, in rhythms and images of unflagging, pistonlike force, the majestic strength of the oppressed, rising equally out of the substances of the poisoned industrial landscape and the intangibles of humiliation. Its language is an extraordinary meld of high rhetoric and illiterate linguistic forms, galvanized by intensity of feeling:

> Out of burlap sacks, out of bearing butter,
> Out of black bean and wet slate bread,
> Out of the acids of rage, the candor of tar,
> Out of creosote, gasoline, drive shafts, wooden dollies,
> They Lion grow.
> . . . .
> From "Bow Down" come "Rise Up,"
> Come they Lion from the reeds of shovels,
> The grained arm that pulls the hands,
> They Lion grow.

JON M. WARNER

They Feed They Lion

Levine's fifth book clearly indicates that he is an outstanding poet. I have a feeling that he has the curse of the poet—constantly wondering about himself in relationship to all things and feeling intensely what his mind sees. This process is a continual source of sadness, of pain, of joy. The subject matter of his poems reflects his curiosity and skill, whether he is walking in the country, recalling Spain where he and his family lived for two years, or thinking while awake in the quiet of the night. His diction and rhythm are simple, yet complex in nuances as in "Cry for Nothing": "Say / your name to stump, / to silence, to the sudden wings / of the air, say / your name to yourself. / It doesn't matter cause / it all comes back . . . burr balls / tapping at your ankles / with their Me! Me! / the fresh weed tongue lashing / at your cheek / to make you cry / for nothing." He must be read.

Reprinted from *Library Journal*, May 1, 1972. Copyright © 1972 by Reed Publishing, USA, Div. of Reed Holdings, Inc.

WILLIAM H. PRITCHARD

They Feed They Lion

The most memorable speaker in Philip Levine's last volume of
poems was a pig who, being led to market, contemplates himself
with some admiration: "It's wonderful how I jog / on four
honed-down ivory toes / my massive buttocks slipping / like
oiled parts with each light step." Haughtily determined to see it
through, he proceeds without evasions, superior to his captor—a
boy who imagines he'll collapse squealing on his side

> or that I'll turn like a beast
> cleverly to hook his teeth
> with my teeth. No. Not this pig.
> ("Animals Are Passing from Our Lives")

This pig means what he says. And with this new volume added
to two of Levine's earlier ones, *On the Edge* (1963) and *Not This
Pig* (1968), it is clear that the poet means it also; his cumulative
work must be taken seriously indeed.

The pig turns up often in *They Feed They Lion*—in "Salami,"
for example, a fine poem that begins with an old Spanish woman
grinding up "pearls of pig eyes," "snout gristle" and "iron of
trotter," along with the requisite parts of sheep and goat to bring
forth eventually "the true and earthy prayer / of salami." But
other undistinguished parts of other animals also exist near the
center of Levine's world, providing him with the gross, natural
facts out of which come spiritual, poetic fulfillments—just
barely. Discovering a fish head while "searching among the
stones for nothing," he is made aware of his own head; then
throwing the fish head into the sea,

New York Times Book Review, July 16, 1972. Reprinted with permission.

             I sniff my fingers
and catch the burned essential oil
seeping out of death. Out of beginning,
I hear, under the sea roar, the bone words
of teeth tearing earth and sea,
anointing the tongues with stone and sand,
water eating fish, fish water,
head eating head to let us be.
      ("To a Fish Head Found on the Beach Near Málaga")

Getting a spiritual lift from dead animals has been one of our century's seedier poetic pastimes (see Richard Eberhart's "The Groundhog"), but Levine means it about the "burned essential oil," means that the eating actually goes on and that in fact we survive by it—"head eating head to let us be." The ambiguity here is of course that while letting us be is a blessing, we're also cursed by it: Please, won't you just let us be.

Levine's best poems are ambiguous, their ambiguity issuing not from cleverly exploited poetic devices, but as a consequence of taking inclusive, Whitman-like attitudes toward the raw materials of life. At times, as in the volume's title poem, the poet's voice is incantatory, concerned with rhetorically exploiting a reader by sweeping him irresistibly along:

Out of burlap sacks, out of bearing butter,
Out of black bean and wet slate bread,
Out of the acids of rage, the candor of tar,
Out of creosote, gasoline, drive shafts, wooden dollies,
They Lion grow.

This is Ford or Pontiac chewing up everything, and the Earth is at it too, "eating trees, fence posts / Gutted cars," obeying the law "From 'Bow Down' come 'Rise Up.'" Eventually the poet includes himself in as possible meat out of the eater:

      From my five arms and all my hands,
From all my white sins forgiven, they feed,
From my car passing under the stars,
They Lion, from my children inherit

From . . .

    . . . all that was hidden burning on the oil-stained earth
    They feed they Lion and he comes.

"Lion" becomes both noun and verb, reaches out to all the
power and waste of a country's used parts, from pigs' trotters to
discarded mufflers; and the poem shocks us with a truth hidden
behind Robert Frost's line—"But waste was of the essence of the
scene."

Even when the scene invites it, Levine avoids moralizing and
refuses to transcend or wish away depressions attendant upon
any American poet who writes, say, about Detroit, 1968:

           A winter Tuesday, the city pouring fire,
           Ford Rouge sulfurs the sun, Cadillac, Lincoln
           Chevy gray. The fat stacks
           of breweries hold their tongues. Rags,
           papers, hands, the stems of birches
           dirtied with words.
                         Near the freeway
           you stop and wonder what came off,
           recall the snowstorm where you lost it all,
           the wolverine, the northern bear, the wolf
           caught out, ice and steel raining
           from the foundries in a shower
           of human breath. On sleds in the false sun
           the new material rests. One brown child
           stares and stares into your frozen eyes
           until the lights change and you go
           forward to work. The charred faces, the eyes
           boarded up, the rubble of innards, the cry
           of wet smoke hanging in your throat,
           the twisted river stopped at the color of iron.
           We burn this city every day.
                                        ("Coming Home")

    The unforgivable landscape is speechless, holding its tongue,
any words dirty ones; while the "you" pausing by the freeway is
a putative poet, struck suddenly to wondering "what came off,"
where it all got lost. In the face of what the language registers

with such accuracy—fantastic and inevitable facts—he remains silent, only faring "forward to work." Thus the pure products of America go crazy, the pig goes to market, and all of us burn this city every day. Philip Levine's acceptance of these facts is strongly poised, beyond affirmation or pessimism, embodied in the stubborn resources of poems: "They feed they lion and he comes."

ALAN HELMS

From "Over the Edge"

Philip Levine's first book of poems (*On the Edge*, 1963) was remarkably good. It demonstrated an already accomplished poet whose strong voice moved through the mostly traditional verse with intelligence, confidence, and an uncanny power to unsettle. Its theme was "the loss of human power" and "the gradual decay of dignity"; its mood was one of almost unremitting pessimism:

> If it were mine by one word
> I would not save any man,
> myself or the universe
> at such cost: reality.
> . . . .
> there is no armor or stance,
> only the frail dignity
> of surrender, which is all
> that can separate me now
> or then from the dumb beast's fall,
> unseen in the frozen snow.
>
>   ("Night Thoughts over a Sick Child")

Since that first book Levine's pursuit of his central theme has worked a big transformation in his style:

> DOWN THE MOUNTAIN
> in Fresno, L.A., Oakland
> a man with three names and no features
> closes my file.

"Over the Edge" first appeared in *Partisan Review* 41, no. 1 (1974). Reprinted with permission.

> The winds
> are weighed, the distance clocked.
> Everything is entered in the book.
>
> ("Thistles," from *They Feed They Lion*)

The skill here is, if anything, more obvious; what's especially new is the immediacy of effect, the almost telegraphic communication of the voice. In its blunt, precise movement it mimics the rhythms of the technology which promotes the poem's insane assumption: the notion that once you've recorded data, you've described a life. The last line triggers the characteristic Levine effect of horror, suggesting by its irrevocable movement the blind tenacity with which the insane belief is held. This small, perfect poem helps reveal the full meaning of Levine's first title. *On the Edge* took us to "the edge of laughter," which is to say the edge of the manageable, the supportable, the tolerable, the barely reasonable. *They Feed They Lion* takes us over the edge into a nightmare world of the wholly mad; a world of

> charred faces, the eyes
> boarded up, the rubble of innards, the cry
> of wet smoke hanging in your throat,
> the twisted river stopped at the color of iron.
> We burn this city every day.
>
> ("Coming Home")

The city is Detroit, the locale of half the poems in the book and the symbol of a technology gone berserk, infecting the lives of its workers like a cancer; a city of ammunition dumps, automobile graveyards, "empires / of metal shops, brickflats, storage tanks, / robbing the air." It's also a city of lonely men and women reduced to parts of themselves, people whose minimal lives are so abraded by despair that it "Don't matter what rare breath / puddles in fire on / the foundry floor. The toilets / overflow, the rats dance, the maggots / have it, the worms of money / crack like whips, and / among the angels / we lie down."

Reversing the dehumanizing tendency whereby we treat people as if they were their "statistics," Levine nominates the oppressed of this refuse world as "angels"; and most of the best

poems in this book are ones in which he speaks in the depressed
voices of those too bewildered and dispirited to speak for them-
selves:

> At the end of mud road
> in the false dawn of the slag heap
> the hut of the angel Bernard.
> His brothers are factories and
> bowling teams, his mother is the
> power to blight, his father
> moves in all men like a threat,
> a closing of hands, an unkept
> promise to return.
>
> ("Angels of Detroit")

As this section concludes, Bernard "cries to sleep." In another
section from the same poem "Nigger / boy's crying in / the shit
house." In "Saturday Sweeping," "Half / the men in this town /
are crying in / the snow." "How much can it hurt?" asks one
poem. For the people of Levine's world, the answer is "More
than we ever expected; more than we thought we could bear."

And their repeated cries would be unbearable, except that
some are of anger as well as sorrow, refusal as well as surrender.
The title poem, the best in the book and one of the most power-
ful poems I've read in years, is a poem of anger in which Levine's
vision carries us to the edge of apocalypse, a poem so urgent and
propulsive in voice as to ignore the "edges" of syntax, logical
relation, propositional sense:

> From my five arms and all my hands,
> From all my white sins forgiven, they feed,
> From my car passing under the stars,
> They Lion, from my children inherit,
> From the oak turned to a wall, they Lion,
> From they sack and they belly opened
> And all that was hidden burning on the oil-stained earth
> They feed they Lion and he comes.

The surging repetition of "They Lion" is like a cry trying to find
shape in language. The passage doesn't make "sense," of course,

since that's one of the points of the poem. It's the kind of poem Barthes would applaud—so wholly engaged that it verges on the act of abolishing itself.

Levine risks a lot with his new poetry; and when his vision is wholly private, then lines, images, sometimes entire poems fail to communicate; sometimes a flat and predictable language seeks automatic response. But when he focuses on the private pains and social ills of others, his best poems oblige us to cry with him. *They Feed They Lion* is not a comforting experience. More important, in its compassion, its skill, and its rare power to disturb our dulled attentions, it is a necessary and a valuable one.

RALPH J. MILLS, JR.

"The True and Earthy Prayer": Philip Levine's Poetry

We live
the way we are
—"The Sadness of Lemons"

The poetry of Philip Levine, from *On the Edge* (1963) to his two latest collections, *Red Dust* (1971) and *They Feed They Lion* (1972), has always displayed technical skill, a dexterous handling of both formal and, more recently, informal modes, and a command of the resources of diction and rhythm. Yet these aspects of technique seem in a way secondary, absorbed as they are by a central, driving intensity peculiar to this poet's approach. Such intensity leads him to a relentless searching through the events of his life and the lives of others, through the particulars of nature as these signify something about the processes of living, the states of existence, in order to arrive not at Eliot's transcendence, Roethke's "condition of joy," or Whitman's ideal of progress and brotherhood (though the sharing of suffering and the common ties of humanity are basic to Levine's attitude) but to the sort of awareness suggested by Yeats's phrase "the desolation of reality": an unflinching acquaintance with the harsh facts of most men's situation which still confirms rather than denies its validity. If this is a difficult prospect, we must acknowledge how familiar it has become of late through the poems of Robert Lowell, David Ignatow, James Wright, Allen Ginsberg, and Galway Kinnell, to mention a few obvious names. In the writing of these poets, as in Levine's, the range of human sympathies, the frankness, perseverance, and sensitivity create of themselves an affirmative, life-sustaining balance to the bleak recognition of religious deprivation, war, social injustice, moral and spiritual confusion.

Levine's early poetry is taut, sharp, formal but gradually alters to accommodate his desire for greater freedom in line length and

---

American Poetry Review, March–April, 1974. Reprinted with permission.

overall construction. A prominent theme of his first book is the reversal or defeat of expectations. Put another way, it motivates a struggle on the poet's part to view life stripped of the vestiges of illusory hope or promise, a type of hard spiritual conditioning which helps to engender his fundamental responsiveness to the dilemmas of the poor, embittered, failed lives of the "submerged population" (the late Frank O'Connor's term) in modern society, a responsiveness that accounts for much of both the energy and the deep humaneness of all his work. A firm grip on existence itself takes priority for Levine from the start, though with it necessarily comes an acceptance of pain and the admission that failure, defeat, and imperfection—but not surrender!—are unavoidable in men's affairs. The penetrating look he gives himself in "The Turning" from *On the Edge* points the direction he follows to maturity, which depends on the realization of flaws as well as the capacity to exist, to continue, made sturdier by this self-knowledge:

> . . . no more a child,
> Only a man,—one who has
> Looked upon his own nakedness
> Without shame, and in defeat
> Has seen nothing to bless.
> Touched once, like a plum, I turned
> Rotten in the meat, or like
> The plum blossom I never
> Saw, hard at the edges, burned
> At the first entrance of life,
> And so endured, unreckoned,
> Untaken, with nothing to give.
> The first Jew was God; the second
> Denied him; I am alive.

Committed to a fallen, unredeemable world, finding no metaphysical consolations, Levine embraces it with an ardor, anguish, and fury that are themselves religious emotions. In a brief comment on his work contributed to *Contemporary Poets of the English Language* (1970) he lists among his "obsessions" "Detroit" (where he was born, did factory labor, and studied), "the dying of America" (a recurrent theme in various guises), and "communion with others," which incorporates its predecessors as well as specifying what is for him a primary poetic impulse. Writing frequently of persons whose lives are distinct yet touch his own, he increases his consciousness and imaginative powers, and a chord of compassion and understanding reverberates within and beyond the boundaries of his poems. This is not to say that Levine puts himself out of the picture or chooses a mask of impersonality, but that his presence in a poem, whether overt or concealed, constitutes an enlargement of personality, a stepping out of the ego-bound "I" into the surrounding life. Paradoxically, he reaches inward, far into the recesses of the psyche, at the same time he reaches outward, thus fulfilling a pattern of movement Robert Bly has long advocated as essential to a modern poetry rich in imaginative potentialities.

Among the poems of Levine's initial volume, this self-extension appears most complete when he adopts the voices of different persons—the Sierra Kid, four French Army deserters in North Africa, the unnamed officer of "The Distant Winter"—to replace his own. Another sort of identification, of a crucial kind for the line of development his work pursues, occurs in the title poem "On the Edge," and also in "My Poets" and "Gangrene." In these instances he does not assume the role of another speaker but takes up the question of a poetic vocation and the destiny of poets in society today. In one shape or another, each of these poems really considers the problem of speechlessness, the lacerating irony of the mute poet imprisoned by circumstances which thwart or oppose his art, making its practice unlikely or impossible. So Levine sorts through the probabilities of his own future. The poet/speaker of "On the Edge" describes himself as the insane, alcoholic Poe of the twentieth century, born, as Levine was, "in 1928 in Michigan." This latter-day Poe plays the part of an observer who doesn't write, only watches the actions and prevarications of nameless people. In the last stanza he repeats a refusal of his art, though we are provided in its statement of alienation, perceptiveness, and silence with a poetry of angry eloquence:

> I did not write, for I am Edgar Poe,
> Edgar the mad one, silly, drunk, unwise,
> But Edgar waiting on the edge of laughter,
> And there is nothing that he does not know
> Whose page is blanker than the raining skies.

This abstention from writing, or persecution for telling the truth by means of it, occupies the other poems mentioned. Levine's effort here is to indicate the need for honest speech, the conditions which militate against it, and the frustrating atmosphere of separateness the poet faces. Thematically, the poem "Silent in America" from *Not this Pig* (1968), Levine's second collection, brings such matters to a critical climax and to a moment of transformation and decision. Though it is not the first poem in the book, dramatically speaking it should be thought of as a pivotal piece, for its procedure and resolution make possible what Levine is doing elsewhere in the same volume: breaking down those barriers which prevent him from entering areas of otherwise lost or unapprehended experience requisite to the poetry he wants to write. At the outset the poet announces his silence, which fashions for him a state of remoteness and solitude that border on anonymity. Watching ordinary things—a sprinkler wetting a lawn—stirs him toward utterance, but he stays quiet. A doctor's examination uncovers no defect. Details of nature engage him with the elusive tracery of their being; still, the animate *something* he notices in trees, water, and flowers defies his wish to name it, and thus his muteness persists. Locked in isolation, Levine now falls victim to inner torments, to his "squat demon, / my little Bobby," a splintered apparition of the self who plagues him with insatiable sexual demands. The poem develops rapidly toward hysteria and derangement until the poet bursts out with a negative cry of resistance. A section ensues in which he articulates the aims of his writing—to give voice to the varied experience of lost, unknown, or forgotten individuals he has met, speaking with and for them—but he is likewise forced to assent to the fact that each person remains finally impervious to total comprehension and communion. The following passage handsomely summarizes Levine's intentions and concerns:

> For a black man whose
> name I have forgotten who danced
> all night at Chevy
> Gear & Axle,
> for that great stunned Pole
> who laughed when he called me Jew

Boy, for the ugly
who had no chance,

the beautiful in
body, the used and the unused,
those who had courage
and those who quit—
Rousek and Ficklin
numbed by their own self-praise
who ate their own shit
in their own rage;

for these and myself
whom I loved and hated, I
had presumed to speak
in measure.
The great night is half
over, and the stage is dark;
all my energy,
all my care for

those I cannot touch
runs on my breath like a sigh;
surely I have failed.
My own wife
and my children reach
in their sleep for some sure sign,
but each has his life
private and sealed.

Levine's anxiety arises from the profoundly felt impulse to put his language, as poetry, in the service of others' lives, in addition to his own. The walls of privacy and individuality he cannot traverse cause him regret and a feeling of loss. Yet, just as surely, he *does* speak for others to the very limit of his abilities, not only here but also in the rest of this book, as well as in his subsequent poetry. If he is unable to appropriate the entirety of another life, like a second skin, it is still possible for him to go with others, moving to the rhythms of their existence and assimilating the details which his imagination requires. This kind of correspondence and kinship receives treatment in the closing section of the poem, where Levine meets a friend, H., in a Los Angeles bar and talks with him. H. is perhaps a writer too; in any event, he is described as doing essentially what an artist does: he creates a world composed of half-real, observed figures and half-fictitious ones who fit in with their actual counterparts, and he lives with them in imagination and sympathy. In the tavern Levine senses the presence of a person of fabulous name, apparently a wholly fictive man, conjured by his mind, who imposes himself no less strongly on the poet's awareness and emotions because of that:

> Archimbault is here—
> I do not have to be drunk
> to feel him come near,
>
> and he touches me with his
> life, and I could cry,
> though I don't know who he is
> or why I should care
> about the mad ones, imagined
> and real, H. places
> in his cherished underground,
> their wounded faces
>
> glowing in the half-light of
> their last days alive,
> as his glows here.

Whatever his self-questioning, Levine clearly cares, and his expressed wish in the next lines merges his own existence with that of such persons as fill the bar, until all seems to become part of poetry itself: "Let me have / the courage to live / as fictions live, proud, careless, / unwilling to die." So he would have his life speak itself as poems do, tenacious of their being. At the conclusion Levine and H. leave the bar and "enter the city." The poet urges his readers to join him, to blend into the mass of humanity thronging the streets in their restlessness, at last to go "beyond the false lights / of Pasadena / where the living are silent / in America." This invitation is as much a definition of his own poetic pursuits as it is a gesture by which the poet makes his reader a partner to what he sees. Levine will invade those areas of the unspoken life and lend them words.

Rich and complex though they usually are, the poems of Levine's first two collections are relatively direct, proceeding by certain logical, sequential, narrative, or other means which provide the reader with support and guidance. Levine never altogether abandons poems of this sort, but even in *Not This Pig* he begins to widen his fields of exploration to include experiences which manifest themselves in irrational, dreamlike, fantastic, or visionary forms, doing so variously in such poems as "The Rats," "The Businessman of Alicante," "The Cartridges," "The One-Eyed King," "Animals Are Passing from Our Lives," "Baby Villon," "Waking an Angel," "The Second Angel," and "The Lost Angel." These pieces prepare the way for the surrealist atmosphere of *Red Dust,* the elliptical, disjunctive composition evident there, and further visible in portions of *They Feed They Lion.* Levine has cited the Spanish and Latin American poets Hernandez, Alberti, Neruda, and Vallejo, in addition to postwar Polish poetry, as having presented new possibilities available to him. The freedom, vigorousness, metaphorical and imagistic daring of these poets plainly has had a tonic effect on Levine's more recent writing, releasing him to new boldness and strength.

So, by any but a narrow or restrictive view, Levine's latest books must be judged extraordinarily successful, exhibiting an access of inventiveness and vision. In *Red Dust* the elements of experience move into different focus; they are less "distanced," talked about, or pointed to than rendered dramatically as the very substance of language and image in the poems. The general character of these poems is also freer, more intuitive, and thus occasionally more difficult, unyielding to logical analysis. From the beginning we find an openness in the structure of poems, in the sense that they are not brought to a tidy conclusion but often end in a startling, seemingly irrational—yet, on consideration, perfectly apt—statement. Here is the final section of "Clouds," a poem which gathers considerable momentum by associative leaping among apparently random details whose disconnectedness actually pulls together a grim portrait of the contemporary world. Over the shifting scenes and figures the aloof clouds travel, absorb, and spill out their rain, giving the poem coherence while at the same time implying a universal indifference to which the poet responds with vehemence in the striking lines at the close:

> You cut an apple in two pieces
> and ate them both. In the rain
> the door knocked and you dreamed it.
> On bad roads the poor walked under cardboard boxes.
>
> The houses are angry because they're watched.
> A soldier wants to talk with God
> but his mouth fills with lost tags.
>
> The clouds have seen it all, in the dark
> they pass over the graves of the forgotten
> and they don't cry or whisper.
>
> They should be punished every morning,
> they should be bitten and boiled like spoons.

In poems of this sort the components are set down in combinations which resist or contradict ordinary rational expectations for them. The reader, thus perceptually thrown off balance, has the option either to give up or give in, and so to see and feel the particulars of experience fused in vivid, evocative ways. Gradually, the shifting shapes, the elisions and abrupt juxtapositions will disclose their significance, if the reader will only accept them on their own terms. As indicated previously, Levine's social and moral preoccupations retain their urgency, but, as in the work of the Spanish-speaking poets he admires, such interests tend at times to be integral with the immediate, elliptical, or surreal orderings of imagery and statement. Frequently now, the poems seek out specific details of landscape, cityscape, even vegetation and animal life, though these directly or obliquely correspond with aspects of human existence. Sensitivity to place—whether Detroit, California, or Spain (where Levine lived for two years recently)—the imagination exercised on what is perceived there, leads readily into poems of large expressive force. The figures inhabiting these pieces may be quite separate and distinct, with Levine himself only a transparent or invisible speaker (though, of course, an indirect commentator, sometimes a savage one), as in "The End of Your Life" or "Where We Live Now"; or they may involve the poet openly, as he tries to define himself and his life, or when he captures a moment's affective resonance, a mood charged with implications, of the kind we observe in "A Sleepless Night," "Told," "Holding On," and "Fist." In "Noon" he draws self and others together beautifully within the frame of a landscape:

I bend to the ground
to catch
something whispered,
urgent, drifting
across the ditches.
The heaviness of
flies stuttering
in orbit, dirt
ripening, the sweat
of eggs.
     There are
small streams
the width of a thumb
running in the villages
of sheaves, whole
eras of grain
wakening on
the stalks, a roof
that breathes over
my head.
     Behind me
the tracks creaking
like a harness,
an abandoned bicycle
that cries and cries,
a bottle of common
wine that won't
pour.
At such times

I expect the earth
to pronounce. I say,
"I have been waiting
so long."   Up ahead
a stand of eucalyptus
guards the river,
the river moving
east, the heavy light
sifts down driving
the sparrows for
cover, and the women
bow as they slap
the life out
of sheets and pants
and worn hands.

In this poem, as in many of Levine's newest, man's common
attachments with earth, his relationship with objects, the hard,
painful climate in which most lives are lived, are evoked through
a skilled interweaving of images, the particulars of the world
suddenly caught up to view, suffused with the "reek of the hu-
man," to borrow a phrase from Donald Davie. "How much
earth is a man," Levine asks in another poem; his answer indi-
cates an indissoluble, fateful bond: "a hand is planted / and the
grave blooms upward / in sunlight and walks the roads." In the
three angel poems from *Not This Pig*, which create a little se-
quence among themselves, the realm of transcendence, of the
spiritual ideal, dissolves or collapses before the spectacle of
flawed earthly reality. What aspects of the spiritual can become
evident belong not to a hidden or remote sphere but radiate, if
possible, from the ingredients of day-to-day mundane affairs.
So, in Levine's work, life is circumscribed by the finality of
death, but this inevitability is countenanced with toughness, sto-
icism, staying power. As he says of his fist in the final stanza of
the poem bearing that title:

It opens and is no longer.
Bud of anger, kinked
tendril of my life, here

in the forged morning
fill with anything—water,
light, blood—but fill.

Between the poems of *Red Dust* and those of *They Feed They Lion* no alterations occur in Levine's attitude toward such matters; two poems, "The Space We Live" and "How Much Can It Hurt?," are even reprinted from the earlier book. In general, however, Levine employs less of the dense irrational or associative manner so prominent in *Red Dust,* though with no loss of concentrated force. The opening poems, "Renaming the Kings" and "The Cutting Edge," for instance, dramatize personal incidents in a direct, sequential way quite appropriate to the experiences. These pieces, along with several others, examine the poet's encounters in the midst of natural settings, with each occasion revealing some facet of a relation between the things of earth and a man—a relation sometimes assuring and harmonious, sometimes disturbing or painful. In "The Cutting Edge" a stone under water gashes the poet's foot; he casts it out of the stream and hobbles away. Later he returns, discovers it, and pauses to wonder before deciding what to do with it:

I could take it home
and plant it in a box;
I could talk about
what it did to me
and what I did to it,
or how in its element
it lives like you or me.
But it stops me, here
on my open hand,
by being a stone, and I send
it flying over the heads
of the fishing children,
arching alone above
the dialogue of reeds,
falling and falling toward water,
somewhere in water to strike
a conversation of stone.

A very different type of "conversation" takes place in "To a Fish Head Found on the Beach Near Málaga," where Levine, walking alone, comes upon the ravaged body and head, hanging by its shred of bone, then confides his "loneliness," "fears," and torments to it. The result of his strange speech makes him sense the contours and characteristics of his own face and head, and, at last, "throw the fish head to the sea. / Let it be fish once more." The poem's concluding lines assert the speaker's comprehension of the unalterable cyclicism of existence, the ironic necessity of destruction for renewal:

> I sniff my fingers
> and catch the burned essential oil
> seeping out of death. Out of beginning,
> I hear, under the sea roar, the bone words
> of teeth tearing earth and sea,
> anointing the tongues with stone and sand,
> water eating fish, fish water,
> head eating head to let us be.

This volume also includes sequences of varying length, as well as groups of obviously connected poems. "Thistles," the longest of them, dedicated to the poet George Oppen, is composed of discrete pieces each of which focuses on a singular occasion, perception, or ambiance of feeling. The same may be said for the shorter sequence, "Dark Rings." These poems are not bound tightly together, though the thistle appears in the first and last pieces of that sequence, and the "dark rings" refer not only to a specific detail in one poem but also to images in most and the mood of all of them. Yet their swift, free, occasionally abbreviated notation and arrangement give an impression of accuracy, deftness, and assurance in the handling of experience. The poems are full of nuances and overtones which linger on. One must place with these sequences most of the poems in the book's second section, dealing with Levine's Detroit life among the automotive workers and the abandoned, hopeless, silent figures we have seen him desirous to know and to speak for. The angels return in this section in shifting but always earthly forms, evanescent protective spirits hovering about the poet, presences in his closet, or incarnate in someone of his acquaintance, as in the fourth poem of "The Angels of Detroit" group. Here "the angel Bernard," trapped and frustrated by the massive industrial system for which he labors and cannot escape, writing poems no one will read, aching for love, release, even death, awakens as always to find himself surrounded by the debris of manufacture, our values and lives rupturing from the shapes of steel and rubber in which we have conceived them:

> At the end of mud road
> in the false dawn of the slag heap
> the hut of the angel Bernard.
> His brothers are factories and
> bowling teams, his mother is the
> power to blight, his father
> moves in all men like a threat,
> a closing of hands, an unkept
> promise to return.
>   We talk
> for years; everything we
> say comes to nothing. We drink
> bad beer and never lie. From
> his bed he pulls fists
> of poems and scatters them
> like snow. "Children are guilty,"
> he whispers, and the soft mouth
> puffs like a wound.
>
> He wants it all tonight.
> The long hard arms of a black woman,
> he wants tenderness, he wants
> the power to die in the
> chalice of God's tears.
>
> True dawn through the soaped window.
> The plastic storm-wrap swallows wind.
> '37 Chevie hoodless, black burst
> lung of inner tube, pot metal
> trees buckling under sheets
> He cries to sleep.

Such a poem gives notice of the incredible strength, the economy and muscle with which Levine endows the majority of his poems. Two of the most amazing and powerful pieces, "Angel Butcher" and "They Feed They Lion," bring the book's second section to a climactic level of prophetic vision; the latter poem is dazzling in its syntactic, linguistic, and dramatic invention, its use of idiomatic effect. But both poems need to be read in their entirety and are too long for quotation here. It remains now simply to say for the purposes of this brief commentary that Levine's poetry, praiseworthy at the start, has developed by momentous strides in the past decade. His new poems make it impossible for him to be ignored or put aside. He stands out as one of the most solid and independent poets of his generation—one of the best poets, I think, anywhere at work in the language. It is time to begin listening.

> Can you hear me?
> the air says. I hold
> my breath and listen
> and a finger of dirt thaws,
> a river drains
> from a snow drop
> and rages down
> my cheeks, our father
> the wind hums
> a prayer through my mouth
> and answers in the oat,
> and now the tight rows of seed
> bow to the earth
> and hold on and hold on.
>
> ("The Way Down")

GEORGE HITCHCOCK

From "A Gathering of Poets"

Philip Levine, on the other hand, has been more fortunate in the critical attention he has received, perhaps because his poetry swims more recognizably within the main stream of American life; students of the *Zeitgeist* have never been at a loss to place *him*. He began as a rather prosaic chronicler of life in industrial Middle America and has progressed steadily, through a number of acclaimed books, to a more imaginative and supple style but with the same fundamental concerns. His latest book (*1933*) is perhaps as a whole his finest achievement although I found no single poem as stirring as his memorable "They Feed They Lion" from his previous collection.

Still, there are splendid pieces here, such as "The Poem Circling Hamtramck, Michigan All Night in Search of You" and the title poem, "1933," a fine elegy beginning "My father entered the kingdom of roots / his head as still as a stone" and ending

> Once in childhood the stars held still all night
>   the moon swelled like a plum but white and silken
>   the last train from Chicago howled through the ghetto
> I came downstairs
>   my father sat writing in a great black book
>   a pile of letters
>   a pile of checks
>   (he would pay his debts)
>   the moon would die
>   the stars jelly
>   the sea freeze
>   I would be a boy in worn shoes splashing through rain

"A Gathering of Poets" first appeared in *Western Humanities Review* 28, no. 4 (Fall 1974).

To me, what is most striking about Levine's poetry is the sense of integrity. The materials of his life are the ordinary ones of a million lives but they are illuminated by honesty and a whole personality. There are few rockets or parakeets in his night; instead, the belching smokestacks of Detroit and the All-Nite diner are the symbols about which his myths gather, but the integrity of the poet is always there and that makes up for a lot. In his more casual moments Levine falls into flatness and—once in a while—banality, but at his best he is very good indeed. And while many poets of his generation seem to have lost their sense of direction, their feeling for the whole life, Levine is steadily getting better. A good sign.

MARK JARMAN

The Eye Filled with Salt

There are two qualities I find remarkable in Philip Levine's poems. One is his tone of voice, which I love and believe more than that of any other poet writing now. It is raised, in a rhetorical sense, just above the conversational tone. At times, it is that of a father telling stories to his children, not lecturing; at others, it is that of a man telling stories to fellow men, never condescending, but speaking directly, making allusions that can be comprehended intuitively, like the gestures, facial expressions, and voice inflections of any good storyteller. Even the rage and agony of poems like "Gangrene" in *On the Edge,* "How Much Can It Hurt" in *Red Dust,* and the great political poem "They Feed They Lion" have for me the tenor of a man who understands oratorical rhetoric but knows that what he has to say is compelling enough to express without it.

The other quality is more difficult to pin down, yet even more important. When reading a poet I am moved or unmoved first by how he says a thing; just what he is saying and how I feel about it comes later, after many readings. As Levine's poetry developed from the tight metrical and syllabic formalism of *On the Edge* to the looser but still essentially syllabic verse of *Not This Pig* to the allusive, Whitmanesque cataloguing of *Red Dust* and *They Feed They Lion,* what he had to say or, rather, what he was *moved* to say was changing, too. Not only is the structure formal in the early poems, but the attitude seems to be an expression of the stance of the previous generation, for which Randall Jarrell in the last lines of "90 North" is a spokesman:

> . . . nothing comes from nothing,
> The darkness from the darkness. Pain comes from darkness
> And we call it wisdom. It is pain.

Kayak 38 (1975). Reprinted with permission.

That's a powerful sentiment, and one that Levine seems to have accepted,

> Today on the
> eve of Thanksgiving, I said
> I will close my eyes, girl-like,
> and when I open them there
> will be something here to love
> and to celebrate. When I
> opened them there was only
> the blank door and beyond it
> the hall. . . .
>
> ("My Poets," *On the Edge*)

and pondered, almost struggling with it,

> One comes for answers to a
> place like this and finds even
> in the darkness, even in
> the sudden flooding of the
> headlights, that in time one comes
> to be a stranger to nothing.
> ("The Cemetery at Academy, California," *Not This Pig*)

and then, not rejected exactly,

> I am what I am,
> Last Sunday's dried peonies
> scattering over your ground.
> I want to blow you kisses
> and I blow you nothing.
> ("After the Revolution," *Red Dust*)

but assimilated and thereby transformed

> Out of beginning,
> I hear, under the sea roar, the bone words
> of teeth tearing earth and sea,

59

AUGUSTANA UNIVERSITY COLLEGE
LIBRARY

anointing the tongues with stone and sand,
water eating fish, fish water,
head eating head to let us be.

("To a Fish Head Found on the Beach near
Málaga," *They Feed They Lion*)

into a vision, rather than a philosophical stance, where pain and
wisdom are so ineffably combined and yet, because they feel
different, so separate, that it is important only to present, as a
storyteller would, and not explain the dichotomy:

How many times has she stared
into those eyes glistening
with love or pain
and seen nothing
but love or pain.

("The Poem Circling Hamtramck, Michigan
All Night in Search of You," *1933*)

The storyteller *presenting* life is the most important quality of
Philip Levine's poetry; it is not the simplistic tantalization pro-
vided by a tale-spinner: it is visionary. Because of his mastery of
this manner, I think *1933* is Levine's best book to date. The vision
is his, the voice is his, and the echoes of influence are no cause,
Mr. Bloom, for anxiety: the strains of Whitman, Neruda, Berry-
man, and George Oppen are not decorative clothing, but muscle
fibers. I would be tempted to call *1933* a climactic book, did I not
know that Levine is still writing good poems, even better ones—
for example, "To My God in His Sickness," which appeared
recently in the *New Yorker*. The fact of his continuing growth and
improvement as a poet moving through middle age makes him
exceptional among his contemporaries. The fact that *1933* deals
with one of literature's great concerns—death and the family—
better than any book of American poetry has ever done, ranks it
and Levine as more than just contemporary phenomena.

1933 is a book with heart and as such could have been a lachry-
mose piece of nostalgia; but when Levine weeps, and he has
never been afraid to speak of crying, the tears are not a blurring

wash of sentimentality, but hard grains of vision: pure salt. Robert Lowell's "Life Studies" was a breakthrough book, yet produced a cold wind that chilled but did not cling; it was "hollow," a word repeated by Lowell many times in those poems. The fine poems about relatives in Merwin's "Drunk in the Furnace" are satiric; the affection is bitter. I can think of one family poem that has *1933*'s greatness of heart, and that is Roethke's "Otto" in *The Far Field*. That is one poem, a terrific one, but *1933* is an entire book of such poems; its wholeness as a book in which the poems work separately or together, like chapters in a novel, is one of its triumphs.

I would like to say something about each of the poems in *1933*, since each is so rich, but that would be nothing more than a reading guide. For this book, which is so exact in its concerns—the death of a father, childhood in the Depression, the coming and continuing presence of World War II, adolescence during that war and adulthood in its shadow—it is better to generalize; I couldn't hope to reproduce the impact of the poems in prose. The range of form extends from beautifully self-contained portraits like "Zaydee" and "Grandmother in Heaven" to the various, all-inclusive arks like "Letters for the Dead" and the title poem. One of the powerful, unifying factors is that in all the poems Levine's voice, even when remembering his perceptions as a child, is that of an adult, an adult who has not only not forgotten what it is like to be a child, but how at five years old as at seventeen one is becoming an adult: the process is one of loss, in this book intensified by the loss of a father, and it is inexorable.

One more thing about *1933* that shows how surely Levine avoids the one pitfall, sentimentality, which could have ruined this book: a dead father is hard enough to write about, especially when he exists in the memory of a five-year-old boy; but his widow, the boy's mother, is even more difficult. "Late Moon," which is about the widowed mother's return home at 2 A.M. from a Detroit beer-garden dance, is one of the finest poems in the book. But for me, the most moving lines about her occur in "1933," the father's poem. They express much that is unforgettable about this book, its candor and affection:

There is the last darkness burning itself to death
   there are nine women come in the dawn with pitchers
   there is my mother
      a dark child in the schoolyard
      miles from anyone
      she has begun to bleed as her mother did . . .

   my mother prays for the horsecart to pass
   my mother prays to become fat and wise
      she becomes fat and wise.

RICHARD HOWARD

Centers of Attention

Comparison, when with others, is said to be invidious because it levels precisely those premises which should be, disparately, started from; when with oneself, comparison is merely . . . inevitable; compared with *They Feed They Lion,* Levine's new book is less splendid, though quite as sordid. What was wonderful about that last book—and what is missing, or missed, in this latest one—is just the conviction of splendor, the just conviction which balances and ransoms the conviction of sordor, the unjust conviction. Poets often suffer from, even exult over, the trough-of-the-wave syndrome in those organized articulations of their *oeuvre* they call their books, their volumes; the crest for Levine was certainly a poem like "Breath," which ended *They Feed They Lion* with these axiological pulsations:

> I give
> the world my worn-out breath
> on an old tune, I give
> it all I have
> and take it back again.

And the trough is here, when Levine apostrophizes "the world" with that same shuddering fall, the urgency of deprivation, that starved energy of shared lives brutalized by displacement, by promiscuous sociability rather than society, by labor rather than work, by agglomeration rather than cities. Addresses to flesh and bone, these poems work by breath, though they do not always "work," as I say—they break down, they break off, they break up:

"Centers of Attention" first appeared in *Poetry* (March, 1975), copyright 1975 by The Modern Poetry Association. Reprinted by permission of the Editor of *Poetry.*

                                          I hold you
        a moment in the cup
        of my voice,

and a moment may not be long enough; the cup runs over and
the world, so accosted, leaks away into the scandalous sands of
profane utterance. And yet. . . . It is so difficult a thing Levine
has undertaken, this balancing act of his, where at a certain
pitch of revering identification "one comes," as he said as long
ago as in *Not This Pig,* "to be a stranger to nothing." And the
more difficult because he does it by breathing, by that systole
and diastole of air taken in and given out, the impulse caught
up and released, which makes any equilibrium a danger, a suffo-
cation even. He wants, preposterously, to bless; he would trans-
form blasphemy into blessing by no more than making the
poem, by no less than uttering it—in all Indo-European lan-
guages, *to do* is initially *to revere,* and Levine's action would
have us know this:

        I am the eye filled with salt,
        his child climbing the rain, we are
        all the moon, the one planet, the hand
        of five stars flung on the night river.
                                          ("Hold Me")

He would have us know that if we are dismembered, we may—
in a total apprehension of magnificence, of terrestrial power—be
remembered. For if it is the *conviction* of splendor which fails in
1933, it is never the assumption. Levine has in fact enlarged his
premises, or brooded upon them till they are the more unmistak-
ably his, and therefore ours, in these indeterminate litanies. He
has breathed the world in and out, he has made the earth itself
the contents of a single infinite and eternal human body, his own:

        I shut my eyes
        and see my own legs stretching off
        like peninsulas, my chest
        and stomach bursting with rocks,
        groves, fields of tall grasses
        with black pools of water underneath.

> I keep them shut. Even the stars
> exploding won't open them.
>
> ("I Am Always")

That is the desperation, then: the apocalypse of closed eyes, whereas (last time round) they had been so observantly open. But I must not mistake an exhalation for a defeat, especially when I am admonished by the poet to such effect: "What I'm really trying to get at," Levine tells one interviewer, "is that American religious experience I see taking place and perhaps the kind of religious experience and sacrifice and violence that a land as extreme and intense as the American west is deserves."

Glints and glimpses, then, of that splendor which asks the terrible questions—"Why does the sea burn? Why do the hills cry?"—at the book's onset, and again, in what we may call (so vehement is the diction, so bitter the enjambments, the lack of solicitude for *keeping*) its on-slaught: "When will the grass be bread / when will the sea winds bring no salt." And a sordid conviction, as I note, that we are indeed judged, that we *deserve* the grim lives and gruelling loves we have let ourselves in for:

> Again at dawn I come home
> to my head on this pillow
> the coverlet frozen
> the fingers hidden, home
> to a name written in water.
>
> ("After")

It is only by pronouncing such *immondices,* as the French call them—the filth of the world which is against the world, which is unworldly—that we can create the world and endow it with our reverence, our informing faith. Levine *names,* and in his fragmentary devotions here he achieves a kind of splenetic salvation, he assumes the world, which is to say he takes it on as a filthy garment, and takes it on, too, as a challenger, "naming / the grains of the sea / and blessing. . . ."

ROBERT MAZZOCCO

From "Matters of Life and Death"

Over the last few years Philip Levine has become so striking a poet that I'm surprised he's not more highly valued than he is. Of course he always wrote forceful poems, but were they always so original? An early admired one, "That Distant Winter," seems now, in retrospect, not to be Levine at all, has varying echoes of Lowell, Jarrell, Trakl, and some of the dramatic properties of Lawrence's "The Prussian Officer," which probably inspired it. Another, equally admired, "On the Edge," sits with the ghost of Weldon Kees, who has haunted the poet elsewhere. But it's when we come to his latest collections, *They Feed They Lion,* published a few years ago, and the recent *1933,* that the particular Levine style and strategy continue almost uninterruptedly from page to page. The fine savagery of the earlier volume is manlier, more immediate in its appeal; the later volume is smoother, craftier, a bit muted, but is an advance, I think, deeper, certainly, and more humane.

Levine's is a daunting, brooding art, often without solace. Scorn and sympathy seem to be there in equal measure, "so much sorrow in hatred," as he says. The bonds of family, work, class, Levine as householder in America, knockabout wanderer in Spain, the wars of man and nature, wilderness and town— these are the different features of a difficult face, "human and ripe with terror"—and with knowledge. Recognition through confrontation, behavior under pressure—obviously these do not come easily to him.

An antagonistic strain, what he calls the "sour afterthought," rubs off on practically everything he touches. Essentially he's a poet of solitude, presents not "the bliss of solitude," Whitman's theme, but solitude as recoil from attachment or obligation, solitude that has him as a poet in middle age ruminating on rem-

New York Review of Books, April 3, 1975. Reprinted with permission.

nants of a boy's dream "of a single self / formed of all the warring selves split / off at my birth / and set spinning." And it is just these selves or their later incarnations—Levine as husband, father, friend—which he keeps discovering or despoiling again and again.

He manages, I suppose, two things probably better than any of his contemporaries, at least those born in the middle or late twenties. The old *mon semblable, mon frère* business of Baudelaire is given renewed American vigor in a number of his poems—for instance, "The Midget," "Baby Villon," "Angel Butcher," parts of "Silent in America." More important, he can create the sense of a milieu, the sound, feel, geography of a place, a time, a people, the flavor of what's been happening among us and what continues to happen, which seem to me almost totally lacking in most other serious poetry today. His portraits, in particular—those in *They Feed They Lion* and *1933*—are troubling, mysterious, delicate, wrathful, constitute a sort of litany of the industrial (Detroit) and immigrant (Jewish) backgrounds which formed him and follow him. They define the poet to himself and his world to us.

Here is Levine's grandmother in "her empty room in heaven," "beautiful Polish daughter / with a worn basket of spotted eggs," with

>. . . a curse

>for the bad back and the black radish
>and three quick spits for the pot.

Here are his uncles and cousins before a funeral in his childhood sitting in the kitchen, seeming "strange / in their serious suits / and shirts, holding / their hands on the table," his mother, with a black fox stiffening at her throat, saying " 'The good die young' / not to me or anyone." Here are the teenagers of the poet's youth, the Angels of Detroit, where the toilets overflow and "the worms of money / crack like whips," the desperate frolics of "long Eddie," the little clown, "the yellows of his eyes / brown on pot," who

never did nothing right
except tell the cops to suck
and wave them off like flies.

Here are the ordinary nightmares of the suburbs, the housewives and their TV sets, "the bullets sucking quietly in their cradles," or the "ice and steel raining / from the foundries in a shower / of human breath," the grundgy roads of the metropolis where "the gates are closing / at Dodge Main / and Wyandotte / Chemical," where the workers are returning to their houses

> to watch the kids
> scrub their brown
> faces or grease
> cartridges for
> the show down.

Here is the world of "Automotive in the city of dreams," where you can learn a job that takes you thirty minutes to learn and then you can work at that job for the next thirty years and then they retire you at fifty or fifty-five and this is heaven, this is life. Here is the black man Luther with his old black Lincoln, "watching the radiator bare its muddy wounds":

> Luther
> rolling his sleeves up
> high and cupping his long
> hillbilly fingers around
> a flaring match, Luther
> cocking his tattoo
> against the black rain and
> the rain of black luck, Luther
> pushing on toward
> the jewelled service station
> of free cokes
> and credit there ahead
> in a heaven of blue
> falling and nothing
> going to make him cry
> for nothing . . .

> ("Cry for Nothing")

Machinery that doesn't work, clothes that fall apart—the old American story growing newer every day. But Levine subverts these sociological images, decor of the depressions, past or present, his "drifters in a drifting crowd," contrasts them with his own pervasive subjectivity, sings as does the midget in the terrible café in Barcelona—"sings of Americas, / of those who never returned / and those who never left."

His poems, moreover, have a startling contiguity to physical detail, invest objects and things with human feelings and human characteristics, a practice once disdained as the pathetic fallacy but which works well for him, as it does more and more in these crazy times for his contemporaries. His descriptive method is a mechanics of action often both natural and surreal, or guardedly hallucinatory in the manner of Latin American verse, though minus the usual blur: stones that gleam with "the warm light of an absent star," "fish head and man head" on a shore in Spain "communing in their tongue," small boats with "orange and scarlet hulls, / unblinking eyes / and bared teeth flashing / on the prows," eventless eventful days among mountains where "the first pale ice plants dot / the slopes like embroidery." These suggest for the poet the weight of human contact, or set him to seek those moments of rest always at the edge of things where

> words become,
> like prayer, a kind of nonsense
> which becomes the thought of our lives, . . .

or where he can create elegies to a damaged past, where "the lie is retold in the heart" and "the scars shine" for good:

> she married and unmarried
> flushed and aborted
> she wrote
> *The jar that stood so high*
> *broke*
> *and fell away*
> she showed the words to everyone
>
> he whispered into the dead phone
> *I'm from Dearborn and I'm drunk*

The tenor and power of the language are often colloquial, yet subtly, sparsely musical too. Musical, I suppose, in the traditional sense that the words on the page always await their proper pitch, can only be arranged in a certain way, deviate from the necessary sequence and the mood is not sustained, the melody lost. And that's important since Levine's metaphors are not always the strongest, his subject matter can seem repetitive or astringent. One really has to *believe* what he says, the way the breath shapes its particular truth. And I do (which doesn't always happen when I read poets).

"Later Still," the demonic "Children's Crusade," and "They Feed They Lion," "Dark Rings," "The Poem Circling Hamtramck, Michigan All Night in Search of You," "Ruth," "Going Home," "Zaydee," "Hold Me," the unusually psalmic, almost apocalyptic title-poem of his latest book, and from earlier collections, "The Horse" and "The Cemetery at Academy, California"—these seem to me pretty nearly perfect in their distillation and achieved cadence, the structure of the poems often clean as a whistle, but the emotions in them deep and dark as a cave.

Levine, though, has one particular fault. Naturally he's a master of *la belle indifférence,* but that sort of stoical orneriness can become, I think, a bit of a trick. A few of the poems, especially those in *They Feed They Lion,* affect an odd air of concealment and exposure, reminiscent of the American thriller, the taut abrupt tone of Bogart with his buried vein of idealism, the Bogart who says, "Don't be too sure I'm as crooked as I'm supposed to be." It's that sort of cockiness, and the threatening calm behind it, that makes him laugh at, for instance, what he calls those "twitch-nosed academic pants-pisser poets" of the fifties, or that has him count a bit monotonously the cost and grit of experience, insisting upon its value even while chafing against it, or has him write declamatory phrases that sound great but don't always make much sense: "I shit handfuls of earth." Still he's obviously a rugged burdened animal. The best of his obsessions seem to me always muscular, always authentic, his characteristic posture being, in fact, that of a horse in harness, moving restively backward or sidewise, who balks but endures.

Whitman saying that "to speak in literature with the perfect rectitude and insouciance of the movements of animals and the unimpeachableness of the sentiment of trees in the woods and grass by the roadside is the flawless triumph of art"—well of course Levine doesn't have that invincibility, lacks the sweep and companionability of Whitman's lines, his orchestrations on the Infinite. Levine is preeminently a poet of the finite, of "one more day" or "one more time," locked in his own sense of fatefulness, his special creed that "each has his life / private and sealed," whether with others or apart from others, locked too in certain recurring emphases, terms, phrases: fingers, moon, horse cart, hankie, black pit. (*Black:* If I had a dollar for every time Levine uses that adjective, I'd have more money than I expect to get on my rebate from Ford.)

Yet though his poems are not inclusive, though they are built on a continual narrowing down of sentiment or comment, the incompatibilities in them—the opposition between grievance and balm, fierceness and tenderness, between himself "made otherwise" by another's pain—do ultimately merge, as they do in Whitman, although not in joyous surrender, but simply of necessity. We learn of the recoveries the poet makes in the dark with the dark, affectionate in his hate, hard in his compassion. Levine is a poet who speaks of "growing up and losing / the strange things we never / understood and settling," yet who is always drawn to what is most strange, most unsettling. He knows that each experience we have had or we remember denies another experience, another life we might have had and might have remembered in its place. He knows too that great heart, skill, and sorrow are the poet's weapons, defining the self negatively by what is let go, positively by what is held on to; and then beyond that there is the twilit other world where the negative and the positive seem to be twins of the same coin, where the poet is both victor and victim, and at times blessed because he is both:

> In May, like this May, long ago
> my tiny Russian Grandpa—the bottle king—
> cupped a stained hand under my chin
> and ran his comb through my golden hair.

Sweat, black shag, horse turds on the wind,
the last wooden cart rattling down
the alleys, the clop of his great gray mare,
green glass flashing in December sun . . .

I am the eye filled with salt,
his child climbing the rain, we are
all the moon, the one planet, the hand
of five stars flung on the night river.

CHRISTOPHER BUCKLEY

Levine's *1933*

The latest collection of poems by Philip Levine, *1933* makes at once a subtle and fantastic departure from his four previous books. The tip of the iceberg, or the most obvious change in Levine's poetry, occurs in his use of imagery. A number of the poems in *1933* are charged by, and pivot on, the fantastic or quasi-surrealistic image—the image influenced partially by Spanish poetry of a Lorca or Neruda. On the other hand, there is a deeper change in attitude, emotion, subject and texture, which Levine's turn in imagistic method brings about. This deeper change is the more subtle, and, in a very real sense, it is an extension of method rather than a "change" per se. A freer style and a more personally accessible stance as regards emotion, increase slightly in each of Levine's books; however, *1933* contains more of these qualities than anything previous. The use of the surrealist image can also be traced to earlier books—(*Red Dust*, 1971, was heavily steeped in the more open surrealistic method). So, while in some sense *1933* is nothing new under the sun, it is something different, something deftly changed. The strength of this volume lies in a synthesis of Levine's tough and yet compassionate vision into hard and real things of the world (the movement inward), and a more clearly enunciated cosmic awareness found in the potentialities of the Lorca-like image (the movement outward). Levine is then able to handle a subject matter consistently more personal and emotional than ever before. To be sure, there are poems in *1933* that rely more on Levine's characteristic acerbic and direct poetic method, and there are those that depend more on the surrealistic image. However, the emotional content and stance of the poems offers and sustains a texture richer than either method alone.

Levine's poetry has always been characterized by a firm and

Margins, September 10, 1975.

tenacious grasp of external objects. His ability to absorb himself in them results in the mind of the poet becoming the thing itself. The identity, or ego centered "I," of the poet becomes transparent and Levine shows us, opens from the inside out, the raw objects of the world. The real marvel is that the reader sees so clearly into things and at the same time experiences an undercurrent of raw and powerful feeling. This emotion is tough and defiant, acute, and yet at the same time it implies compassion for everyone with similar experiences. Very early in his career Levine said that he wanted a poem that would be harsh, natural, and somehow powerful without employing a heightened vocabulary. The poems of his first two books, *On the Edge* (1963) and *Not This Pig* (1968), not to mention the titles themselves, are incredibly lean and biting—they drive directly to the bitter heart of experience.

Levine continued this direct and fiercely empathetic vein, still handling a variety of subject matter, into his fourth book, *They Feed They Lion* (1972). Occasionally the subjects of the poems would be autobiographical, about his sons or wife. But most often Levine would show us ourselves in terms of the external objects of the world. In "Renaming the Kings," rocks relate as mythic elements of the earth, relate in human pain, myth and blood, like sons. Levine uses the power of all the used parts of our country—the gas stations, junked cars, slag heaps, and burning stacks of Detroit. He gives us the clarity from within and he gives it to us straight and hard—he is defiant.

1933 shifts the subject matter of his poems and the imagistic manner in which he deals with it. It is almost totally autobiographical, heavily centered on the poet's personal experience with family or the absence of family. We are not shown things, objects, the hard realities of the world, so much as we are shown experiences and people. Subsequently, these poems are more highly personal, lyrical. These poems are still lean, athletic, but there is a change in attitude—we have Levine's highly sensitive ear and gift for language, but there is more compassion than anger.

An interesting comparison between *1933* and Levine's first book, *On the Edge,* arises in the different images of the father or fatherhood. 1933 is the year Levine lost his father and in a way the central emotive focal point of the book. But his view of his father is tender, poignant, replete with dramatic detail that renders the emotion without sentimentality, but nevertheless tender. At once, we have the emotion of the child for father and the father for child—we have the personal and the metaphysical. The image of fatherhood in "Night Thoughts over a Sick Child" (*On the Edge*) is one of anger and defiance. This change, concomitant with the change in imagistic method/treatment of concrete detail, is probably best explained by Levine himself. Levine spoke of this shift in attitude in an interview with poets Glover Davis and Dennis Saleh in late 1971, which later appeared in *American Poetry Review.*

I want to be a poet of joy as well as suffering. If you look at *On the Edge* you find poetry of someone on the edge, on the edge of despair, the edge of breakdown, on the edge of his culture, of his own life. The image of fatherhood in that book is the image of the father, scared, hovering over the sick child, and furious at creation for afflicting the child. I think later I'm more likely to cherish the child no matter what he is.

This turn in emotional attitude, the more gentle texture of Levine's new poems, is most easily seen in the last part of the title poem, "1933."

> my father opens the telegram under the moon
>   Cousin Philip is dead
>   my father stands on the porch in his last summer
>   he holds back his tears
>   he holds back my tears
>
> Once in childhood the stars held still all night
>   the moon swelled like a plum but white and silken
>   the last train from Chicago howled through the ghetto
>   I came downstairs
>   my father sat writing in a great black book
>   a pile of letters
>   a pile of checks
>   (he would pay his debts)
>   the moon would die
>   the stars jelly
>   the sea freeze
>   I would be a boy in worn shoes splashing through rain

The view of the father is specific, accurate, but tender—there is great compassion, "he holds back his tears / he holds back my tears," "he would pay his debts." The poem ends on an emotional tone of solitude, abandonment, personal anguish, but there is no anger or defiance at the world. Levine is not angry with his father for his absence but rather offers us a vision of a father we can cherish with him. We have the image, almost archetypal, of an emotional communion we all desire and we all lose.

Also in this poem and in all of the poems of *1933*, the rhythms are not as driving and tight as before, the forms not as strict. A natural and graceful line length and rhythm reinforce the material and its more subjective topics. The rhythms and lines do in fact relent. The reader is not overwhelmed and overpowered as he was in the magnificent title poem of *They Feed They Lion*. But these poems have power, a subtle power of genuine empathy— one arising out of a larger vision of the human condition. Their power comes from the sense of life they give forth—a sense that arises from intense feeling for the major phases of existence, love and death.

In the same interview mentioned above, Levine referred to the freer and more open forms he was using after returning from Spain. The implication was that he abandoned the more formal structures for more natural forms fitting the content that arises more and more out of the subconscious:

> I think that what I was beginning to learn, not just to articulate, but to learn, was that there were things in me that would create poems and I would just have to follow them, and I began to write less from a sense of identifying myself, "This is Philip Levine! This is the way he structures a poem." I was sort of listening to things as they came out and I followed them.

The change in attitude and the extension of rhythmical and structural methods alone are not enough to create nuance in a more or less subject-mainstream of contemporary verse, i.e., autobiography. Where Levine really succeeds in the poems of *1933* is in combining the aforementioned changes with the touches of surrealist image and symbol. This style of symbol enables Levine to go from the personal to the metaphysical—to give us the emotive content of a situation and then spiral it outward through the image to a larger consciousness. Levine moves all collective experience in empathy toward his vision. This final imaginative movement outward, effected through the surrealist image, helps to objectify essentially subjective energies and experiences. This movement sheds any trace of sentimentality and raises autobiography to contemporary myth, to a larger consciousness emblematic of our history.

I would emphasize that these poems have surrealist "touches." This is to say that they are not surrealist poems, but rather that a few well-chosen images integrate with the direct narrative imagery to give us something new. A fine example of this skillfully handled imagery occurs in the section of the title poem from *1933* quoted earlier. From the narrative of the child watching his father write, facing the future of his loss, Levine moves us to the overwhelming implication of death and loss: "the moon would die / the stars jelly / the sea freeze." In the last line Levine combines the personal image of the boy and the archetypal element of the rain to convey the emotion of abandonment as well as the depth of his vision of our relation to the universe/void. The moon dying, the stars going to jelly, etc., are not the usual Levine imagistic moves, not the profound *concrete* images of his earlier work. And I have chosen the term surrealistic because that is the closest word, generically associative, to *how* the images function. However, while I feel that this type of image has been influenced by the Spanish surrealist poetics, I in no way feel any of the images in *1933* are in debt to that movement. For example, I find very few images as radically disjunctive as many of Lorca's. Even when Levine does arrive at images of sharply juxtaposed realities, these are all tempered and qualified by an essential emotional tone rather than by fantasy or singular vision.

A good specific image to examine, indicative of this shift in imagery, is that of the river. In "Alone," a poem from *They Feed They Lion,* the poet is "following a broken trail of stones / toward the deep and starless river." In the last poem in *1933,* "Hold Me," the river blends with another image and takes a more inclusive stance: ". . . we are / all the moon, the one planet, the hand / of five stars flung on the night river." In both instances the final movement of the poem is outward toward the symbolism of an emotional state signified by the surrounding landscape. But in the first poem we stay on the earth, beautifully concrete and tied down. In the poem from *1933* we move out to the stars with the planets, we approach the cosmos.

In the opening poem of *1933,* "Zaydee," Levine begins with this type of image. He invokes the larger elements and aspects of the earth, gives them a shade of surrealism to support and accent the sense of loss: "Why does the sea burn? Why do the hills cry?"

In his poem "War," Levine again uses this technique. The images are grounded in possibly the hardest of all realities, the particulars of war and their effects on the people at home as well as the bleeding soldier. The more surreal and almost translucent image comes in at the end of the poem. The reader is given a vision wherein the workers go out of factories and movies back into their lives, but not into life. They are transformed, almost into death itself, they move as shades or ghosts.

> December 1942
> a bleeding soldier in a torn jacket
> waits at the back of a diner
> no one asks him anything
> dead horses blaze in the cold, wheels
> lock, crates of secret wings slide forward
> in the guarded hallways children stand
> for hours holding their metal trays
> downtown the workers sleep in the movies
> their heads hung back over the seats
> their mouths wet and calling
> when the darkness spreads from the factories
> oiling everything, they waken
> not as ghosts of women
> black and white, dancing in tears
> but as themselves and go out
> into the streets past the beer gardens
> where the sisters burn like salt
> and they remember nothing

What Levine accomplishes in *1933* in extending his methods is to focus on an event or object and at the same time to extend the vision. One of my favorite poems in the book is "Once in May,"

in which the imagery appears to be very direct, specifically focal-
ized, and yet at the same time becomes translucent, delicate,
ethereal. There is a communion with the larger aspects of nature.
Standing in the water the night arrives with the moon and stars
and in a moment of epiphany the poet is annointed by them all.
He touches life almost at an elevated or psychic level of energy.
At the same instant he is reminded of death and/or mortality and
the force of life beyond that mortality by the fish and the fisher-
man. By the conclusion of the poem the poet knows that the
earth is not all there is, only a part.

> Once in May the earth seemed
> all there was, all
> there had to be, and I waited
> at the sea's edge not counting
> anything, and after a while
> walked in, my white pants darkening,
> my shirt going soft, fountain pen,
> billfold, letters, notes,
> small change all slipped away
> and I was no one, a boy
> laughing at the hidden stars,
> a boy jeered by a mob
> of Spanish boys. I stood
> all afternoon under heaven
> with water in my pockets,
> salt in my socks, naming
> the grains of the sea
> and blessing the kids,
> until the face of the waves
> deepened and the winds came
> shuddering in and I huddled
> under a blanket and sang.
> The moon rose slowly
> showing its broken face,
> the ring of stars climbed
> to the tips of my fingers,
> one bright planet crowned my hair
> and hummed until dawn.
> The sea gray and sliding,

small boats coming in,
the men tired, gray, unloading
hake, merluza, squid in handfuls,
sea bass, prawns, sword fish,
great finned flat fillets,
the cold meats of the deep.

There are poems in *1933* that lean more to the direct visceral discovery of Levine's earlier books ("Letters for the Dead"), and occasionally a poem that favors the more surreal environment of *Red Dust*. But by and large, all the poems have been tempered by a new attitude and method—one more visionary with a latitude encompassing personal subjects and elevating autobiography to a universal awareness. Levine's new style is subtle and brilliant— it is highly personal and yet somewhat fantastic. Levine synthesizes the concrete and the cosmic and produces "the one planet, the hand / of five stars. . . ."

CHERYL WALKER

From "Looking Back, Looking Forward"

To move from Robert Penn Warren's *Or Else* to Philip Levine's *1933* is to shift from a rural to an urban landscape. Here everything means more than it means not in the way of eternal verities but in the way of Detroit junkyards burning souls black beyond recognition. Suddenly there are people going to work, a poor couple driving across Ohio eating cold candy bars; there are rats and all-night car lots. "A strange star / is born one more time."

Although Levine's landscapes are apt to be grimier than Warren's, the pace of his poems quicker, less reminiscent, Levine is also looking backward here. Like Warren, he too is retracing his steps in hope of finding "the sacraments we waited for," which, however, in Levine's world cannot be recaptured between ticks of the clock. Instead they

> go gray
> little flat sacks of refuse
> and no one can look
> or look away

I must say that I don't find this book as impressive as Levine's last collection, *They Feed They Lion*. Nothing here so good as that "Salami," made of

> Stomach of goat, crushed
> sheep balls, soft full
> pearls of pig eyes,
> . . . .

"Looking Back, Looking Forward" first appeared in *The Nation*, September 13, 1975. Copyright 1975 by The Nation Company, Inc. Reprinted with permission.

mountain thyme, basil,
paprika, and knobs of garlic.
And if a tooth of stink thistle
pulls blood from the round
blue marbled hand
all the better for
this ruby of Pamplona,
this bright jewel of Vich,
this stained crown
of Solsona, this
salami.

Too much of *1933* is an exploration of territory already explored.
Haven't we all had those strange, difficult fathers, those mothers
trapped in strange difficulties? Why didn't they teach us more
about ourselves then? Why can't they teach us more now?

But where Levine is good in this book, in "Grandmother in
Heaven," for instance, or "Ruth" or "Death Bearing," he fulfills
the promise of *They Feed They Lion*. His shuttle passes outward
toward pattern, toward destiny, and turns back, catching at the
knot in the silk. He is always specific but never trivial. His
incidents capture in a small space with unusual power both War-
ren's mysterious experiential hover and the hawklike snap of the
vertebrae so characteristic of contemporary poets. Here is the
end of "Goodbye," which describes a little boy's confrontation
with death, his waking to the presence of uncles and cousins, "all
the beds empty and made / but mine." We never know precisely
who it is who has died, but Mama—"with long black gloves /
coming out her sleeves / and a black fox / stiffening at her
throat" says: "The good die young." After the boredom and
strain of the funeral, in the first light of the following day:

I opened my eyes
and the gauze curtains
were streaming.
"Come here," the sparrow said.
I went. In the alley below
a horse cart piled with bags,
bundles, great tubs of fat,
brass lamps the children broke.

I saw the sheenie-man pissing
into a litle paper fire
in the snow, and laughed.
The bird smiled. When I unlatched
the window the bird looked back
three times over each shoulder
then shook his head.
He was never coming back inside,
and rose in a shower
of white dust above
the blazing roofs
and telephone poles.

It meant a child
would have to leave the world.

CALVIN BEDIENT

From "Four American Poets"

The drama of Levine's career lies in his movement away from his origins—industrial and Jewish immigrant, bereft and skeptical—toward American romanticism, that faith of the senses in an intimate bigness beyond even the bigness of the land. From Detroit, a "city pouring fire," to "the one stove of earth"—such has been his progress.

"The first Jew was God," he wrote at the outset, in *On the Edge* (1964); "the second / Denied him; I am alive." History had left him nothing, so it seemed, except a legacy of horror, such as the horse that survived Hiroshima "without skin, naked, hairless, without eyes and ears, searching for the stableboy's caress." Like the classic American he was beginning anew, but not trustingly. Quite the contrary: "And I say 'balls,' / the time will never come," says one of the tough burned poems of *Not This Pig* (1968), "nor ripeness be all." Would he turn to bite the boy who led him to market? "No. Not this pig."

Yet by the third volume, *Red Dust* (1971), he was saying, "A man has every place to lay his head." In this poem and that, one could see forming the vast innocence, the sensuously crucified mysticism, of the romantic. The more Levine came to know of time and death the more he loved and was warmed by the "one stove"—and the more he needed to save things from its consumption. In words from his next volume, *They Feed They Lion* (1972), he developed the "ferocity of pig driven to holiness." He fed he lioned. His subject, when he could get past his finite griefs, was "the one poem born / of the eternal and always going back."

In *1933* the "one poem" consists, in part, of the natural world, its usual American form. The triumphant instance is "Once in May"; then "the earth seemed / all there was, all / there had to

Sewanee Review 84 (1976). Reprinted with permission.

be," and the poet stood with water in his pockets, salt in his socks, "naming / the grains of the sea."

> The moon rose slowly
> showing its broken face,
> the ring of stars climbed
> to the tips of my fingers,
> one bright planet crowned my hair
> and hummed until dawn.
> The sea gray and sliding,
> small boats coming in,
> the men tired, gray, unloading
> hake, merluza, squid in handfuls,
> sea bass, prawns, sword fish,
> great finned flat fillets,
> the cold meats of the deep.

The murderous variety of the many, the irrefragable One—both press their reality upon him. His poem simply bears it, stretched between pain and ecstasy.

But for Levine (and here he is exceptional as a romantic) the "one poem" is also human beings, above all his family. He is with Whitman and James Agee, his spiritual distinction an immense tenderness for those who have come near him. The romanticism of *1933* lies in part in remembered love—in love that time has transmuted into ecstasy. So it is, for instance, in the final poem, "Hold Me":

> In May, like this May, long ago
> my tiny Russian Grandpa—the bottle king—
> cupped a stained hand under my chin
> and ran his comb through my golden hair.
>
> Sweat, black shag, horse turds on the wind,
> the last wooden cart rattling down
> the alleys, the clop of his great gray mare,
> green glass flashing in December sun. . . .

And then, suddenly, space calls together the above and below and time closes back on itself, on a child defying mortality, separation, loss:

I am the eye filled with salt,
his child climbing the rain, we are
all the moon, the one planet, the hand
of five stars flung on the night river.

So in parts of *1933* Levine turns back to his childhood as to the gate to sempiternity. Back to 1933, when his father died, and back to the subtly doomed subsequent years. And indeed he finds he is "always a boy swimming up / through the odors of beer and dreams / to hear my name shivering / on the window. Beside me mother / curls on her side. . . ."

Then, again, he is not that boy, any more than he can really climb the rain: "The table is cleared of my place / and cannot remember." He enters a bedroom and his father, it may be, looks up but sees nothing. "Was I dust that I should fall?"

Once he was diffuse enough to confuse himself with others and now, in making this family album, he is the many in search of the one he may have been, the one in search of the many he was. And if finally, in the closing lines, he succeeds in being borne up by the past, it is only by having first been weighed down by it, painfully, throughout the book. Memory, *1933* shows us, is the least if the last of romantic kingdoms, because the ally as well as the adversary of separation and death.

Levine's manner has altered with his matter—indeed has at last become part of it. At first, rather than merging with, rather than transforming its subjects, it presented them. If poetic enough by conventional standards, his voice had a clothes-hanger stiffness, the intentionality of a diagram: "I have not found peace / but I have found I am where / I am by / being only there, / by standing in the clouded presence of the things I observe."

Gradually Levine learned to entice the reader into his words, so as to dream them. And finally he could write a line as bafflingly simple and right, as inexhaustible, as "his child climbing the rain." How grasp such a line except with a thrill of the emotional imagination?

Levine developed a unique manner of plain emotional language and braced rhythms. He was spare with adjectives, so that old romantic properties—dawn, moon, stars, roots, stones, sun, ocean, trees, darkness, burning, angels, snow, rain, eyes—emerged with a contemporary astringency. The thrifty procedure gave an effect of precision. Once perfected in *They Feed They Lion,* the result was both chaste and lyrical. And as in these lines on his father it could turn the ordinary into miracle:

> Dusk is a burning
> of the sun.
> West of Chowchilla
> The Lost Continent of Butterflies
> streams across the freeway.
> Radiators crusted,
> windshields smeared with gold
> and you come on
> rising into the moons
> of headlights.
>
> ("Losing You")

In *1933,* with its hazards of nostalgia, the style occasionally lapses, it is true, into the infantile, the fey—as in "Why do the hills cry?" and "After the water bled / the toad grew a shell" and "the stars are burned eyes that see." The mode pretends the wonder that is elsewhere painstakingly earned. Yet for the most part the style is unusually pure, with a mature taste behind it, the pathetic element subtly risked and judged. "And a breeze woke / from the breathing river"—such is its typical tenor, reticently oracular.

Levine's words now join those before them as if this were the sweetest pleasure, with a pull and affinity and satisfaction of contact like magnetism. The poet's ear for sequence has become impeccable. A few simple words, a little alliteration or assonance, some clearly delineated rhythms—somehow from these humble ingredients again and again a consummate irresistible order is formed.

No one has managed short lines better or broken them with a surer hand. Here is a passage on fishing boats from "One by One":

> All afternoon
> they steamed on the sand
> and the fishermen dozed
> in the buzzing shade and woke

blinking in the first
chill winds. Now
in the deepening rose
of day's end, they slide
into the breakers and bob out
to meet the moon.

Almost every line-break justly emphasizes the local meaning.
Typically the sinuous syntactical forms play the short lines for a
raised yet restrained lyricism. And the pauses yield a suspense
that is like the awaiting of a revelation.

The chief limitation of the manner is its undying poignancy.
Telling us over and over how all life excites and hurts in the same
way since it is all caught up in the same coming and going, it
makes the volume virtually "one poem" but by proving much of
a sameness. The poems, too, are cut alike. They linger among
memories and close either in imitation of death or, conversely,
with an absolving embrace of all that has been, is now, or will
be. Monotony is avoided only by frequent changes of scene and
cast and by the continual creative pilgrimage of the language.

On the other hand the holding power of Levine's taut manner
is so great that he can risk the "flung" structures which his love
of the "one poem" incites. His poems reflect the indetermination
of memory. They feel their way. A few—"I've Been Asleep,"
"Harvest," "One by One"—juxtapose adventure and death, plea-
sure and pain, uncompromisingly, in separate sections. The pro-
cedure is interestingly bold but not quite satisfying: we cannot
make the ends meet; the parts remain fractional. The more tradi-
tional structure of "Once in May" merges contraries without
annihilating them, and here we feel the striking iron of vision.

I wish that Levine would cease starting poems over near the
end, as in "Bad Penny" (which yet ends wonderfully) and "War"
(which ends in an apocalyptic bash). The practice seems to elbow
aside what has already been composed. For the rest, even his
most innovative structures pay their way, uncertain as their neces-
sity, their triumphs, may be. In all *1933* is at once daring and
exquisite: an extraordinary volume.

STEPHEN YENSER

Bringing It Home

Auden once observed that every poem testifies to a rivalry between Ariel and Prospero. Ariel urges the poet to make "a verbal paradise, a timeless world of pure play" that affords some relief from the historical world with all its dilemmas and suffering. Prospero, concerned more with truth than with beauty, exhorts him to reveal life as it really is, to bring us face to face with "the problematic, the painful, the disorderly, the ugly" and thus to "free us from self-enchantment and deception." While any poem will owe something to each of these advocates, it is usually possible to decide whether a poem and occasionally whether a poet is "Ariel-dominated" or "Prospero-dominated." Few have listened as attentively to Prospero as Philip Levine. Ariel sometimes draws him aside, but Levine is too much a product of the fallen world to be comfortable for long in the realm of "pure play."

"If you want to die you will have to pay for it": Charon's caveat, as set down by Louis MacNeice, could be inscribed above the exit from the world of Levine's poems. Inhabited by exhausted blue-collar workers and derelicts, desperate young toughs, convicts, and bone-weary housewives, it is all bleared and smeared with toil and pain. Selections from Doré's *Inferno* illustrations might have accompanied the poems in Levine's most recent and grimly impressive volume. Here people wake to "the cold anger / of machines that have to eat"; there a harmless old bum gets a beating from the cops; near by, "Covered / with dust, rags over / their mouths," farm workers "go out in open trucks / to burn in the fields." For Levine, the plight of the man in "Waiting," convicted on the testimony of a lying witness and sweating out the ninth year of his sentence, merely exaggerates an all too common condition.

Parnassus: Poetry in Review 6 (1977). Reprinted with permission.

Since that condition is political, so is much of Levine's poetry, as he had to insist in a recent *Partisan Review*. His interviewer, admiring Levine's work and wanting to save it from itself, suggested that poems about lonely, depressed people who want to give up but find themselves enduring need not be political. Levine responded that "an accurate depiction of people's lives as they are actually lived" (Prospero's means precisely) must itself be "a political act" in our society. He continued:

I mean, what are the sources of anger in a lot of the poems that I write and that a lot of people write? The sources of anger are frequently social, and they have to do with the fact that people's lives are frustrated, they're lied to, they're cheated, that there is no equitable handing out of the goods of this world. A lot of the rage that one encounters in contemporary poetry has to do with the political facts of our lives.

The American poets who might subscribe enthusiastically to that statement seem to me comparatively few—Allen Ginsberg, Imamu Amiri Baraka, and in certain moods Robert Bly, Galway Kinnell, Adrienne Rich, Robert Lowell—and none sounds much like Levine. When he speaks of "the agony of living" he is thinking chiefly of the life of the working class in a system in which "the people in power have no compassion." While his own compassionate skepticism saves him from being narrowly partisan, Levine is our notable heir to the radicalism of the 1930s, a descendant of Henry Roth who has read Neruda and Vallejo closely.

He said in the same interview that he gets "ideas that encompass more than one poem at a time, that almost reach out to the idea of the whole thing" that he wants to write about in a book. Thus Buenaventura Durruti, the leader of the left wing of the anarchist movement during the Spanish Civil War, to whom Levine dedicates *The Names of the Lost,* stands at the center of this volume. My guess is that the cover photograph—of a line of men, faces half-shadowed, marching through a desert—pictures Durruti's column. Levine follows his dedication, in any case, with an epigraph—*"and the world he said is growing here in my heart this moment"*—that echoes Durruti's comments in an interview published in the Toronto *Star* in September, 1936. Since they help us to see Durruti as Levine does, they warrant fuller quotation here. The interviewer had just warned that a leftist victory might leave all of Spain in ruins, and Durruti replied:

> We have always lived in slums and holes in the wall. We will know how to accommodate ourselves for a time. For, you must not forget, we can also build. It is we who built these palaces and cities, here in Spain and America and everywhere else. We, the workers, we can build others to take their places. And better ones. We are not in the least afraid of ruins. We are going to inherit the earth. . . . We carry a new world, here, in our hearts. That world is growing this very moment.

He was to die soon in the defense of Madrid, perhaps shot by one of his own men, and within a few years Fascism had all but choked out that new growth everywhere in Spain.

Prospero counsels realism; Levine's epigraph is no declaration of faith. Seen in the light of many of these poems, it might even be read as a bitterly mocking epitaph, not only for Durruti and the *anarquistas* but also for the vision behind the movement. Levine recalls Durruti's vow in a derisive passage in "Gift for a Believer." In a friend's vision Durruti whispered that he would never forget his comrades "who died believing they carried / a new world there in their hearts"—but when Durruti died, "he forgot." Levine knows how lesser exigencies paralyze conviction: later in this poem he tells how he once swore never to forget an early, radicalizing experience at the Chevy plant, and yet eventually "the memory slept, and I bowed / my head so that I might live." If Durruti's faith survives today, he implies, it survives as tenuously as the wretched garden at the end of "Autumn Again," where "Down the oiled path of cans / and inner tubes in the field / by the river" a young mechanic struggles to keep his beans and herbs alive.

The garden recurs so often in *The Names of the Lost* that it becomes a unifying element closely related to the *"world growing here in my heart this moment."* The poet's wife almost always appears tending her plants ("New Season," "Autumn Again," "The Falling Sky," "Another Life," "My Son and I"), as though she embodied Durruti's spirit, or as though the growth he envisioned depended upon such steady, intense devotion. Levine's own detachment from the family garden reminds us that he has little faith in a new world, and the advent of the "New Season" seems to bear him out. While "the future grows / like a scar," the garden, so painstakingly cultivated each day, suffers at night the slow fury of the snails: "the rhododendrons shrivel / like paper under water, all / the small secret mouths are feeding / on the green heart of the plum." Surely Levine is playing those lines against the memory, continually imperiled, of Durruti's words. But of course—and from this qualification spring both the tension and the occasional self-righteousness in this book—Levine does finally remember. Nullifidian though he might be, he has his own plot, as the poems prove. His grafting of irony on to idealism is an attempt to develop a sustaining belief. As he says in "For the Poets of Chile," "Someone / must remember it over / and over, must bring / it all home and rinse / each crushed cell / in the waters of our lives."

The need to bring it all home, in both senses, shapes a number of these poems, including "For the Fallen," a moving elegy for Durruti, and "And the Trains Go On." In "For the Fallen" Levine remembers not only the Spanish Civil War but also his relationship to it, which he could not then have known, as a boy of eight. He first focuses on the burial of Durruti (Joaquín Ascaso was the President of the Council of Aragon, another anarchist leader) and then cuts to an image of himself, on the threshold of learning, less from history books than from the working people he grew up among, something about exploitation of labor:

> The comrades must have known
> it was over, and Joaquín
> Ascaso, staring at the earth
> that had opened so quickly
> for his brothers, must
> have whispered *soon*.
> Soon the boy rose
> from his desk and went
> into the darkness
> congealing in cold parlours
> or in the weariness
> of old pistons, in the gasps
> of men and women asleep
> and dreaming as the bus

stalls and starts on the way
home from work.

Technically austere, as befits both the scene and Prospero's tem-
perament, this passage is nonetheless subtly put together. The
images in its narrow gauge lines flow as smoothly as in a film.
Like much of his work, it calls up Eisenstein, some grainy black
and white silent picture (for Levine's work is unusually chiaros-
curist, his people rarely speak), the point of its montage unmistak-
ably political. The covert analogy between the uneasy sleepers
and the poorly running engine implies and implicates a society in
which people with dreams but no power become worn parts in
the machinery. As the boy rises from the desk, years pass; and
with the unobtrusive shift in tense the past dissolves into the
present, elegy into indictment. Levine sometimes considers Dur-
ruti's acts alms for oblivion, but he cannot forget their pertinence.

This volume's title, just near enough paradox to snag the
attention, joins these barely reconcilable feelings. It derives from
"And the Trains Go On," a highly concentrated meditative lyric
which grows from memories of riding the rails with an unidenti-
fied companion some twenty-five years ago. Levine starts in the
past tense, then shifts to present and future tenses in combination
with images drawn from the Korean War to conjure the future,
and finally modulates into a present tense that recovers the past.
These taut lines get us from the second to the third phase:

> When I lie down at last to sleep
> inside a boxcar of coffins bound
> for the villages climbing north
> will I waken in a small station
> where women have come to claim
> what is left of glory? Or will
> I sleep until the silver bridge
> spanning the Mystic River jabs
> me awake, and I am back
> in a dirty work-shirt that says *Phil,*
> 24 years old, hungry and lost, on
> the run from a war no one can win?

In some contexts that river would seem too felicitously named to
be true; here, coupled with the silver bridge that links past and

future, the name is too obliquely accurate to have been invented. Quietly magical as that transition is, the poem's real achievement is its conclusion, where Levine and his friend come "back the long / tangled road that leads us home":

> Through Flat Rock going east
> picking up speed, the damp fields
> asleep in moonlight. You stand
> beside me, breathing the cold
> in silence. When you grip
> my arm hard and lean way out
> and shout out the holy names
> of the lost neither of us is scared
> and our tears mean nothing.

These lines bring the past incident rushing into the present, thus accomplishing in small one of the book's aims, and they image the movement into the future. Wearing his "dirty work-shirt," Levine seems already one of the lost whose names these poems shout into the darkness. Besides the men killed in Korea they include all of those whose lives have been wasted in futile political struggles—who have died in other wars, like Durruti, or who have been worn down by iniquitous systems, like Levine's Uncle Joe, or warped by them, like the black convicts. The tears "mean nothing," since they can change nothing, and that is what they mean.

The lost began to haunt Levine in *On the Edge* (1963), although he did not yet know they were to be his abiding subject. Looking at "An Abandoned Factory, Detroit," he lamented, in painfully mimetic, mechanically regular lines

> the loss of human power,
> Experienced and slow, the loss of years,
> The gradual decay of dignity.
> Men lived within these foundries, hour by hour;
> Nothing they forged outlived the rusted gears
> Which might have served to grind their eulogy.

This stanza might drug us into a sort of awareness; the first volume's more interesting poems, not all political, try to shock us into it. "Gangrene" does so as literally as possible. Beginning with a description of electrical and other tortures of political prisoners, packaged in fussy syllabic stanzas, it then rounds on the reader, *ipso facto* "secretly thrilled by / the circus of excrement." "Think of the colossal brutality, cruelty and mendacity which is now allowed to spread itself over the civilized world. Do you really believe that a handful of unprincipled placehunters and corrupters of men would have succeeded in letting loose all this latent evil, if the millions of their followers were not also guilty?" So the more circumspect Freud in his self-vindication forty years earlier. For the American who might really believe himself innocent, Levine juxtaposes "Gangrene" with a searingly objective poem about a horse flayed alive by the bomb dropped on Hiroshima. In various ways, "L'Homme et la Bête," "Small Game," and "The Turning" serve the same end: Levine means to strip the reader of his own integument of moral pretension.

"Political facts" motivated many of the poems in *Not This Pig* (1968), but frequently Levine's animus took the form of satire on bourgeois conformity, viewed once more as the spiritually bankrupting price of admission to the system. The title "Barbie & Ken, Ken & Barbie" gives away that poem's game immediately. In "Obscure" Levine portrays a woman who lives in pathetic dread of never mothering "civic children" whose names would be "real" to her because she would be "reading them in the evening / during station breaks." In his advice "To a Child Trapped in a Barber Shop" he ridicules shibboleths that enshrine bourgeois values. "So don't drink / the Lucky Tiger, don't / fill up on grease," he warns, "because that makes it a lot worse, / that makes it a crime / against property and the state / and that costs time." Though he be a Jew, the child might find himself delivered the next morning into the hands of a teacher like the Miss Jennings of "Who Are You?," who will teach him to play " 'Here / Is the church, there the steeple.' " At best he might eventually withdraw, like the man in "Heaven," a rendering of the Ariel-dominated poet, who took to his room in a time of war to build a paradise for his "mad canary," complete with a "network of golden ladders." He was certain to be hunted down and "laid off"—"and it would do no good / to show how he had taken / clothespins and cardboard / and made each step safe."

"Heaven" is an eerie, softly-hued poem, but these others,

although smooth enough—no, partly because so smooth—seem thin and dated as old coins. The poem with the wonderfully skewed title, "Animals Are Passing from Our Lives," will always seem newly minted. A parable of the blinkered "progress" of the consumer society, it fascinates both because of its framing concept (how many poets would dream of adopting the point of view of the first little pig in the children's game?) and its execution of detail. Nothing could be more right, descriptively or politically, than the conjunction of "my massive buttocks slipping / like oiled parts with each light step" and the butcher's "pudgy white fingers / that shake out the intestines / like a hankie." Everyone will remember the last lines, where the pig senses that the boy driving him along believes

> that at any moment I'll fall
> on my side and drum my toes
> like a typewriter or squeal
> and shit like a new housewife
>
> discovering television,
> or that I'll turn like a beast
> cleverly to hook his teeth
> with my teeth. No. Not this pig.

What works so well, even to overcome the merely serviceable first simile and the confusingly extended last, is the flat refusal to act unpredictably. How better to leave us to our own devices?

But such a poem is a tiny territory discovered and fully exploited at once, just as "Heaven" is an enchanting island to which one does not return. "The Midget" might stand for Levine's entrance into a country large and potentially productive as the Spain in which it is set. The poet is accosted, in a workers' bar in Barcelona once frequented by Durruti, by a midget who will not be bought off or discouraged by pleas to be left alone. As in a bad dream, the midget insists on intimacy, begs Levine to feel him where he is "big where it really counts," and finally crawls into his lap to sing drunken songs of "fabled Americas." The workers pay and leave, the odd couple are left alone, and now the poet sings lullabies to "this late-born freak / of the old world swelling my lap." Few poems deal as ruthlessly with our attempts to dissociate ourselves from the world's grief or dramatize as convincingly our utter moral defenselessness in the face of the claims of the poor and powerless. The heads of all our international conglomerates should be made to read it every night after saying their prayers. Levine has never shaken that obstinate midget. His paradoxical image of potency was prophetic: from such narrow circumstances, whether in Spain or the United States, most of his finest poems have come. As early as "Silent in America" in this second volume he could say that he "had presumed to speak" for the lost, for the laborers he had worked with in Detroit, and more generally "for the ugly / who had no chance, the beautiful in / body, the used and the unused, / those who had courage / and those who quit."

Levine's home turf is the urban setting, so it makes whimsical sense for *Not This Pig* to be dedicated in part to "the cities that are here, Detroit, Fresno, Barcelona." But often in *Red Dust* and throughout *Pili's Wall,* both published by small presses in 1971, Levine explored the rural areas of the country of the spirit that he had settled in. Two of the best poems in *Red Dust,* which now looks rather like a preparation for *They Feed They Lion* and must be slighted here, were reprinted in that later volume. None of *Pili's Wall,* a sequence of ten lyrics, has ever been reprinted, * perhaps because the accompanying photos would pose a problem in a larger edition. Its limited printing is a pity, but one has to approve the decision not to publish the poems alone; for although they never refer to the wall's graffiti, reproduced in the photos, the two media come to seem inseparable. Levine never quite says so, but it seems that Pili, a "Spanish girlchild," chipped these figures into the wall. They are her poem at the same time that they inspire Levine's, which is also primitive, elliptical, out of perspective—and written in a tight free verse rather than the syllabics that predominate in the earlier volumes.

Through most of the sequence Levine assumes Pili's point of view, while she in turn merges with the elements of her small but inexhaustible world: a lost and frightened dog, a weary shepherd, even the wall itself, as in section VII, the germ of "They Feed They Lion":

Pili's Wall appears in *Selected Poems, 1984.*—ED.

Out of saying No
No to the barn swallow, No

to the hurled stone
No to the air

out of *you can't*
to the crying grain, *you won't*

to the lost river
of blackening ivy

out of blind
out of deaf, closed, still

I stand and stand and stand into
this wall.

While the syntax of this section owes an obvious debt to Whitman, the definition of self in terms of gritty negation is pure Levine. Again, the identifications at the heart of the sequence recall "There Was a Child Went Forth," but only Levine could so vitalize a wall that it could give a detailed, inventive account of its birth. In section IX we learn how the wall's "seed" gradually became a "fist / tightening into / a turnip / with one hard eye" and then changed again, "broke the dried crust," and rose into the air, its "stiff back . . . humping," to stand in the morning "like a row of windless corn / never to be / eaten." The concluding negative, Levine's cachet, is more positive and specific than that in "Not This Pig." In this context of "the low houses of the poor" and a hardscrabble life the wall embodies the refusal of those who built it not to exist.

The force that drives the wall up also powers the rough beast in the ferocious, exhilarating title poem in *They Feed They Lion* (1972), but here the focus is once more on the city:

Out of burlap bags, out of bearing butter,
Out of black bean and wet slate bread,
Out of the acids of rage, the candor of tar,
Out of creosote, gasoline, drive shafts, wooden dollies,
They Lion grow.

The tremendous compression corresponds to the constraint of the energy Levine at once eulogizes and stands in awe of, like Michaelangelo's slaves, their bodies straining to free themselves from the marble. And like the sculptures, the poem catches moments at which raw material converts itself into raw power, and it too elicits a kinaesthetic response:

> From the sweet glues of the trotters
> Come the sweet kinks of the fist, from the full flower
> Of the hams the thorax of caves,
> From "Bow Down" come "Rise Up,"
> Come they Lion from the reeds of shovels,
> The grained arm that pulls the hands. . . .

Or perhaps we should take our cue from the black dialect it draws much of its strength from and think of it as a sort of apocalyptic jazz. In any case, Levine's Lion is plainly a later, fiercer version of his wall and an earlier, more joyful version of the world growing in the workers' hearts.

Someone is always asking whether the good political poem is possible in the United States today. An affirmative answer can only be concrete, and to confront the question with "They Feed They Lion" or "For the Fallen" (or Lowell's "For the Union Dead" or Kinnell's sixth poem in *The Book of Nightmares*) is to expose a pseudo-issue. Of course "They Feed They Lion" celebrates latent power at least as much as it condemns oppression, and its union of labor and nature (as in "caves," "reeds," and "grained") augurs something closer to the proverbial inheritance than to revolution, but it is not the less political on those accounts—though it might be the more visionary. If an accurate depiction of the lives of the undeservedly poor and luckless is a legitimate criterion (and I take "accurate depiction" to exclude sloganeering and stereotyping), this volume contains a host of other fine political poems. Here we have Luther, whose pregnant wife is delivering early and whose "old black Lincoln" (what else?) has broken down:

> Luther
> cocking his tattoo
> against the black rain and

                         the rain of black luck, Luther
                         pushing on toward
                         the jewelled service station
                         of free cokes
                         and credit there ahead
                         in a heaven of blue
                         falling and nothing
                         going to make him cry
                         for nothing.

                                        ("Cry for Nothing")

Once again the negative—and how well Levine has listened to
Luther's speech—amounts to an affirmation, as in its own small
way the perfect placement of "falling" does. Or there is the
Spanish stone cutter's thirty-six year old retarded daughter, mak-
ing her "Salami" from an increasingly wondrous list of ingredi-
ents, ending with "dried cat heart, / cock claws." She is solid and
undiscriminating as earth itself. Or there is the Cuban woman in
"The Angels of Detroit," or Lemon in "Detroit Grease Shop
Poem," or a half dozen others.

    In spite of the harshness of the lives depicted, these poems are
all laced with a certain delicacy, which in strange combination
with repugnant subjects generates some of Levine's most original
work. At one end of the spectrum is "¡Hola Miguelin!," a lovely
lyric about a young Spanish neighbor just risen from love-
making, which is all delicacy except for its last line's hint of a
frisson. At the other end is "The Children's Crusade," an inscruta-
ble tale in which a little girl who is an accomplice in the gruesome
murder of her father wears, very precisely, "silver ignition keys
hooked in her / pierced ears." Somewhere between them is the
astonishing "Angel Butcher." Set in a celestial abbatoir, it re-
counts a ritual execution by the speaker of a fellow angel, Chris-
tophe, who "wants to die / like a rabbit." After preliminary courte-
sies, Christophe is arranged as though for a portrait:

                                                    I can
                         feel my lungs flower as the
                         swing begins. He smiles again
                         with only one side of his mouth
                         and looks down to the

dark valley where the cities
burn. When I hit
him he comes apart like a
perfect puzzle or an
old flower.
                And my legs
dance and twitch for hours.

As Christophe comes apart, Levine's puzzle completes itself, and
we realize that one reason Christophe smiles with only one side
of his mouth is that the other side is the butcher's (whose own
legs "dance and twitch"). Another reason is Christophe's wry
anticipation, for if "They Feed They Lion" is Levine's "Second
Coming," "Angel Butcher" is his "Dialogue of Self and Soul,"
its "dark valley" being analogous to Yeats's ditch and its burning
cities Levine's special object of love and hate.

But Yeats's Self praises life as he has known it, and to the
extent that Levine does likewise his anger at its political facts
must be affected. His discontent can afford only so much nostal-
gia. In *1933* (1974) Levine's emphasis shifted. As he said in the
interview, this volume is "less aggressive" than its predecessor. It
includes a number of his best realistic vignettes, but as its title
hints, its wistfulness at least balances its rancor. When "Grand-
mother in Heaven" unpacks her market basket item by item,
"with a little word for each, a curse / for the bad back and the
black radish / and three quick spits for the pot," each plosive and
stress serves a loving reminiscence. "Zaydee," about Levine's
grandfather—crook, fruit vendor, stove factory worker, aging
midwestern Autolycus who speaks like a god from a cloud of
English Oval smoke—shapes the political facts of Levine's early
life into a nearly Edenic world. "At the Fillmore" sketches a
wartime romance at the dance hall, and neither the background
presence of "the wards of the wounded" nor the appropriately
stripped down tercets can subdue its lyricism. The woman daw-
dles in the ladies' room and feels her longing and tipsyness, "this
warmth / like the flush of juice / up the pale stem / of the
flower." It is enough to make you feel more strongly about
efflorescence.

Yet Levine's nostalgia encourages the soft and the sentimental.
Sometimes one cannot believe—or does not know how to

believe—his claims, as when he says in "1933" (the year of his father's death) that "Once in childhood the stars held still all night / the moon swelled like a plum but white and silken." The standing still of the stars is patently symbolic and the image of the moon hardly calculated to substantiate the "Once." In "Once in May" he recalls that he stood "all afternoon under heaven / with water in my pockets, / salt in my socks, naming / the grains of the sea." But it is no more clear what that too familiar "naming" might really mean than it is where else he might have stood on the beach. At such moments Prospero yields the floor to Ariel, but Ariel, flustered and out of practice, blurts out the first thing that comes into his head.

Nostalgia perhaps breeds another kind of self-indulgence in "Letters for the Dead," an ambitious elegiac poem 350 lines long which is crisply written, particular at every step, yet confusing as a whole. The problem is simply that it needs the fleshing out one often gets at readings. The relationships among its people remain stubbornly obscure, and the reader is so bedeviled by ambiguous second person pronouns that he can hardly tell how many people are involved. What is the purpose? I am not certain, but the vivid obscurity gives one an especially strong sense of being privy to an intensely personal transaction. For some readers the poem will prove the exceeding tolerance of Mill's definition of successful poetry as "feeling confessing itself to itself in moments of solitude." Yet one values just this quality of seeming "overheard" in Levine's recent political poems. They spurn what Mill called "eloquence"—"feeling pouring itself forth to other minds, courting their sympathy, or endeavoring to influence their belief, or move them to passion or to action." "And the Trains Go On" and "For the Fallen," far from having designs on us, allow us to eavesdrop on meditations. If occasional obscurity were the expense of the mode, it would be worth the price.

The Names of the Lost often reworks the political themes of *They Feed They Lion* in the elegiac manner of *1933*. The two meet in "Another Life," when Levine, who has earned the right if anyone has, asks "how many men, dying, passed me / the blood of their voices, the spittle / oiling their groans." This poem's lost person is a black man, Levine's age and like him born in Detroit, but "white haired" and "toothless" and a four-time loser now in

Folsom, where Levine taught a writing course. The man rambles on about his prison terms and other things:

> about the poem he can write will follow
> me all the way home, try my chair,
> eat from my plate, take my voice
> until I'm the one walks all night
> in the rain, gets stopped by the cops
> at dawn, and with the sky reddening
> spread my arms and legs against the car
> and feel the gloved hand
> slide over my balls and pause
> and go on, leaving nothing.

The transition is flawless. If it is impossible to say whether the frisking is Levine's experience too or just the convict's, that seems to be the point.

At exactly this point one has to voice a reservation. The question—which threatens to raise itself even in the case of "I was the man, I suffered, I was there"—is whether the identification does not trivialize the experience it means to bring home, whether the technique has not subverted the subject. The final image means something for the convict that it cannot mean for Levine. He confronts the difficulty in "For the Fallen": "Look at your hands. They / are not scarred by / the cigarettes of the police." But then "For the Poets of Chile" opens with these lines:

> Today I called for you
> my death, like a cup
> of creamy milk I
> could drink in the cold dawn,
> I called you to come
> down soon.

Could any poem accommodate this passage? It might illustrate one problem with Mill's concept of poetry, which does not allow for the awareness of audience that can cut the grease of mawkishness that often films over conversations with the self. When Levine concludes with an image of the daughter of a slain political prisoner setting the breakfast table with "the tall glasses / for the milk" that she and her mother must drink each morning, the easy symmetry and the presumptuous equation betray whatever emotion has survived the opening lines.

Levine's rhetorical questions can also lead him to the brink of the bathetic. In "To My God in His Sickness" he asks: "Can the hands rebuild the rocks / can the tongue make air or water / can the blood flow back / into the twigs of the child." One imitates the rhetoric of Job's God at his own peril. These lines leave a faintly embarrassed impression of self-consciousness. Or take the passage in "Ask the Roses" where Levine demands: "Has anyone told the sea it must count / its tears and explain each one / has anyone told the blood / how long it must crust the sheets." Isn't this really a way of making witty images, a means of setting in motion a machine that can process, in the name of suffering, any material that comes to hand?

Still, such moments are rare in this volume. Besides "And the Trains Go On," "For the Fallen," and "Gift for a Believer," *The Names of the Lost* contains several other poems nearly as compelling, including "New Season," "My Son and I," "On the Murder of Lieutenant José del Castillo by the Falangist Bravo Martinez, July 12, 1936," and "No One Remembers." A few others, such as "A Late Answer" and "Wednesday," are admirably done though more modest attempts. The latter begins unassumingly:

> I could say the day began
> behind the Sierras,
> in the orange grove the ladder
> that reaches partway
> to the stars grew
> a shadow, and the fruit
> wet with mist put on
> its color and glowed
> like a globe of fire. . . .

There might be a touch of expediency in the sudden reduction of the grove to one orange, but the fusion of the rising sun and the fruit combines with the knowing overstatement about the ladder to work wonders. Even the line break after "grew" contributes its gram to the delicate balance between the sanguine will to action and the ironic recognition of limitation—or, to use the more dramatic terms of "They Feed They Lion," between " 'Rise Up' " and " 'Bow Down.' "

References to rising and falling run throughout this volume ("You," "Let It Begin," "Another Life," "Gift for a Believer," and "For the Fallen," for example), and the tension between the impulses they embody—parallel to that between remembering and forgetting—is at its very heart. A section of "For the Fallen," where Levine transports us to the cemetery in which Durruti is buried, will serve as synecdoche:

> You
> can go down on your knees
> and pray that the spirit
> of men and women come back
> and inhabit this failing flesh
> but if you listen well
> your heart will ask
> you to stand, under
> the fading sun or
> the rising moon, it
> doesn't matter, either
> alone or breathing as you
> do now the words
> of the fallen and the slow
> clouds of diesel exhaust.

Within the intricate local counterpointing, we might take as summarizing lines the two on "the fading sun" and "the rising moon," where the attribution of "rising" to the weaker "moon" nearly redresses the slight imbalance caused by the stronger position of that second adjective. In the sentence as a whole, the foreknowledge of the futility of rising up nearly frustrates the urge to do so. The standing must be accomplished, after all, within sight of "the fallen." And the "heart" (again one remembers Durruti's words) is saddled with the "failing flesh."

Not that bowing down is to be despised. On the contrary, the endurance it represents has often approximated heroism in Levine's work. The first poem in the first volume ends with a lone bird arrived too early in March who, "Frozen, holds on and sings"; in "The Way Down" in *They Feed They Lion* "the tight rows of seed / bow to the earth / and hold on and hold on"; and in "Gift for a Believer" Levine's wife "kneels / to the cold earth and we have bread." But it is no longer so clear to him that "From 'Bow Down' come 'Rise Up.' " "For the Fallen" and this book in general admit the near impossibility of that transition, either for the individual or society. Lacking the dynamism of "They Feed They Lion," "For the Fallen" might not be as immediately appealing, but it just might be more accurate, a poem Prospero could approve more quickly—as well as a harder one to write, or at least to be felt through, to have brought home.

If few others in this volume can stand with the prodigious poems in *They Feed They Lion,* we must remember that we do not have the right to expect such poems and can only be grateful when they appear. Perhaps not even Levine has the right to expect them. Randall Jarrell told us that a good poet is "someone who manages, in a lifetime of standing out in thunderstorms, to be struck by lightning five or six times." Levine has already been struck at least that many times, and Lord knows no one is more likely to continue standing out in thunderstorms.

ROBERT PINSKY

The Names of the Lost

The power to look around and see, and the strength of a living syntax, have distinguished Philip Levine's work at its best. In *Not This Pig* (1968) and *They Feed They Lion* (1972), he awakened and moved readers with poems meant to be read. That is high praise when so much recent poetry seems sealed off from what people see, or how people might speak when moved—sealed off either by coy mannerism or by the standard poetic diction of a *chic* reticence: that tongue of a place where the dusty Stone of your blood eats Light like the snowy breathing of Water, *et cetera*.

Into that antiseptic, surrealist kitchen came Levine's recognizable pig:

> It's wonderful how I jog
> on four honed-down ivory toes
> my massive buttocks slipping
> like oiled parts with each light step.
>
> I'm to market. I can smell
> the sour, grooved block, I can smell
> the blade that opens the hole
> and the pudgy white fingers
>
> that shake out the intestines
> like a hankie.

This does not explain God's ways to man, but it is human, and a real animal, part of an American terrain which Levine has seen with unglazed eyes. The material itself invites literary cliché: the lower-middle-class Detroit of Levine's childhood; the

New York Times Book Review, February 20, 1977. Reprinted with permission.

abattoirs, grease-shops and smeared rivers that are part of the country; the sweet, uneasy California suburb that is another part. The list itself is a cliché, but Levine can overcome that because like the pig these things are not seen as "material," but as life; the poet's prejudices are political and moral, not literary.

That said, it must be admitted that Levine's work is uneven, and that its failing is the maudlin. I understand the maudlin to be not a degree of feeling, or even a kind of feeling, but the locking of tone into a flaw or groove, running there without the capacity for modulation of emotion: a single, sustained whine, piercing but not penetrating. In other words, if Swinburne used the same adjectives for a sunset and a woman, Levine sometimes uses the same ones for a dead fish and a lost war. (The poems not directly of America often draw on Levine's experience of Spain, particularly Barcelona and its enduring aftermark of the Civil War.) As with women and sunsets, there may be good reasons for using the same terms, but the reasons must be thought out and felt through, somehow.

What staves off the maudlin in any art is continuity of thought, a sustained choice to speak with all of one's mind. The best poems by Levine meet that intellectual risk, or make peace with it, as in (for example) "Silent in America," "Animals Are Passing from Our Lives," "Baby Villon," "Salami," "They Feed They Lion," all from the two volumes I have named. The volume before this new one, *1933*, disappointed me, seemed duller because the poems had become more impressionistic and orphic, less rather than more willing to make the mind known.

To be more specific: I cannot say, amid the technologies of death, deliberate and inadvertent, that America, Barcelona, the world, are any less horrible, or less fit objects for elegy, than Levine says. But often his horrors feel too much the same; to grow old, to drink bad water, to bomb Dresden, to eat sick animals, to be shot by Fascists, if they are understood too similarly have been understood too simply.

The new poems of *The Names of the Lost* renew and heighten the accomplishments and conflicts which I have tried to outline here. The mood is (as the title implies) more obsessively elegiac than ever; one of the most moving poems, "Gift for a Believer," with its closing echo of Hopkins ("two palm-fulls the sky gave us, / what the roots crave, rain"), is a kind of prayer to escape from the wan hope of elegy, into a political anger. Other political or near-political poems ("For the Poets of Chile," "For the Fallen") are less deeply felt, for me, than the forthright, personal elegy of "New Season," where the themes of mourning and survival are not themes but the strands of a life, and where the syntax, rhythm, details, give the poem clarity and proportion.

On the other hand, as in *1933,* the tendency to hold a poem together from its beginning to end only by a thin, vibrating wire of emotion seems extended. Is it odd or inappropriate to find poems deficient in *thought?* The monotony of feeling, and repetitiousness of method, produce a dark, sleepy air not so different, after all, from the Stone-Breath-Light-Snow surrealism. With the exceptions of "New Season" and "Another Life," the poems of *The Names of the Lost* are both more vatic, and looser, than earlier work: if not quite trivializing the mood of *They Feed They Lion,* then making it more formulaic. This weak, forced passage is from the new book's "Ask the Roses":

> There are tall reedy weeds by the fence
> the fallen oranges in my neighbor's yard
> blacken and spread like shotgun wounds
> Down south in L.A. they are pouring
> milk back to the sewers
> Has anyone asked the cows
> has anyone told the sunset
> it will be on tv or the child
> that her breasts filled with plastic
> will sell fried chicken
> Has anyone told the sea it must count
> its tears and explain each one

And this fierce catalogue is from "They Feed They Lion":

> Out of burlap sacks, out of bearing butter,
> Out of black bean and wet slate bread,
> Out of the acids of rage, the candor of tar,
> Out of creosote, gasoline, drive shafts, wooden dollies,
> They Lion grow.

It is hard dealing to quote a writer against himself, but Levine has earned and undertaken the hardness of high standards.

RICHARD HUGO

Philip Levine: Naming the Lost

Philip Levine knows a few things so well that he cannot forget them when he writes a poem, no matter what compositional problems might arise. He seldom tells us anything we don't already know but what he tells us is basic to the maintenance of our humanity, and fundamental to perpetuating our capacity for compassion. If I were dictator of the world long enough to pass a few laws, two of those laws would be: (1) at least once a year, everyone must view the films taken at Hiroshima immediately after the bombing; (2) at least once every six months, everyone must read a book of Philip Levine's poems aloud. That wouldn't necessarily make us better people, but it might make us hope we won't get any worse, and want to be the best we can be. . . .

Here are a few things Levine knows well: to the heart, in time relationships transcend values ("On the Birth of Good and Evil During the Long Winter of '28," p. 9). Levine's world is at least as old as religion. The professional is outlawed. It is the amateur who discovers "7000 miles from home" that she who "bruised his wakings" can, on this cold day after her death, be forgiven for the wool cap she knitted long ago, whose very color once seemed despicable.

We did not return love when it was needed. When we realize that failure it is too late and we must live with the resultant regret. We did not accept the essential relationships that provided our sense of self. When we understand that, it is too late and self-acceptance remains painfully difficult. ("The Secret of Their Voices," pp. 10–11.)

People hurt each other in lasting ways. The ways we help each other seem trivial and transitory in contrast. Time and memory and accumulated experience make the helpful acts as permanent as the hurtful ones. ("No One Remembers," pp. 14–17.)

American Poetry Review, May–June, 1977. Reprinted with permission.

Levine's poems seldom fail to remind us of important things about ourselves we should not forget. *The Names of the Lost* is the third powerful book Levine has given us in the past five years. Give him a saliva test. The title might be so-so for some poets, but it is ideal for Levine. He has been naming the lost for a long time. Not just lost people but lost associations and feelings.

Levine's method of writing depends to some extent on the ear of the reader to get into the poems. Few of his first lines are grippers: "Nine years ago, early winter," "Beyond that stand of firs," "In a coffee house at 3 A.M.," "It is Friday, a usual day," but they are immediate enough that we faintly sense something is going on, and we faintly sense that feelings are involved in the terse sounds of the words even when the words seem to be only narrating, conveying information or setting the scene. In a lesser poet this would be starting too far upstream, at the beginning of things rather than in the middle. For the reader it seems like getting a running start, then becoming aware that the race has already begun, long ago. The feeling seems to precede its source.

In a way, Levine's technique corresponds with his vision of the world in which grief is presumed the perpetual condition of humanity, there long before the individual has experienced anything to grieve. When something happens that causes us grief, we are already in good grieving condition because we have been practising a long time.

Since Levine can write as if feeling precedes experience, he can command a wider range of subjects than many poets. By wider range, I mean his subjects can vary in the intensity of their relationship to him. (In their natures, his subjects are similar.) He can invest as much feeling in poems about the poets of Chile or a man killed in Spain when Levine was eight years old in Detroit, as he can in poems involving relatives, friends, and personal experience.

No poem in this fine collection is disappointing and almost every poem seems to be the best when reading it. My favorite, "And the Trains Go On," pp. 64–65, is a poem of great faith and it immediately precedes the final poem, "To My God in His Sickness," a somewhat grim parody of John Donne's "Hymne to God my God in my sicknesse." If Levine is solely responsible for the arrangement of the book, he may still consider the faith he has found in the power of words, in the power of naming, secondary to the religious faith he has lost in the face of an unjust world. If that is necessary to keep poems of such emotive force coming, let's not try to set him straight.

"And the Trains Go On" is a sort of microscopic Odyssey. The speaker is on the run from a self and a situation he could not bear, "The run from a war no one can win," and finds himself in a bizarre, cruel, and despairing world. At first he and a companion are "at the back door / of the shop" and a "line of box cars / or soured wheat and pop bottles / uncoupled and was sent creaking down our spur. . . ." Already what is given ("was sent") is a world used, empty ("pop bottles"), and spoiled ("soured wheat"). The old man who steps from the box car certifies the negative heritage with mock gentility—"and tipped his hat. 'It's all yours, boys!'" The speaker wonders "whose father / he was and how long he kept / moving until the police / found him, ticketless, sleeping in a 2nd class waiting room / and tore the cardboard box / out of his hands and beat him / until the ink of his birth smudged / and surrendered its separate vowels." So the speaker has no doubt about the outcome. In this brutal world we lose not only our meagre possessions but our beginnings and our names to civilization's authority. Though the speaker never sees the man again, his vision is so relentless and fixed that the man's fate is determined in detail.

With the mention of "2nd class" the scene has shifted to Europe. Levine senses in the more immediate heritage, the historical heritage. He writes in some historical depth anyway, despite the immediacy of emotions and images. What civilized authority can do to the mind is revealed in the next event in the poem. A dog is wandering in the Milan railyard. A boy makes a perfectly reasonable explanation: the dog is "searching for his master." But the boy's grandfather "said, 'No. He was sent by God / to test the Italian railroads.'" The boy can still believe in the desirability and need for affectionate and supportive relationships. The grandfather has cynically accepted a bizarre explanation, involving phony religiosity, the deity's direct interest in the state, and a presumed unimportance of humanity.

This unimportance of humanity on the scale of civilization's values is reinforced by the next image. The speaker sleeps in a "box car of coffins bound / for the villages climbing north" and wonders if he will waken when "women have come to claim" dead husbands, sons, lovers, "what is left of glory." Or will he sleep through that and not waken again until he is back in the States, crossing the Mystic River, which is in Massachusetts? Levine takes the poem out beautifully, "back the long / tangled road that leads us home," but now his companion is you, and me, and it is also him, the self he ran from, "in a dirty workshirt that says *Phil*" (the only person named in the poem). And if we, you, I, Levine, can "lean way out / and shout out the holy names / of the lost neither of us is scared / and our tears mean nothing." We can go home (accept the self we ran from) with the certainty, the poet's certainty, that our words (their names and ours) are all we can give, and if we can share in that, then we have transcended our grief and redeemed our loss.

This is one of the most moving poems I've seen. In its capacity to touch and affect, I believe it rivals Yeats's "Easter, 1916," and like "Easter, 1916," we find ourselves in a world where "motley is worn" or if not motley, then its industrial work-shirt counterpart. It is a world that doesn't hear and doesn't care. Levine's poems are important because in them we hear and we care. They call us back to the basic sources of despair: the dispossession, the destitution, the inadequacy of our love for each other. And they call back again that we can triumph over our sad psychic heritage through language and song.

Given the emotional depth of Levine's poems, one is inclined to avoid prolonged explorative analysis. Not that it would be ruinous, the poems are too tough for that, but that it would seem secondary, if not trivial—like program notes to a splendid concert. But at least one poem in this collection lends itself to discussion because it is somewhat revelatory of Levine's psychic process involved in the act of writing. More than most of his poems, it shows how his writing grows out of ways he feels about himself and his relations with the world.

LET IT BEGIN

Snow before dawn, the trees asleep.
In one window a yellow light—someone
is rising to wash and make coffee
and doze at the table remembering
how a child sleeps late and wakens

drenched in sunlight. If he thinks
of a street, he knows it has gone,
a dog has died, a tulip burned
for an hour and joined the wind.
With the others I drift, useless,
in the parking lot while the day-shift
comes on, or I stand at the corner
as the sun wakens on a gray crust.
The children pass by in silent knots
on the way home from the burial
of the birds. The day has begun.
I can put it away, a white shirt,
unworn, at the back of a drawer,
but my hands are someone else's—
stained, they shine like old wood
and burn in the cold. They have joined
each other in the fellowship
of the shovel. I stood in the temple
of junk where the engine blocks
turned and the nickle-plated grills
dripped on hooks, and though
steel rang on the lip of the furnace
and fire rose out of black earth
and rained down, in the end
I knelt to cinders and ice. I stared
into the needle's dark eye
so the peddler could mend his elbow
and gasp under his sack of rags.
Now the cat pulls on his skullcap
of bones and bows before the mouse.
Light that will spread the morning glory
burns on my tongue and spills
into the small valleys of our living,
the branches creak, and I let it begin.

(pp. 33–34)

Levine feels that loss, like the imagination, is the final equal-
izer. The man "thinks of a street" and knows three losses, the
street, a dog, and a tulip, equal in value now they are gone, equal
because they are gone. In a world where loss predominates, the

yellow light in the window is as good a beginning as dawn which comes now, not to waken the child but to wake itself on the gray industrial crust of the city. The speaker is "useless" (dawn does not need him), one of the many third shift workers who "drift in the parking lot." The aimlessness of their existence is as gratuitous as the snow that starts this poem, this day. You come off shift and it's just there: "Snow before dawn, the trees asleep."

The workers are "children" bound together in "knots" of an innocence they've inherited. The innocence of an existence that dims the senses, minimizes experience and limits possibilities. They are silent as the birds who are buried in silence once dawn is complete and their song is ended. When childhood is over and they could no longer wait for sunlight to drench them awake, but had to obey the call of the alarm clock, their impulse to song (poetry?) drained away.

The speaker can't be part of the middle class and knows it. His white shirt can be put away, unworn, for good. In Levine's case, very much for good, his and ours. But neither is he part of the working class. His hands are worker's hands, but they are not his, even though "they have joined each other in the fellowship of the shovel," a union (labor union?) of dubious worth. The sentimentality seemingly built into certain "of" constructions is ideal for nailing down a sarcastic phrase—my garden book of memories.

He is not of the working class because he cannot identify with accomplishment, the engine blocks, the grills, the steel and fire of the plant, that "temple of junk." Given the deterioration of religious values by industrial values that in turn are inadequate substitutes, the poet kneels not to abandoned Gods of the past, nor to the gods of the present, progress, civilization, the end products of manufacturing. He kneels to the end products of the whole process, cinders and ice, the two ways it can end, according to Frost. Levine will not break off his love affair with the finality of loss.

He stares into the "needle's dark eye" not for mystical purposes, the try for "inscape," but to prolong and perpetuate the suffering of the forlorn, the deprivation of humanity, the quotidian despair. The eye of the needle could be the gate of the biblical city, "dark" suggesting what cities have become, but the word "mend" suggests that whatever its metaphorical past it is now just a needle.

If that were all Levine was saying in this passage, he would be guilty of no more phoniness than is normal to a poet. He would be saying, I'll keep you patched together, your elbow mended, so you can gasp under your sack of rags and I can write "and gasp under his sack of rags." In a way that *is* what he is saying. But of course he is also trying to save the rag man (and you, and me) from oblivion. By prolonging our suffering, Levine is giving himself a chance to finish the poem, but he is also prolonging us.

The cat bows to the mouse because the cat needs the mouse just as the poet needs the rag man. The "skullcap of bones" suggests the death of religion, and the act of kneeling is not a religious act, but an aesthetic one. Because the poet has insight, he is not part of what he sees and realizes a certain powerful advantage, the advantage of the cat over the mouse. He gives up the advantage to write the poem.

Levine has remained a child and kept alive his impulse to sing. The dawn that drenched him awake still burns in him, on his tongue, in his words. The "it" he lets begin is the dawn, the life that belongs to all of us and is all we have, the poem itself. He not only shouts out the holy names of the lost, he shouts out the holy names of the living. And we are not lost. That's a big beautiful cat at our mousy feet.

Levine may very well believe that imagination and loss are not just close allies or forces that mutually trigger each other, but one and the same. One of our able critics should enlighten us on this in the years ahead. Those of us who are not critics should read Levine not for whatever literary advance he could be making but because he reminds us of what we are in a time it is important that we don't forget. And whatever we are, hopeful, hurt, angry, sad, happy, we should forget least of all Philip Levine's poems. They attend us and our lives in profound, durable ways. I believe he is deservedly destined to be one of the most celebrated poets of the time.

STANLEY PLUMLY

The Names of the Lost

The names of the lost are legion. Teddy Holmes, Uncle Joe,
Tatum, Ray Estrada, David Ber Prishkulnick, Harry Levine,
José del Castillo, the brothers Durruti, Jaroubi, Billy Ray, Gor-
don, the poets of Chile, not to mention the son, the wife, the
mother and the father of Philip Levine's own family. There are
theme poets, idea poets, image poets, language poets, but the
kind of visceral commitments Levine is stuck with are those that
must engage, at the moment of empathy, an actual antagonist,
somebody in person. Somebody named. In this, his fifth full
book of poems, Levine is more of a people poet than ever, a
proletariat qualification less revisionist than revolutionary. The
antagonist relationship—that act of directly, and dramatically,
addressing himself to someone, living or dead—is his most im-
mediate access to his larger material and statement, his center of
gravity for whatever else holds ground.

> When the streetcar stalled on Joy Road,
> the conductor finished his coffee, puffed
> into his overcoat, and went to phone in.
> The Hungarian punch-press operator wakened
> alone, 7000 miles from home, pulled down
> his orange cap and set out. If he saw
> the winter birds scuffling in the cinders,
> if he felt this was the dawn of a new day,
> he didn't let on. Where the sidewalks
> were unshovelled, he stamped on, raising
> his galoshes a little higher with each step.
> I came as close as I dared and could hear

The Ohio Review 18 (1977). Reprinted with permission.

> only the little gasps as the cold entered
> the stained refectory of the breath.
>
> ("On the Birth . . .")

The stained refectory of the breath: Levine's people are his passion, in the total sense. His poems invariably begin in local drama and adumbrate from there. And the dramatic situation invariably involves losses, all the little, as well as the literal, deaths. Hence the naming, the recounting, of those losses by means of who has suffered them. Yet the continuing distinction and power of Levine's poetry is that he rarely calls attention to himself as potential victim. The authority of his voice, his presence in a poem, is based in his reliability as a witness, that feeling of the truth being rendered one-to-one, without the intervention of self-consciousness. Nor are his antagonists to be type-cast for pity. It is the nature of real grief to work itself out to the other side of itself, to the fullness of the emotion, even unto joy. *The Names of the Lost* is full, "the world growing here in my heart this moment." The volition of its energy is toward light—"As light enters the morning glory / I feel the heart of the tree swell / and grow into mine, as light falls / through the tunnels of branches / that lead back the way I came / I rise from this grave and go"—toward the illumination of a tone, the reconciliation of a struggle.

The so-called "moral imagination" consistently runs the risk of moral superiority. Levine avoids the potential danger by refusing to draw clear conclusions and by resisting the polemics of politics (even at the most tempting moments, such as "To My God in His Sickness") at the expense of the person whose story has become his. The imagination, in and of itself, is subversive, and poetry is already a political act: Levine's drive is toward the testament, even the sacrament, his art can be. Whether the setting is Trumball Avenue, the stock yard at Folsom Prison, or his own garden, Levine's losses illuminate because they are never simply personal, nor simple-mindedly public.

> Tonight, after dinner,
> after the long, halting call
> to my mother, I'll come out here
> to the yard rinsed in moonlight
> that blurs it all. She will not

                    become the small openings
                    in my brain again through which the wind
                    rages, though she was the ocean
                    that ebbed in my blood, the storm clouds
                    that battered my lungs, though I hide
                    in the crotch of the orange tree
                    and weep where the future grows
                    like a scar, she will not come again
                    in the brilliant day.

                                                    ("New Season")

"Everyone brings some piece / of himself to the table," he says in "Autumn Again." Levine is the host, as those others, those names, are the host, as the bread itself is host. It is difficult to read this poet without the implications of ritual, the invocation of the religious. His raw materials are so raw—"and ran down to the Detroit River / to baptize ourselves in the brine / of car parts, dead fish, stolen bicycles, / melted snow"—and the intensity of his vision so demanding the result is bound to be a major tension, and inevitable transformation, the bread into word, the dumb dark into the knowing light. Nearly every title here suggests the rhythm of the seasons, the fundamental patterns of dying and new birth, the juxtaposition of "a globe of blood" against "a globe of fire." And nearly every poem seeks to maintain, in the manner of the supplicant, some balance between hubris and humility.

Book by book, Levine has become the singular poet of his generation. If in the new work some of the places are by now familiar—Fresno, Detroit, Barcelona—the names are indeed changed, and not just the names of the lost, be they Spanish revolutionaries, Chilean poets, Black prisoners, one's own family, or oneself. Like any vital poet, Levine is renaming our experience, complete with contradictions, as something whole, a total passion, as something connected, broken, and bound up again. In "New Season" Levine draws the parallels along genealogical lines: his teenage son, prime combatant "in the wars of the young"; his mother, "70 today, the woman / who took my hand and walked me / past the corridor of willows / to the dark pond where one swan / drifted"; and the poet himself, about to tell the son "the story of my 15th spring"—all share the past as much as each will perfect the common future. Levine wants his son to understand what all fathers want all sons to understand, just as he, in the progress of the poem, is coming to an understanding through the person and example of his mother. In the garden again:

> My cat Nellie,
> 15 now, follows me, safe
> in the dark from the mockingbird
> and jay, her fur frost tipped
> in the pure air, and together we hear
> the wounding of the rose, the willow
> on fire—to the dark pond
> where the one swan drifted, the woman
> is 70 now—the willow is burning,
> the rhododendrons shrivel
> like paper under water, all
> the small secret mouths are feeding
> on the green heart of the plum.

In a poem later in the book, an older son comes to believe that his father too is dying. Typically, Levine does not allay his son's fears—"from all the lives I've lost"—no more than he compromises the truth for the sake of compassion in dealing with the locked-up and lucked-out of the world. His perception is fierce, his language sometimes incandescent, his class all working. Enjambment, that cornering device, is his favorite technical resource. The speed of his connections, as one reality turns toward its larger, myth-making counterpart, is meant to take away our breath. But the pacing of his poems should not blur the size of the space they cover. This book is well-traveled—from Folsom to Nimes to the "*futbol* stadium / of Santiago" to New York to Levine's own California backyard. Its cause lies less in the injustices it inveighs against than in the condition it celebrates. Finally, Levine's people are fixed in the long, tragic perspective. The interconnections may be global; they are also rooted, like the rain, to the earth.

IRA SADOFF

From "A Chronicle of Recent Poetry"

At a time when much American poetry has become *self-conscious*, exploring the psyche almost to the point of narcissism, Philip Levine, one of our finest poets, continues to write poetry that explores the relation between self and other, between the personal and social worlds. His poetic ancestors are the most vulnerable and feeling Spanish surrealists, Vallejo and Hernandez, and he uses many of their poetic devices in his work: the catalogue, repetition, and the interrogative. Levine is also a born storyteller, and he uses his narrative gifts in his latest book, *The Names of the Lost,* to name, to call back, the metaphoric and literal dead, to tell their stories, stories which they could not tell themselves. Dealing with subjects often excluded from poetry, Levine explores the railroad and steel worker, the street black, the young Polish girl swimming in a polluted river, and the political revolutionaires of Chile, Italy, and Spain. For, in a sense, these are the people who haunt him, from whom he can't escape:

> did they come hand
> in hand through
> the bare wood halls
> to sway above my bed
> and call me back
> to the small damp body.
> ("The Secret of Their Voices")

A number of poems serve as dedications to political revolutionaries, those who have lost their lives in causes not yet won; Levine cries out for explanations, a sense of moral justice, really,

Copyright © 1977 by The Antioch Review, Inc. First appeared in the *Antioch Review* 35, nos. 2–3 (Spring–Summer 1977).

to compensate for their tragedies. These poems are often melancholy, powerful, though occasionally a little sentimental. But it is the memory of the poet's own Detroit childhood, where political realities take on a haunting particularity, that calls forth his greatest powers, his descriptions of the nobility and harsh realities of urban life: "The moon gone dark / the smoke of the rolling mills, / the switch engine quiet / in the iron sheds," and, speaking of his compatriots, the manual laborers, "They have joined / each other in the fellowship / of the shovel." In another of his strongest poems, "Belle Isle, 1949," the poet creates a reverie, recalls a moment of illumination and vulnerability with a young Polish girl:

> We stripped down in the first warm spring night
> and ran down into the Detroit River
> to baptize ourselves in the brine
> of car parts, dead fish, stolen bicycles,
> melted snow.

The poem allows for a brief interlude of lives touching, of communion, before returning to the sense-deadening rituals of everyday life.

Memory, then, becomes an important center for the book. To remember, to recall, is to honor the "lost," the dead, to learn from, if not recover, the past. As he says in "To the Poets of Chile": "Someone / must remember it over / and over, must bring / it home. . . ." Memory is also central because the book begins, in a Job-like fashion, to question the irrevocable process of time, the process which leads us only to death. The personal obsession of the book (and of Levine's previous and brilliant book, titled *1933*) becomes the justification of loss: the loss of those we love and those who touch our lives, and our own inevitable death. In one of the most moving poems of the book, "No One Remembers," Levine recalls his uncle Joe, a strong and cruel man who believed too much in his own personal power, but who also had the capacity for tenderness; ultimately Joe cannot rely on his façade of manhood to face death:

> You think because I
> was a boy, I didn't hear,

you think because you had
a pocketful of loose change,
your feet on the desk,
your own phone, a yellow car
on credit, I didn't see
you open your hands
like a prayer and die
into them the way a child
dies into a razor, a black hair,
into a tire iron, a chain.

The Names of the Lost creates a process of discovery, beginning by questioning the inevitability of loss: "Shall I ask / how many men, dying, passed me / the blood of their voices, the spittle / oiling their groans." And is it possible that the poet himself, with strong memories of his youth and a history with the woman he loves, "will come at last / to dirt and stone and love them?" Gradually the book attempts to move toward acceptance. Speaking of his mother, he says, "If I held her head now / it would be clay," and he realizes the process of time cannot be halted:

Nothing I can say will stop
the great bellied clouds
riding low over the fences
and flat wooden houses
of this old neighborhood
of keeping the late roses
from shredding down to dust

("The Falling Sky")

Still, there is a dialectic between community and decay, imagistically between blossoming and burning, a link between him and the past, personally and politically. As for the future, "which grows like a scar," Levine fears these connections will be lost; this fear is usually confronted when dealing with his own son, to whom he carries, via the fables of story-telling, the lessons of the past. Levine mourns, in another strong poem, "My Son and I": "We are Americans / and never touch on this / stunned earth where a boy / sees his life fly past / through a car window," and asks, "Why / do I have to sit before him / no longer his father, only / a man?" In the same poem he accepts the inevitability of loss, answering the poem's questions: "Because the given / must be taken, because / we hunger before we eat, / because each small spark / must turn to darkness."

Finally, by the end of the book, in "And the Trains Go On," he returns to the necessity and limitations of his need to bring the past forward, in a beautiful passage:

> . . . When you grip
> my arm hard and lean way out
> and shout out the holy names
> of the lost neither of us is scared
> and the tears mean nothing.

JAY PARINI

From "The Small Valleys of Our Living"

I take my title from a poem in which Philip Levine sees the modern poet in a diminished but not inglorious rôle, a descendant of Isaiah, whom the angel of the Lord touched on the lips with a coal to bring forth prophecy: "Light that will spread the morning glory / burns on my tongue and spills / into the small valleys of our living, / the branches creak, and I let it begin." Given the intractable nature of poetry today, any generalization may well boomerang, but few readers will quarrel with Levine's modest assertion. We have learned to expect less from our poets, it seems; for, as Auden said repeatedly, poetry makes nothing happen. . . .

We do, however, need the poems of Philip Levine. He is one of our necessary voices, a poet who has consistently evinced the desperation of the lost, failed, and powerless. Lines from his first book, *On the Edge* (1963), come to mind.

> Touched once, like a plum, I turned
> Rotten in the meat, or like
> The plum blossom I never
> Saw, hard at the edges, burned
> At the first entrance of life,
> And so endured, unreckoned,
> Untaken, with nothing to give.
> The first Jew was God; the second
> Denied him; I am alive.
>
> ("The Turning")

"The Small Valleys of Our Living" first appeared in *Poetry* (August, 1977), copyright 1977 by The Modern Poetry Association. Reprinted by permission of the Editor of *Poetry*.

This typical early Levine persona will not give in to despair. Whatever happens, he confirms the ultimate I AM. Like the pig in "Animals Are Passing from Our Lives," his characters kick and squeal, even while smells of the chopping block sour the air. He is the poet confirming a life force which no amount of failure can repress at last.

Levine takes his subjects from his own past, his childhood in Detroit, his family, Spain. His poems recreate the sense of place and time with a density and specificity all his own. They can be difficult, hellishly so; but the difficulty comes, not from wilfulness or inattention, but from the complex emotional terrain which Levine explores. There is less obscurity than before, I should add, in *The Names of the Lost,* which represents this poet's best work to date. The varied personae have, for the most part, disappeared. Levine consolidates his imagination here with a fresh urge to praise the things of this world in spite of the terror and cruelty everywhere in evidence around him.

The Spanish Civil War provides a setting for a good many of these poems, and Levine handles this potentially hazardous subject with restraint and a somewhat eerie control. Among the finest of these poems is "On the Murder of Lieutenant José del Castillo by the Falangist Bravo Martinez, July 12, 1936":

> When the Lieutenant of the Guardia de Asalto
> heard the automatic go off, he turned
> and took the second shot just above
> the sternum, the third tore away
> the right shoulder of his uniform,
> the fourth perforated his cheek.

He presents the scene with a vividness undiminished by the tone of detachment. We realize what has happened along with the ambushed officer, and the second shot takes our breath away with his. The narrator's objectivity wheels the scene into a timeless arena, partly the result of an inverted bathos: "The pigeons that spotted the cold floor / of Barcelona rose as he sank below / the waves of silence crashing / on the far shores of his legs, growing / faint and watery." As ever with Levine, lines grip and claw for attention; yet he manages to weld the poem into a

complex whole in the magnificent last lines, where he raises the
tone suddenly. Here is the language of elegy in full bloom:

> . . . There is more
> to be said, but by someone who has suffered
> and died for his sister the earth
> and his brothers the beasts and the trees.
> The Lieutenant can hear it, the prayer
> that comes on the voices of water, today
> or yesterday, from Chicago or Valladolid,
> and hangs like smoke above this street
> he won't walk as a man ever again.

In "My Son and I," one of the most haunting poems in the
collection, father and son meet at 3 A.M. in a coffee house in New
York, a rendezvous of generations, bizarre because they meet as
strangers, although the blood-line pulls them together. The son
thinks his father is dying:

> . . . He's dressed
> in worn corduroy pants
> and shirts over shirts,
> and his hands are stained
> as mine once were
> with glue, ink, paint.
> A brown stocking cap
> hides the thick blond hair
> so unlike mine. For forty
> minutes he's tried not
> to cry. How are his brothers?
> I tell him I don't know,
> they have grown away
> from me. . . .

The father knows he comes before his son "no longer his father."
He does so because "the given / must be taken, because / we
hunger before we eat, / because each small spark / must turn to
darkness."

"The Falling Sky" evokes a dream-world wherein the figures

move in a strange weather, a climate of exhaustion. It approximates Eden after the Fall, but there is still something positive recognized by the poet, what he calls "the glory living gives us."

> Last night while I slept
> someone woke and went
> to the window to see
> if the moon was dreaming
> in the October night.
> I heard her leave the bed,
> heard the floor creak
> and opened my eyes a moment
> to see her standing in all
> the glory living gives us.

He doesn't say how much glory this is, of course; but that anything at all approximates glory in the rubble of his characters' lives amounts to optimism! We see here what Wallace Stevens in *Of Modern Poetry* called "The poem of the mind in the act of finding / What will suffice."

In "A Late Answer," perhaps the central poem in this new book, Levine concludes:

> . . . Somewhere
> the sea saves its tears
> for the rising tide, somewhere
> we'll leave the world weighing
> no more than when we came,
> and the answer will be
> the same, your hand in mine,
> mine in yours, in that clearing
> where the angels come toward us
> without laughter, without tears.

The scene recalls Milton's Adam and Eve on their last journey through paradise: "They hand in hand with wand'ring steps and slow, / Through Eden took their solitary way." The theological underpinning is missing from Levine, but the elegiac note persists. "To My God in His Sickness," the last poem in the book, denies the possibility of redemption: "though my grandmother argues / the first cause of night / and the kitchen cantor mumbles his names / still the grave will sleep." The title, which parodies a famous poem by Donne, bristles with nuances. If God is alive, he must be sick. Sick-ill or sick-nasty? I think the latter, for Levine offers a world where "A rabbit snared in a fence of pain / screams and screams." The poet wakes up to his childhood, but "it's not a dream." Writhing in his sleep, he images "this America we thought we dreamed / falling away flake by flake / into the sea." The poem whirls its fragments around the still center of Levine's dispassionate voice, cutting across time. The speaker answers Moses at one point; at the end he claims: "I was a friend to the ox and walked / with Absalom. . . ." This book confirms Levine as one of our essential poets. His dark vision is central to our experience in this century, and *The Names of the Lost* will be read for a long time to come.

SYDNEY LEA

From "Wakings in Limbo"

Philip Levine's characters are specifically not the masters of their need. The opening passage of *The Names of the Lost* signals that it will be filled with wakenings, but not into home:

> When the streetcar stalled on Joy Road
> the conductor finished his coffee, puffed
> into his overcoat, and went to phone in.
> The Hungarian punch-press operator wakened
> alone, 7000 miles from home, pulled down
> his orange cap and set out. If he saw
> the winter birds scuffling in the cinders,
> if he felt it was the dawn of a new day,
> he didn't let on . . .
>
> ("On the Birth of Good and Evil During the
Long Winter of '28")

The punch-press operator is literally—as so many of Levine's lost are metaphorically—a Displaced Person, his life and mind mysterious. Does he expect or even want revelation, the dawn of a new day? We don't know; hence the poet's own frustration, for he at least yearns to transform this gritty tableau.

But Levine moots his general desire to make large changes, to forge grand significances, by honestly presenting all that stands in the way. Neither breast-beater nor self-styled vatic, he reveals the perilous longings of the Inquiring Spirit, Coleridge's Mariner, say, or Milton's Satan, and he confronts the full implications of the latter's famous contention that "the mind is its own place." It is as if some god had indeed fated the heirs of such subjectivism always to lack a home. *The Names of the Lost* is appropriately filled with rebels and/or wanderers like "The Survivor":

Chicago Review 30 (1978). Reprinted with permission. In his essay Lea compares Levine's *The Names of the Lost* with Robert Pack's *Keeping Watch.*—ED.

> . . . Home is here,
> you say; your hand reaches
> out and touches nothing.
> Russia, New York, back,
> that was your father; you
> took up the road, moving
> at dawn or after dusk . . .

A poet's titles are telling, and Levine's include "No One Remembers," "For the Fallen," "For the Poets of Chile," "And the Trains Go On." He is a master of the tragedy of transience and alienation, of the wide meeting of souls. For him, even the family is unfamiliar: he frequently tells us that his children "have grown away"; under "The Falling Sky" (one of the most moving pieces) his wife is "growing smaller, / darker." Or

> She is deaf and works
> in the earth for days, hearing
> the dirt pray and guiding
> the worm to its feasts . . .
>
> ("My Son and I")

The very closest associate is almost uncanny, so that all fellows are strangers, all moments of tenderness exquisitely tenuous, like this one in a train yard:

> When your head dropped to your chest
> I parted your fingers
> and drew the cigarette out
> and smoked it.

With some ardor, one sees in this at least a furtively ritual gesture, yet when the poet wakes

> You were gone, brother,
> the face I never saw in darkness
> gone, the cigarette gone,
> and I haven't touched you since.
>
> ("You")

For Levine's lost, the mind *is* its own place, a fact which persistently vetoes the poet's wish for a revealed wholeness and community. For Levine, "everyone brings some piece / of himself to the table, / and the old wood groans" ("Autumn Again"). In "New Season" Levine and his son visit a garden spot where together they have planted a plum tree. This is not a yielding Mother Earth; the poet recalls "digging / . . . through three feet / of hard pan." His son's hands are "glazed with callus," and his manners are adolescently violent: "He flicks two snails off a leaf / and smashes them underfoot," talking of "the wars of the young . . . / . . . ready to fight for nothing, hard." Levine summons recurrent loss and strife, not peaceable continuity, from his reading of the landscape: he runs together his senile mother, the Detroit riots of '43, the feebleness of his aged cat, and ends by undercutting even the durability and gentle gradualism which another poet might attribute to nature.

> . . . the willow is burning,
> the rhododendrons shrivel
> like paper under water, all
> the small secret mouths are feeding
> on the green heart of the plum.

That burning willow subtly reminds us of Levine's urge for revelation—his search for some means to integrate and ennoble this frankly sordid and fragmented instant—but the poem acknowledges its unattainability. The search for a cohering Truth is vitiated by things-as-they-are: the foliage shrivels like paper under water, and we cannot miss the bitter implications for Levine's own writings. It is the bitterness that closes his volume in "To My God in His Sickness," for this sickness is that He does not exist, that there *is* no transcending Principle to gather up and redeem the names (or the poems) of the lost. Levine anticipates a great blank page.

It takes a vigorous poet to carry on, once having assumed this perspective, or at least to do so without lapsing into self-pity and sentimentalism; and it takes restraint, as for example in "On the Corner," in which Art Tatum and his bass player are "talking Jackie Robinson." "Can't / believe how fast / he is to first," says the blind Tatum. "Wait'll / you see Mays," says the bass player without cruelty:

> The gutters swirled
> their heavy waters,
> the streets reflected
> the sky, which was
> nothing. Tatum
> stamped on toward
> the Bland Hotel, a wet
> newspaper stuck
> to his shoe, his mouth
> open, his vest
> drawn and darkening.
> I can't hardly wait, he said.

It is impossible to overpraise either the tact that gives the poem its pathos or its author's respect for human valor, even among the apparently lost. Tatum avoids despair, appears sturdy, and his character in turn both heightens and dignifies the pathos here. Such instances are common in *The Names of the Lost:* one thinks of the jauntiness of a railroad bum in "And the Trains Go On":

> . . . Once, when I
> unsealed a car and the two
> of us strained the door open
> with a groan of rust, an old man
> stepped out and tipped his hat.
> "It's all yours, boys!"
> and he went off, stiff-legged,
> smelling of straw and shit;

of the vitality in a falsely convicted prisoner ("Waiting") whose

> . . . letter ends,
> as always, with a poem, this one
> of Ginny, "greener than goose manure
> piled five feet high";

of even the villainous Uncle Joe in "No One Remembers," a child- and women-beater who nonetheless once

> picked me up and said
> my name, *Philip,* and held
> the winter sun up
> for me to see outside
> the French windows of
> the old house on Pingree . . .

The good poets all have some humanity, at least in their writings, which checks self-vaunting in the interest of compassion for the humblest, the most lost, of their fellows. And even the most lost of their utterances are quickened by that sympathy for their fleshly fellows:

> old words, lost truths
> ground to their essential nonsense
> I lift you in my hand
> and inhale, the odor of light
> out of darkness, substance out of air
> of blood before it reddens and runs
> ("To My God in His Sickness")

WILLIAM STAFFORD

A Poet with Something to Tell You

One way to get the immediacy of Philip Levine's poetry is to imagine overhearing it, maybe from the other side of a door, so that the strange *onwardness* of the language can snag you without the distraction of knowing it is poetry. Listen to this part of "No One Remembers," from *The Names of the Lost:*

> You think because I was a boy, I didn't hear, you think be-
> cause you had a pocketful of loose change, your feet on the
> desk, your own phone, a yellow car on credit, I didn't see you
> open your hands like a prayer and die into them the way a
> child dies into a razor, black hair, into a tire iron, a chain. You
> think I didn't smell the sweat that rose from your bed, didn't
> know you on the stairs in the dark, grunting into a frightened
> girl. Because you could push me aside like a kitchen chair and
> hit where you wanted, you think I was a wren, a mourning
> dove surrendering the nest.

Philip Levine's messages to the world can be lined out this way, as prose, to demonstrate how easily this current poetry has pulled up alongside us and begun to deliver its immediately available communication—direct, uncluttered, nonesoteric. This kind of poetry—and Philip Levine is demonstrating it at its best year after year—doesn't require any background of culture from T. S. Eliot's "tradition," or even from the assumed centrality of the American Standard Background, as in Lowell's early work.

Levine's work quietly appropriates the direct language of prose while maintaining a readiness to gain from the frequent bonuses that lurk in syllables and cadences in the lingo of talk. There is an immediate, coercive drop onto common experience, the opposite of scholarly allusion. But there is a kind of unfold-

Inquiry, June 26, 1978. Reprinted with permission.

ing and controlled tenacity about the sentences as they go down the page. Here is the end of the poem quoted above, this time by the lines as Philip Levine formed them:

> The earth is asleep, Joe,
> it's rock, steel, ice,
> the earth doesn't care
> or forgive. No one remembers
> your eyes before they tired,
> the way you fought weeping.
> No one remembers how much
> it cost to drive all night
> to Chicago, how much
> to sleep all night in a car,
> to have it all except
> the money. No one remembers
> your hand, opened, warm
> and sweating on the back
> of my neck when you first
> picked me up and said
> my name, *Philip,* and held
> the winter sun up
> for me to see outside
> the French windows of
> the old house on Pingree,
> no one remembers.

One shouldn't claim too much for these unspectacular lines, or try to force admiration for an art that depends, after all, on little, sustained satisfactions. But when the quietness and consistency of a book like *The Names of the Lost* can recur to you as you rove through other books, you begin to know that a voice has established itself in your life. And you go back, wondering why it is when "No one remembers" that you remember. You find again a certain bittersweet flavor.

That flavor comes, it seems to me, from a distinctive inward complexity in our time. For Levine, and for many, many others today, the world is an unfeeling place. People brush on by, and forget. And we are surrounded by violence and foreshadowings.

How can people be this way? And yet, it is only by our feelings that we identify "unfeeling." If the feelings didn't exist, there would be no reaction, no realization. In such a world, justice is a continent always being discovered by taking soundings. That continent comes into being as we read writers like Philip Levine. The tradition behind these individual talents is just the widely available tradition of being alive, of having relatives, of experiencing cold, hunger, fulfillment, loss, redemption. The places and people in these poems are there—inevitably—for all of us. They are the elements of our lives made clear, enhanced by art, and returned to us. In light of such poems we see better where we are now.

Levine is one of the many in this current tradition-of-being-alive. Many poets now do it his way—coming at experience with language validated by everyone's feelings about talk.

And sometimes his poems seem strange. I can't account for why they work: there are elements in each one not yet encompassed in critical theory. For example, in a poem called "Waiting," the reader finds a constant stretching toward particulars that are so incidental that they need not be explained, but so meaningful to the speaker that he must mention them:

> You sit
> at the window above the windswept yard
> treeless forever, and you pray
> for us all, for the lying witness
> left in a ditch, for the stolen car. . . .

Any example may be forced under some critical formulation, but the effect of reading Levine is that of finding ourselves surprised by a move that carried us beyond what we knew, or where we have been, or where we expected to go.

Philip Levine is exploring, taking soundings. In such writing, even though people and places are nearby and the language is the language of talk, there can be many surprises. And when he does range into world events, his lines catch up occasional accelerations, recurrences at odd places, glimpses that allow ordinary phrases to go telescopic. A good example is found in "For the Poets of Chile" (also from *The Names of the Lost*). He remarks that ". . . someone must / stand at the window . . . / remembering how once / there were voices. . . ." And speaking of "Victor, who died / on the third day," he ends with the living:

> Victor left a child,
> a little girl
> who must waken each day
> before her mother
> beside her, and dress
> herself in the clothes
> laid out the night
> before. The house sleeps
> except for her, the floors
> and cupboards cry out
> like dreamers. She goes
> to the table and sets out
> two forks, two spoons, two knives,
> white linen napkins gone
> gray at the edges,
> the bare plates,
> and the tall glasses
> for the milk they must
> drink each morning.

It was Ezra Pound, I believe, who said that poetry should be as well written as prose. To test whether Levine has something to tell you, regardless of how it is placed on the page, here is "On the Murder of Lieutenant José del Castillo by the Falangist Bravo Martinez, July 12, 1936," printed as a news account:

When the Lieutenant of the Guardia de Asalto heard the automatic go off, he turned and took the second shot just above the sternum, the third tore away the right shoulder of his uniform, the fourth perforated his cheek. As he slid out of his comrade's hold toward the gray cement of the Ramblas he lost count and knew only that he would not die and that the blue sky smudged with clouds was not heaven for heaven was nowhere and in his eyes slowly filling with their own light. The pigeons that spotted the cold floor of Barcelona rose as he sank below the waves of silence crashing on the far shores of his legs, growing faint and watery. His hands opened a last time to receive the benedictions of automobile exhaust and rain and the rain of soot. His mouth, that would never again say "I am afraid," closed on nothing. The old grandfather hawking daisies at his stand pressed a handkerchief against his lips and turned his eyes away before they held the eyes of a gunman. The shepherd dogs on sale howled in their cages and turned in circles. There is more to be said, but by someone who has suffered and died for his sister the earth and his brothers the beasts and the trees. The Lieutenant can hear it, the prayer that comes on the voices of water, today or yesterday, from Chicago or Valladolid, and hangs like smoke above this street he won't walk as a man ever again.

JAY PARINI

Award-Winning Poems

Philip Levine may be the best of the generation of poets that grew up during World War II, came of age in the 1950s, and has been writing for twenty years or so. He is certainly among the handful of poets without whom contemporary poetry in America would be much the poorer.

These fairly extravagant claims sound all the more so given Levine's relative obscurity until his second book, *Not This Pig,* appeared in 1968, and indeed, it was not until the *New Yorker* and Atheneum gave him a wide audience that Levine, in a sense, discovered himself. His last book, *The Names of the Lost,* appeared in 1976 and established his presence as a poet of originality, moral concern, and vision. And now *Ashes* and *7 Years from Somewhere* (winners of the National Book Critics Circle Award for poetry) confirm everything we had hoped for: a necessary voice, prodigious in volume, consistently good and entirely sui generis.

Ashes reprints thirteen poems from an earlier book, now out of print, and contains thirteen new ones. An autobiographical poet in the explicit sense, Levine invokes the industrial images of a Detroit childhood, of working-class family tensions, of travels in Spain and elsewhere. He can describe a scene with the accuracy that accompanies a bright inward vision:

> From the high hill
> behind Ford Rouge, we could see
> the ore boats pulling
> down river, the rail yards,
> and the smoking mountain.

"Award-Winning Poems" first appeared in *The Nation,* February 2, 1980. Copyright 1980 by The Nation Company, Inc. Reprinted with permission.

> East, the city spreading
> toward St. Clair, miles of houses,
> factories, shops burning
> in the still white snow.
>
> ("In the New Sun")

As seen here, Levine writes with an informal clarity and an idiosyncratic tone that combine conversational cadences with an unusual lyric tautness.

Levine moves from description to revelation in his best work, beginning with a vivid image, transforming the image into a resonant symbol. Nature, as Emerson told us, is the symbol of the spirit; for Levine, nature includes factories, transmission shops, gas stations, railroads—all the detritus of urban-industrial living—in addition to the green hills of pastoral verse. Whatever his setting—and the variety will astound—we soon learn to recognize the cadence, the dreamlike atmosphere, the strange weather of aloneness characteristic of his voice. His short lines and abrupt enjambments verge on prose, but they can veer of a sudden into lyric intensity rarely seen these days. Consider the end of "Ashes":

> Do you want the earth to be heaven?
> Then pray, go down on your knees
> as though a king stood before you,
> and pray to become all you'll
> never be, a drop of sea water,
> a small hurtling flame across the sky,
> a fine flake of dust that moves
> an evening like smoke at great height
> above the earth and sees it all.

7 Years from Somewhere fills to the same brim as Ashes. The same landscapes occur, similar situations, but the whole book feels even more thoroughly *achieved* than some of Levine's early books. It is as if a corresponding inward intensity of vision has finally met and equaled the brightness of his external vision. There are poems of childhood, such as "Milkweed," a beautiful lyric which in its final stanza moves beyond simple recollection

into an awareness of natural cycles. The poet revisits a scene where, as a child, he cut down milkweeds with a carved wooden sword:

> Two days ago I walked
> the empty woods, bent over,
> crunching through oak leaves,
> asking myself questions
> without answers. From somewhere
> a froth of seeds drifted by touched
> with gold in the last light
> of a lost day, going with
> the wind as they always did.

Or in "Snow," for instance, he recalls snow falling in a Detroit street, saying "the snow / which has been falling for hours / is more beautiful than even the spring / grass which once unfurled here / before the invention of steel and fire." A late Romantic, Levine refuses the traditional consolations; he knows that the past cannot be recovered, nor the dead revived; he looks instead to the redemptive power of imagination, which is like the snow in "Snow," at once "nothing" and something of great importance:

> It has no melody or form, it
> is as though the tears of all
> the lost souls rose to heaven
> and were finally blessed
> with substance and the power of light
> and given their choice chose then
> to return to earth, to lay their
> great pale cheek against the burning
> cheek of earth and say, There, there, child.

So Levine says, "There, there child," for his poems offer us the consolation of achieved form, which is something. Like Robert Frost, another late Romantic, he knows that "earth's the right place for love," that love is unlikely to go better elsewhere. We can be grateful for Levine's presence among us.

142

ROCHELLE RATNER

The Two Faces of Philip Levine

Take One: Philip Levine is one of the finest poets writing today, a poet who takes risks, reveals his past, the intimate details of his life. He has the ability to turn trivialities into events of real importance. His is vital, extremely well-crafted poetry.

Take Two: Philip Levine is the poet of academia, a poet who writes and writes and says nothing. He's similar to W. S. Merwin in that with *They Feed They Lion* (1972), he hit upon an extremely strong statement and has since written book after book of similar theme, differing only here and there in image. The poems are hollow, with tricks of extremely astute phrasing to hold the reader's attention.

Both readings are partially accurate. The simultaneous publication by Atheneum of two books, *Ashes: Poems New and Old* and *7 Years from Somewhere,* gives us a good chance to view a large portion of his work in perspective.

On the surface, Levine's poetry is extremely personal, intense dramatic monologues probing what it means to love, to be part of a family. But it's personal in a roundabout way, with "you," "he," or "she" used over and over again. And because the person isn't named, we're quick to assume the emotion applies universally.

Levine has also become America's most powerful poet of despair. So much so that it's beginning to seem his poems are written by formula. They fit too easily now into the pattern he's come to handle so masterfully: long poem, fairly short lines, few if any stanza breaks, all running together to be more or less summed up by the last few lines.

After reading *They Feed They Lion,* I went back and read all Levine's earlier books. What impressed me most were his technical abilities, and the way that each book varied from the one before it. What strikes me now about the thirteen early poems

Soho Weekly News, September 27, 1979. Reprinted with permission.

reprinted in *Ashes* is not their style so much as the attempt to be less personal. Still, when read here, in contrast to newer poems, they can't help but be viewed as personal. And that Levine would choose to include them in this collection says something to me about the way he now views his poetic development. In *Ashes* the remnants of his working-class childhood carry through an identification with the workers, the oppressed, he meets now, as if in a romanticized attempt to call back his childhood. Yet when I reread *They Feed They Lion* (1972) or *1933* (1974), where the attempt was essentially the same, I found no feeling of romanticism. That only comes when the observation itself begins to fail him.

I've read *7 Years from Somewhere* numerous times now, and I'm just beginning to understand it. By the second reading I'd jotted down in my notes that "a poem like 'Let Me Be' gets me angry. Levine places this poem near the conclusion of an autobiographical series, but midway through he talks about being arrested for drunk driving four times and spending months in jail, happy there with his children coming on weekends. Is he being ironic? Nothing in the other poems prepares us for this."

On this reading I can see that this book is Levine's attempt to break away from his past work, to create a more fictional, wished-for autobiography. Born in 1928, he couldn't have been in the army in 1943 as he claims in "I Could Believe," and this first poem sets the tone for the rest of the book. In his striving to identify with others, he at last becomes them, as in "Your Life." These are contrasted with poems like "Asking," where he goes back to a point in his life and asks how it could have been otherwise if he had allowed that situation to change him. In "Let Me Be," where the situation is too far removed to be believable, his weaknesses hang out all over. But perhaps that's his greatest strength in other poems—the fact that he can combine memory with fantasy. He's at the beginning of something new in his work, something he hasn't yet mastered, but which I hope he'll take further. He's too good a poet not to.

RALPH J. MILLS, JR.

"Back to This Life":
Philip Levine's New Poems

Issuing two collections of poems by an American poet in mid-career at the same time is an unusual gesture for a New York publisher these days, even for one so firmly supportive of the art as Atheneum, but this publication must surely say something about the high reputation Philip Levine has established since the appearance of *They Feed They Lion* in 1972. Other motives may be discerned as well. In *Ashes* Levine reprints thirteen poems from his decisive Kayak volume in *Red Dust* (1971), interspersing them skillfully with nineteen recent pieces to achieve a considerable unity. In *7 Years from Somewhere* the poems, all of them new, possess even closer relations with one another. Finally, there are numerous important ties between the two books: echoes, resonances, and repetitions that are linguistic, thematic, imagistic. Of course, it would have been possible to combine all this work under a single set of covers, but something would have been sacrificed, a certain breathing space from which the separate groups of poems benefit.

Anyone who has followed Levine's brilliant development will recall the sharp-edged, elliptical, often associative or surrealist manner of the poems in *Red Dust,* which were a crucial step away from his previous writings—though there were visible foreshadowings in *Not This Pig*—and were indicative of an acquaintance with Spanish and Latin American poets. Like them, Levine has a social conscience, moral indignation and disgust, an ability to identify with the poor, the failed, those trapped for life by wearying, grinding, unfulfilling labor. As his poems have steadily revealed, he knows this type of experience from the inside, has held such jobs and seen them eat out the substance of family and

New England Review 2 (1979). Reprinted with permission.

friends. It is no surprise to observe him maintaining an interest in these materials right into his latest work, and he still treats them with energy and freshness. But the style of the *Red Dust* poems stands out as more jagged and fierce, wilder in its imaginative "leaps," to borrow Robert Bly's term, among images and objects, than that of many (though not all) of the newer pieces in *Ashes.* Two examples of this earlier style must suffice. The initial one consists of the final section from "Clouds":

> You cut an apple in two pieces
> and ate them both. In the rain
> the door knocked and you dreamed it.
> On bad roads the poor walked under cardboard boxes.
>
> The houses are angry because they're watched.
> A soldier wants to talk with God
> but his mouth fills with lost tags.
>
> The clouds have seen it all, in the dark
> they pass over the graves of the forgotten
> and they don't cry or whisper.
>
> They should be punished every morning,
> they should be bitten and boiled like spoons.

And here is the opening stanza of "How Much Earth":

> Torn into light, you woke wriggling
> on a woman's palm. Halved, quartered,
> shredded to the wind, you were the life
> that thrilled along the underbelly
> of a stone. Stilled in the frozen pond
> you rinsed heaven with a sigh.

Loss, frustration, despair, and fury alternate among the poems of *Ashes,* whether Levine's concentration is on elements of his own life or the lives of others. But the author's great compassion and tenderness are present to match those qualities too. Framing the book is the figure of the poet's father, whom he lost when a small boy. That is one of the "little deaths" of which he perceives one's existence to be composed. In the poems of both books Levine frequently views himself under various forms as dying and being reborn within the compass of an individual lifetime; this becomes a way of dramatizing the stages, alterations and mutations that he has undergone and will continue to undergo, even with his actual death, a theme taken up more fully in *7 Years.* "Now," he says, "I must wait and be still / and say nothing I don't know, / nothing I haven't lived / over and over, / and that's everything."

But if "you can howl your name into the wind / and it will blow it into dust, you / can pledge your single life, the earth / will eat it all," as he notes in the title poem of *Ashes,* still that wind and earth are just about all Levine can discover to come back to. He seems to have little faith in a redemptive power. So, at the end of the same poem, he offers his own moving act of reverence for the world, though its consolation lies only in the lyrical power of the writing itself:

> Do you want the earth to be heaven?
> Then pray, go down on your knees
> as though a king stood before you,
> and pray to become all you'll
> never be, a drop of sea water,
> a small hurtling flame across the sky,
> a fine flake of dust that moves
> at evening like smoke at great height
> above the earth and sees it all.

While in the beginning poem of *Ashes,* called "Father," he dismisses his dead parent after finding him only in himself and his own grief, Levine is much more positive in the concluding piece, "Lost and Found," which reunites father and son, the middle-aged poet with the child he once was, and confirms in a stronger, less qualified fashion than the passage above an enduring human bond, with the natural world its context:

> Now he
> is home, the one I searched for.
> He is beside me as he always
> was, a light spirit that brings

me luck and listens when I speak.
The day is here, and it will last
forever or until the sun fails
and the birds are once again
hidden and moaning, but for now
the lost are found. The sun
has cleared the trees, the wind
risen, and we, father and child
hand in hand, the living and
the dead, are entering the world.

7 Years from Somewhere, which contains nothing but recent work, shows more coherence; many of the poems are of that tall, columnar kind Levine has been writing of late, with swift-paced, often relatively short lines and simple, direct, sometimes repetitive diction and imagery. The repetition is obviously part of the linking between different poems. It is impossible in a brief review to do more than point to the fact of complexity, of intertwining motifs and recurrent concerns in this pair of books; the poems merit long, careful discussion. *7 Years,* however, seems to push even further the poet's confrontation with the fundamentals of existence, especially with death. "I Could Believe," the first poem, starts with fantastic, romantic speculations which then carry Levine into the projection of an alternate life for himself (though this life is not itself romantic and may have parallels, in its dates, with his father's), but everything settles down to "dying" at the finish, as if to announce a central preoccupation for the remainder of the volume. Yet the dead in the poems of *7 Years* belong to the world perhaps even more completely than in the poems of *Ashes.* With the remarkable sequence "Ricky," a commemoration of a young friend of Levine's sons who died by drowning, the poet envisages the boy's "breath passing through dark water / never to return" to its owner, but at the close, synonymous with his spirit, that breath flows everywhere, "nothing could contain it." Similarly, the dream of the "City of God" fashioned by the Spanish revolutionaries Levine has often celebrated and mourned is given up with their last breath to the air, though it is received in turn by others who sustain the life of the dream. The essence of being never departs the world: poem after poem returns us to the "place," the "life" "no one promised" which is yet "like no other." In prayerful lines from "Words" he seeks absorption in the totality of lives and things, a moment of visionary identification and realization with a strange resonance of the gospel maxim that the one who loses his life shall find it:

>   I want
>   you to lead me to
>   the place within me
>   where I am every
>   man and woman, the trees
>   floating in the cold haze
>   of January, the small
>   beasts whose names
>   I have forgotten, the ache
>   I feel to be no
>   longer only myself.

These are all, of course, hard-won affirmations of existence. "No one / said it would be easy," Levine states flatly and irrefutably in the final line of a poem. The attentive, sensitive reader cannot avoid perceiving what intense emotion, deep suffering, and rending joy have been distilled into the apparent effortlessness of this poet's style; he can merely imagine the cost. I should like to quote here one poem, "In the Dark," in its entirety, believing it will serve better than any comment to illustrate the characteristic movement of Levine's lines, his beautiful dispositions of language and artful simplicity—and everything working toward the terrible, cumulative force of the completed piece.

>   1.
>
>   Each hour of this life
>   I see the darkness
>   more clearly, see how
>   it lives in the shadows
>   of the wild phlox, how
>   it climbs the valley ash
>   at dusk and finally crowns
>   the leaves, how it rises

then slowly from the grass.
The trees are still. I
hold my breath that one
moment and suddenly
tiny fires blur the sky
but cannot make it light.

2.

The woman who sleeps
beside me is dreaming
of something I can
never touch. When I touch
her shoulder she turns,
her damp cheek bathed
in the first soft light
of a day begun like
no other. She says
my name, one hushed
long syllable than means
I have entered again
the single presence she holds.

3.

Once, as a boy, I
climbed the attic stairs
in a sleeping house
and entered a room
no one used. I found
a trunk full of letters
and post cards from a man
who had travelled for years
and then come home to die.
In moonlight each one
said the same thing: how
long the nights were, how
cold it was so far away,
and how it had to end.

I have barely touched here on the richness, artistry, and imaginative achievement of these books.* Published simultaneously, they ought to be read together rather than apart, and of course in relation to Levine's preceding work. It appears to be the author's clear intention that the poems gathered form something close to sequences; while each can satisfy individually, all share internal ties. Again Philip Levine has proved himself one of our finest, most valuable poets, and one with whom every serious reader of poetry must come to terms.

---

*A small criticism. In 7 Years from Somewhere there are grammatical lapses in a few places which should have been caught: "neither . . . or" appears twice; murmurs is spelled "murmers"; in the last line of "Toward Home" there is a split infinitive which makes for an awkward ending; and in "Words" the pronoun "who" is used instead of "which" to refer to "words."

DAVE SMITH

From "The Second Self"

Who does not know the poems of Philip Levine? Can there be any point to reviewing his two new collections, *Ashes* and *7 Years from Somewhere,* if there is no radical, visible change? Maybe one simply likes what one likes, for my opinion is that I would as soon stop reading as give up Mr. Levine's poems. Still, what accounts for such delight? Especially when I have not altogether dismissed objections. Some have said he has written the same poem for years, that he lacks variety and vision. True, many of his poems possess one doleful cadence. True, his vision is such a relentless denunciation of injustice that he has occasionally engaged in reductive oversimplifications. For example, the political underbelly of *The Names of the Lost* comes uncomfortably close to cadres of the good, the bad, and the ugly. His prose piece, "To My Brother on the Death of a Young Poet" (*Antaeus* 30/31), seems irresponsibly blindered thinking and is, I think, reprehensible. Mr. Levine has a polemic streak which makes some of his work strident, manipulative, and at least ungenerous. And, some note, there is a level of violence in his poems few poets equal, whether it be objectionable or reflective. In spite of these objections and others, I cannot help believing his poetry is nearly a national treasure and many of the new poems are as good if not better than anything he has written.

Ashes contains thirteen poems from the long out of print *Red Dust* (Kayak, 1971) and nineteen new poems. The former have been characterized as surreal by way of the Spanish, an influence Mr. Levine admits. The analysis is based on images and phrasings, rather than entire poems, which are more dreamlike and associative than rational and linear. For example, "Blood runs to the heart and finds it locked"; or "rifles are brooding / in the closet"; or "the grave blooms upward / in sunlight and walks the

American Poetry Review, November–December, 1979. Reprinted with permission.

roads." I suspect there is less surrealism here than a vitally alive and active landscape whose every particle possesses the ability and need to express itself and a nearly symbiotic integrity. Another way of saying this is that Mr. Levine seems to have an extraordinary capacity to sense and give witness to a man's relationship with all that exists. He is no painter of mindscapes nor a primitivist nor a canting ecologist, though dream life, fundamental states of being, and an impure world matter greatly to him. He is distinctly American, a consumer and a mensch. When he writes, "The clouds go on eating oil," he indicts industrial greed as well as projects an emotional abuse beyond individual proportions. But it is the activity of his metaphor, its visual accumulation and poisoned ingestion, which causes a visceral rather than a mental response. He does not, even in *Red Dust,* rely very much on flashed and extra-worldly conjunctions but on the charged interaction of all things which he so acutely feels.

Importantly, Mr. Levine's poems always begin and remain grounded in a single, highly receptive consciousness which is a man's alone. The language, the figures of speech, the narrative progressions of this consciousness are never so private, so obscure, so truncated as to forbid less sophisticated readers. Though he takes on the largest subjects of death, love, courage, manhood, loyalty, etc., he brings the mysteries of existence down into the ordinarily inarticulate events and objects of daily life. His speaker and subject is the abused and disabused spirit of the common yet singular self. He risks the maudlin, the sentimental, the banal, and worse because he cannot live in the world fully enough; because the world is so much with us all we must sing or die of its inexpressible presence.

For me, Mr. Levine has been writing this way throughout his nine books, granted the shift from regular verse after *Not This Pig* and some slight reorientation after *Red Dust.* With *They Feed They Lion, 1933, The Names of the Lost,* and now *Ashes* and *7 Years from Somewhere,* he has shown increased technical control, a growing mastery of image and phrase, a deepened power to dramatize the suffering and potential of each moment. But there is no radical change in "a man alone, ignorant / strong, holding the burning moments / for all they're worth." The style of a man's poem need not change in pace with Detroit's assembly lines. It might be said that Mr. Levine has a formula and I would answer that we should all be so fortunate, for what he has is a style patiently developed to fit his need to speak the hurt and the joy that in all of us remains unshaped and embryonic. The point is:

> What would it mean to lose this life
> and go wandering the hallways
> of that house in search of another self?

If we can speak strongly and accurately enough our own love of life and hatred of diminishment, we may speak for all our selves. In such poems as "Toward Home," "Andorra," "Planting," "Let Me Begin Again" and others, Mr. Levine has moved well past caricature and glibness, past concern for anything but the honest reality he can forge in words. He not only speaks for us but as if he is us. A poet of main force, like the sun, he speaks the individual communion of "every / man and woman" contained in the imagination. He is wise, proud, eloquent, and excellent because, like Durer, he is *himself* and more. Here is the voice of poetry in "Lost and Found":

> He is beside me as he always
> was, a light spirit that brings
> me luck and listens when I speak.
> The day is here, and it will last
> forever or until the sun fails
> and the birds are once again
> hidden and moaning, but for now
> the lost are found. The sun
> has cleared the trees, the wind
> risen, and we, father and child
> hand in hand, the living and
> the dead, are entering the world.

PETER STITT

From "The Sincere, the Mythic, the Playful: Forms of Voice in Current Poetry"

Because lyric poetry is spoken in a direct and seemingly intimate voice, it is by its very nature a personal form of utterance. Such recent movements as confessionalism have sometimes led us to believe that lyric poetry, being personal, is also inherently sincere. In the sense that the poet means what he or she says, of course, poetry (except for the ostensibly ironic) is generally sincere. But in the sense that the poet is writing about his or her *own* life, feelings, and thoughts, poetry is never necessarily sincere. In one way or another—whether it appears only in the form or also in the content—artifice must be a component of the poem, and artifice is inevitably a dilutant of absolute sincerity. Without art there would be no poem; artificiality forms the musculature of poetic structure, and when a writer cuts too close to the white bone of unadulterated truth, it is the fiber of art which is damaged. A literal poem, one which shows no figurations, neither comparisons nor transformations, no renderings of fact into metaphor, is a poem in which the artistry is dead.

In terms of content, Philip Levine has always written a poetry that is generally both personal and sincere, a poetry based on the facts, feelings, and experiences of his own life. On one day last year, Levine published two books which, between them, illustrate both directions that this kind of verse can take. The poems in *Ashes* (many of which first appeared in Levine's 1971 volume, *Red Dust*) show everywhere signs of the transforming power of the artistic imagination; the raw materials of experience and emotion

The Georgia Review 34 (1980). Copyright 1980 by The University of Georgia. Reprinted by permission of *The Georgia Review* and the author.

have been converted, through metaphor, through music, into poetry. In *7 Years from Somewhere,* on the other hand, the writing is generally flat, the poems literal. At his best, Levine has always been a rhetorician, ever willing to set the devices of poetry working for him; it is a disappointment to find these elements so lacking in his most recent poems. One's sense of disappointment is all the more acute given Levine's obviously strong sense of commitment to his material. The poems are all, in one way or another, elegies—some lament the passage of time, the coming of age; some lament the deaths of friends, heroes; some lament the progressive passing of the poet himself, the loss of his childhood and youth. These are affective subjects, possessed of considerable power in and of themselves. It is understandable that Levine often relies on this inherent strength to carry his poems, but the results here are not compelling. "Words," for example, tells how time takes its toll on a family; the speaker seems to be trying, but failing, to extricate himself from a sense of depression. The poem ends: "My wife will say nothing / of the helplessness / she feels seeing her / men rocking on / their separate seas. / We are three people / bowing our heads to / all she has given us, / to bread and wine and meat. / The windows have gone / dark, but the room is / quiet in yellow light. / Nothing needs to be said." The form of this poem is, in a curious way, appropriate to the subject; both reveal an endemic emptiness.

Elsewhere there is an altogether direct and artless expression of excess emotion, artistically unjustified, as in these lines: "I did cry. I put my hands between / my legs, alone, in the room I came / to love because it was all the room / I had, and pitched forward and cried / without hope or relief, for myself." The poems in this book are generally narrative in form and often epiphanic in structure; in poem after poem, the speaker tells of incidents in his life which led to one revelation or another. Many are good poems too—like "Peace," "Let Me Begin Again," "You Can Have It," and the title poem "7 Years from Somewhere"—but none is as good as even the average poem in *Ashes.* There is a progression evident in Levine's work from the lush rhetorical intensity of his earlier poems to the relatively plain style of these later volumes. But Levine's natural voice is not well suited to the plain style, and that is why there is so much flatness in *7 Years from Somewhere.*

Ashes embodies a stylistic compromise. The pounding rhythms and insistent repetitions of the early work are largely absent here, with the formal emphasis being placed upon Levine's figurative imagination. The ability to double, to see one thing within another, to spot the latent form lurking in the block of stone—always notable in his work—is the chief feature of *Ashes*. As many critics have demonstrated, metaphor is a complicated and elusive literary device, virtually impossible to pin down and describe in all its many forms; but it is the essence of poetry, an essence of life. One kind of metaphor, sometimes called surrealism, involves ascribing to an object characteristics which in nature that object could not possess. Metaphorically, we might call this a kind of synesthesia, which itself allows a stimulation to be registered by the wrong sense, as hearing the scent of a rose or tasting the color blue. Levine's poem "Noon" is built of such metaphors; we read of "The heaviness of / flies stuttering / in orbit, dirt / ripening, the sweat / of eggs"; "the villages / of sheaves, whole / eras of grain / . . . a roof / that breathes." Each of these figures is an expression of the oppressiveness of a hot noontime; "At such times," says Levine later, "I expect the earth / to pronounce"— as indeed it has. The poem ends on a similar transference of function: "the women / bow as they slap / the life out / of sheets and pants / and worn hands." This sort of thing can easily become too clever, but here the purpose is admirably served.

Elsewhere Levine's images can be close to the purely descriptive, the literal, but still work brilliantly because of their profusion; for example, this stanza from "Clouds": "Morning is exhaustion, tranquilizers, gasoline / the screaming of frozen bearings, / the failures of will, the TV talking to itself." The relative literality of these lines prepares us well to appreciate the metaphorical power of this later depiction of the clouds: "In their great silent pockets / they carry off all our dead." In his best poems, Levine reinforces his images with, and places them within, an insistent rhetorical flow. "How Much Earth" attempts to show man's inherent mortality through a metaphorical description of the progress of his life; it is an example of Levine at his recent best:

Torn into light, you woke wriggling
on a woman's palm. Halved, quartered,
shredded to the wind, you were the life
that thrilled along the underbelly
of a stone. Stilled in the frozen pond
you rinsed heaven with a sigh.

How much earth is a man.
A wall lies down and roses
rush from its teeth; in the fists
of the hungry, cucumbers sleep
their lives away, under your nails
the ocean moans in its bed.

How much earth.
The great ice fields slip
and the unbroken veins of an eye
startle under light, a hand is planted
and the grave blooms upward
in sunlight and walks the roads.

The texture of Levine's poetry has ever been emotional, revealing a strong commitment both to his subjects and his art. The feeling in this poem verges continually on the edge of an extreme, as is shown in certain crucial words ("torn," "shredded," "thrilled," "stilled," "rush," "fists," "startle") and in many phrases. This kind of verbal, imagistic intensity is central to Levine's art, and the retreat from it (and from metaphor) in *7 Years from Somewhere* is unfortunate. Happily, *Ashes* shows him easily in command of his full powers; it is a stunning book from one of our most powerful and masterful poets.

STEPHEN YENSER

From "Recent Poetry"

The black and white photo on the cover shows an empty vase and a couple of bunches of flowers, weighed down by rocks, resting on a stone slab covered with graffiti. We cannot know whose grave it is. No formal inscription appears, and the graffiti include at least two names, one clumsily spraypainted and barely legible, the other done with a marker and partly cropped from the photo. But then perhaps the ambiguity makes its own point, since the one name is Durruti and the other is Ferrer Guardia and they both died fighting for the same cause. As a circled *A* scrawled over Durruti's name suggests, it could be the grave of the Spanish Anarchist movement.

Philip Levine has frequently paid tribute to the Anarquistas. He dedicated his preceding book, *The Names of the Lost,* to Durruti, the leader of the radical wing of the Iberian Anarchist Federation, and several of those poems elegized Durruti and his comrades. "Francisco, I'll Bring You Red Carnations," one of the finest poems in *7 Years from Somewhere* (published simultaneously with *Ashes,* a collection of new and older poems), honors Francisco Ascaso, another powerful figure in the FAI who died in combat. Set in a cemetery in Barcelona, it surveys "the three stones / all in a row: Ferrer Guardia, / B. Durruti, F. Ascaso" and then focuses on the latter. The swift, clean development represents Levine at his best:

> For two there are floral
> displays, but Ascaso faces
> eternity with only a stone.
> Maybe as it should be. He was
> a stone, a stone and a blade,

Reprinted from *The Yale Review* 70 (1980), copyright Yale University.

the first grinding and sharpening
the other.

Although this is the only poem here that deals explicitly with the
Spanish Civil War, one feels that it marks a center, that this
gravestone and whetstone is the omphalos of Levine's world. As
his earlier work testifies, from his point of view, that war no
more ended in 1939 than it began in 1931. It was instead a crucial
part of a continuing political struggle. We always find "The poor
packed in tenements / a dozen high; the rich / in splendid homes
or temples."

Those lines refer ironically to the graves and mausoleums, but
the metaphor instantly reverses itself. Levine wants us to see that
Barcelona also qualifies as a "city of the dead." Suffocating in
"industrial filth and / the burning mists of gasoline," it could be
hell—and at the same time any city in which, as he put it in an
interview several years ago, "people's lives are frustrated, they're
lied to, they're cheated, there is no equitable handing out of
goods." His native Detroit appears in the same infernal light.
"The Gift" summons up its Stygian "river black at night / with
darkness or with oil / or both, gleaming with the lights / of all
the fires that burned / beside it." In "The Life Ahead" he remem-
bers even more pointedly Detroit's "dark streets awash / with
oil" and one in particular "that led to hell." In this far-flung
urban Hades, the workers serve interminable sentences at hard
labor and even undergo a certain torture: the people in the steel
factories work on "with sudden gasps / of breath crying out even
over the roar / of the huge descending presses." Not that they
inspire pity alone. The Barcelona laborers in "Hear Me" have the
fierce, contemptuous strength of folk heroes:

> If God
> cared he would send an old crone
> to waken each of them and whisper
> that in work is salvation, and
> there would be great laughter,
> for they have become work.
> That one who is still only a boy
> is first the ringing of a hammer
> on steel. If you put your ear

to his chest you will hear the music
of salvation breaking his heart.

Strong as they are, however, and because they are so strong,
their lives travesty Ascaso's "dream of the city / of God, where
every man / and every woman gives / and receives the gifts of
work / and care." Much as he admires the Anarchists, Levine finds it hard to
share their meliorism, because his disillusionment goes so deep.
Capitalism simply epitomizes an indifferent universe, purposeless
unless its purpose is to frustrate change. "The farmer / and his
horse slowly / plowing the field they / plowed the day before"
could serve as an emblem for his life and the other monotonous,
pointless lives he sees all about him. "And there I was, going /
nowhere and seeing nothing," he recalls in "Left on the Shore," a
poem about entering middle age. In "The Face" he is still "going
nowhere," and in "Let Me Begin Again" he longs to "go back to
land after a lifetime / of going nowhere." In "The Last Step" he
realizes that while we all have certain "companions / for a time,"
"nothing goes / the whole way." Perhaps we should hear that last
clause in two senses. Rather like Teufelsdröckh, he steadily con-
fronts *das ewige Nein* of existence.

But the negative, as Carlyle's figure discovered, cuts both
ways. Or it is the stone on which Levine hones the knife of his
own spirit. "Dawn, 1952," which concerns his refusal to join the
army during the Korean War, records that early instance of his
negation of negation: "But I said, No, no, I will not go, and /
they let me go, knowing I was nothing." The anticlimactic repeti-
tion of "go" stresses his fecklessness, but the refusal still trans-
forms the nugatory into something. "You Can Have It" passion-
ately commemorates a more profound rejection on a night over
thirty years ago: "My brother comes home from work / and
climbs the stairs to our room. / I can hear the bed groan and his
shoes drop / one by one. You can have it, he says." Levine recalls
with sardonic hyperbole that both of them worked so hard that
they never lived that year of their lives: "In 1948 in the city of
Detroit . . . no one walked the streets or stoked a furnace, / for
there was no such year." But that's all right with him. He would
gladly trade in that year and much more besides, he tells us in
touching paradoxes:

I give you back 1948.
I give you all the years from then
to the coming one. Give me back the moon
with its frail light falling across a face.

Give me back my young brother, hard
and furious, with wide shoulders and a curse
for God and burning eyes that look upon
all creation and say, You can have it.

It would be easy to make too much of the affinity with Carlyle, but such passages rhyme in spirit with the famous repudiation: "The Everlasting No had said: 'Behold, thou art fatherless, outcast, and the Universe is mine (the Devil's)'; to which my whole Me now made answer: '*I* am not thine, but Free, and forever hate thee!' " Levine's vehement denials also affirm the human by rejecting the inhuman. This renunciation of creation is the dream of the city of God in negative.

In these poems affirmation always springs out of the stoniest ground. "Words" begins almost predictably with the poet, "alone, searching / again for words / that will make / some difference / and finding none." A poem about the need to overcome alienation, it ends with the grim reality of a typical evening at home and the inexorable negatives. Like his father before him, Levine's son will come home from work exhausted, "slump before his dinner," and "say / nothing of how much / it costs to be 18." His wife "will say nothing / of the helplessness / she feels seeing her / men rocking on / their separate seas." As the three of them bow their heads not in prayer but "to bread and wine and meat," the windows go dark, "but the room is / quiet in yellow light. / Nothing needs to be said." It is a vibrantly equivocal last line. Like the words never discovered at the beginning, the prayer would make no difference if uttered. But these three know one another's suffering, and their silence itself constitutes a mutual blessing. When he yearns earlier in the poem to have "to rise above / nothing," he is pleading for the communication withheld at dinner. Yet it is precisely the nothing said that he does rise above in the end.

His carefully devised details call little attention to themselves in Levine's poems, most of them outfitted in the same homely prosodic uniform: short free verse lines often recklessly enjambed and rarely divided into stanzas. Because the verse is so insistently serviceable, one expects little subtlety elsewhere, but some of these poems owe their strength to it. "Andorra" sets a scene in the mountains, in the past tense, and then shifts into the future. When Levine repeats and complicates the process, his purpose begins to clarify itself:

> The man I was
> smiles into the light, young
> and full of hope. He will leave
> the bridge and lean down to splash
> the freezing water on his face
> and shake his head as though he
> were saying No! No! to everything.
> He is awakening to a day as pure
> as new snow, a day like no
> other, cold and black at the edges
> and elusive as light at the center,
> a day on which he will climb
> high above the village and sing
> in his cracked voice to everyone
> and no one.

He finishes in the present tense, as the figure in his memory climbs on "out of sight." The poem bids farewell to that former self, "full of hope," but the carefully chosen tenses make it a fuller statement. As the young man "is awakening," something like his feeling returns to the older man; and as the one moves out of sight, the day on which he "will climb / high above the village and sing" has just arrived again. This "cracked" song, with its "No! No! to everything," rejects cynicism as much as it does ingenuousness. Levine lives in this penumbra between disillusionment and faith. In the homage to Ascaso, the dream of the new life "goes on in spite of the slums, . . . in spite of all / that mocks it." But at least as often he believes that the dream cannot go on, and poem after poem has to prove all over again the will to continue.

Sometimes I wish he were less like that farmer who must keep on plowing the same field. Yet our very familiarity with his spiritual struggle enables his details to say more than they do. The parabolic title poem recounts a touring incident in north Africa, when Levine and his wife came to a place where "the bridge / had washed out." When he remembers wondering, "can we go back / and to what?," we sense parallels with both the rift between the bitter older poet and the sanguine young man and the discrepancy between the actual world and the city of God. Back then, some "dirty, green / eyed Berbers" appeared miraculously out of nowhere. One mysteriously took Levine's hand, and then the Berbers told them to "double / back" and they would find a bridge. But today is another story, the same old story:

> the smell of bourbon
> and sweat and another day
> with no bridge, no old city
> cupped carefully in
> a bowl of mountains,
> no one to take this hand,
> the five perfect fingers
> of the soul, and hold it
> as one holds a blue egg
> found in tall grasses
> and smile and say something
> that means nothing, that
> means you are, you
> are, and you are home.

So the volume ends with negations: "no bridge, no old city," "no one," "nothing." Or nearly ends that way. For no one can read this poem without feeling that it supplies the missing bridge— the bridge from the nowhere of the present to the dreamlike "somewhere" in the past, from the "bombed-out American / city" to the "old city" that (like Jerusalem) presages a new one. It is not for "nothing" that Levine coaxes us into recombining his metaphors so that the mountains cup the old city as carefully "as one holds a blue egg." Over the course of this last sentence, the lost experience increasingly, wondrously asserts itself until, with the importunate tenses in the last lines, the past is present. Because the dream persists in spite of all that mocks it, "the world we made / and will never call / ours" can be "home" by the poem's end. In such unexpected ways, Levine's terse, flinty, bitterly eloquent poems keep convincing him (and for this we must be grateful) that they are worth the writing.

WILLIAM MATTHEWS

From "Wagoner, Hugo, and Levine"

Philip Levine's *Ashes* is a miraculous amalgamation of new and old poems. Wagoner has collected poems (Indiana University Press) through 1976, and Hugo has selected poems. We'll have to wait, in Levine's case, until he huddles with Atheneum's Harry Ford, his exemplary editor, to have in one book a large view of Levine's continuous achievement. But this book serves as a hint. Half the poems are from *Red Dust,* published by George Hitchcock's Kayak press in 1971 and long out-of-print, and half are recent. Without checking my copy of *Red Dust* or the copyright page of *Ashes,* I couldn't surely place poems in either group, Levine's work is so obsessive, consistently good and continuous. And yet, once you know which are which, you can see the improvement, the steady development.

All of his work does seem to be one body, one thing. Or a dust or oil or ash that comes from one thing being used up, or many things being used up so that they reduce themselves to one thing. "The long lines of diesels" is the book's first line, and the book describes throughout the world using itself up to go on being the world.

Some of the poems are set in Spain, which turns out to have a palpable connection to Fresno, where Levine has lived so long:

> . . . red dust, that dust which
> even here I taste, having eaten it
> all these years.

It's the dust of work, of getting up and going to work, eating work in order to eat dinner, and how the world doesn't care

Ohio Review 26 (1981). Reprinted with permission. Levine's *Selected Poems* came out in 1984.—ED.

about and is poorly served by the endless frictions of our survival. Here's the beginning stanza of "Fist" (1971):

> Iron growing in the dark,
> it dreams all night long
> and will not work. A flower
> that hates God, a child
> tearing at itself, this one
> closes on nothing.

It's matter itself, the fool's gold of industrial life, that resists industrial life, sated and smug and glowing and lazy (*pig iron,* it's called in one of its manifestations); it's as if matter fed *us* to the refining fires. Thence the title, *Ashes.*

That time is irrecoverable is a powerful urge to lyric poetry, but Levine's fascination with work results in a sense of time different from that in most lyric poetry. Many of his poems are about waking up, the long day, the world sped along by the relentlessness of time but the job, somehow, both heroically and stupidly, remaining the same. "We are the dignified / by dirt," Levine says in "Making It New," not out of a Steinbeck sentimentality for numbing work, but because he sees work to be quixotic, a kind of biological joke we become human by playing on ourselves, and thereby join the rest of the world we might otherwise hold ourselves wrongly above—grasses, gulls, ores, and debris.

There's something degrading, to borrow a trope from Hugo, about all this dirty dignity, and that may explain the splendid truculence in Levine's poems. A poem called "Father" ends:

> I find you
> in these tears, few,
> useless and here at last.
>
> Don't come back.

If the inheritance is this drab and usual response to time—working to make ashes—then, say the heirs, to hell with it and don't come back. What an elegy!

And there are these lines from "Starlight," a poem about a
father and a son.

> He has found nothing, and he smiles
> and holds my head with both his hands.
> Then he lifts me to his shoulder,
> and now I too am there among the stars,
> as tall as he. Are you happy? I say.
> He nods in answer, Yes! oh yes! oh yes!
> And in that new voice he says nothing,
> holding my head tight against his head,
> his eyes closed against the starlight,
> as though those tiny blinking eyes
> of light might find a tall, gaunt child
> holding his child against the promises
> of autumn, until the boy slept
> never to waken in that world again.

How rapidly Levine can move, the way our inner lives move,
from truculence to tenderness, and back, and back and forth.

What are the ashes? Cinders from industry, the ashes of the
dead, trees that will be burnt, the footnotes of fire.

Behind David Wagoner's poems we can sense the sky above
Gary, Indiana, glowing, and behind Richard Hugo's poems we
can hear the dust being pushed from one part of White Center
to another. For Levine it's his native Detroit that he carries
everywhere, like an urn of ashes. The second stanza of "Fist"
reads:

> Friday, late,
> Detroit Transmission. If I live
> forever, the first clouded light
> of dawn will flood me
> in the cold streams
> north of Pontiac.

Endurance is his theme, as reconciliation is Wagoner's and accep-
tance is Hugo's. How do we live, our best poetry begins by
asking, and ends—though none of these poets is near an end, all

three in their fifties only—by telling us how we get by. Here's the third and final stanza of "Fists":

> It opens and is no longer.
> Bud of anger, kinked
> tendril of my life, here
> in the forged morning
> fill with anything—water,
> light, blood—but fill.

Concurrently with *Ashes,* Atheneum published a book consisting entirely of new poems, *7 Years from Somewhere.* The problems of matching the *Red Dust* poems to newer poems in *Ashes* were well solved, but they made the book less various than its companion.

There's a story famous in poetry circles about one of Levine's readings—so famous that it doubtless bears no resemblance to what actually happened. In the middle of a reading Levine looked up at this audience and confessed that this wasn't his real face, he was wearing a mask. And he reached up and grabbed his face with his hands, and his face was so plastic and mobile (I picture a thin Buddy Hackett) that he almost convinced his audience he was twisting a mask from his face. The story ends there, and what I've always wanted to know is how reader and audience regathered themselves to go on.

The Levine of that anecdote is more visible in *7 Years from Somewhere,* which begins with a poem called "I Could Believe."

> I could come to believe
> almost anything, even
> my soul, which is
> my unlit cigar, even
> the earth that huddled
> all these years to
> my bones, waiting
> for the little of me
> it would claim. . . .

And later in the poem the speaker could believe this:

and my mother would
climb into the stars
hand over hand,
a woman of imagination
and stamina among
the airy spaces
of broken clouds,
and I, middle aged
and heavy, would
buy my suits by
the dozen, vested ones,
and wear a watch chain
stretched across my
middle. . . .

And fifty-eight lines later the speaker ends:

except
for the dying I could
believe.

Another poem begins "I did not know your life / was mine,"
and another "Let me begin again as a speck." The range of
rhetorical and dramatic situations Levine finds for himself in
these poems is important, since the relentlessness of time and
work, his beloved subjects, could induce in him a relentlessness
of poetic means. That unswerving confrontation is practically
his hallmark, of course, but who among the few poets as accom-
plished as those I've considered in this brief review isn't fearful
of his strengths? I'll end by quoting the third and final stanza of
"In the Dark."

Once, as a boy, I
climbed the attic stairs
in a sleeping house
and entered a room
no one used. I found
a trunk full of letters
and post cards from a man
who had travelled for years

and then come home to die.
In moonlight each one
said the same thing: how
long the nights were, how
cold it was so far away,
and how it had to end.

HELEN VENDLER

From "All Too Real"

Philip Levine is, though it may seem odd to say so, in the same camp with Rich, believing that realism is the only credible base for verse (even his allegories are painstakingly tailored to a realist origin, a realist frame, and a realist linear progression). Often Levine seems to me simply a memoir-writer in prose who chops up his reminiscent paragraphs into short lines. Here he is on the subject of his first suit, a brown double-breasted pin-stripe with wide lapels:

> Three times I wore it formally: first with red suspenders to a high school dance where no one danced except the chaperones, in a style that minimized the fear of gonorrhea. . . . Then to a party to which almost no one came and those who did counted the minutes until the birthday cake with its armored frosting was cut and we could flee. And finally to the draft board where I stuffed it in a basket with my shoes, shirt, socks, and underclothes and was herded naked with the others past doctors half asleep and determined to find nothing.

An American fifties' autobiography—is there any compelling reason why it should be called poetry? Certainly it is not notably improved by being cut into the short lines in which it appears in this volume of poetry:

> And finally to the draft board where
> I stuffed it in a basket with my shoes,
> shirt, socks, and underclothes and was
> herded naked, etc.

Levine's line breaks (unlike Williams's and Ammons's) are not particularly witty or arresting. Levine's notion of a poem is an

New York Review of Books, December 17, 1981. Reprinted with permission.

anecdote with a flush of reflexive emotion gushing up at the end, like "that flush / of warmth that came with knowing / no one could be more ridiculous than I," with which Levine ends the tale of the brown suit. Levine does attempt poems of mythical or symbolic status, but he is not happy without his clenched toe-holds of circumstantial evidence. He is entirely aware of the division in himself between "items" on the one hand, and yearnings on the other; and he mocks his own notion (a still ineradicable one in him) that "poems"—*real* "poems"—are about love or the rose or the dew, and are sonnets "in fourteen rhyming lines."

He writes a somewhat petulant account of this affliction in a poem of thirteen adamantly unrhyming lines called "Genius." In it, he first enumerates a characteristic list of his sordidly and surrealistically realistic "items" ("An unpaid water bill, the rear license / of a dog that messed on your lawn," etc.) and then says that with these images "a bright beginner could make a poem / in fourteen rhyming lines about the purity / of first love or the rose's many thorns." This opposition of the squalid and the rhapsodic seems to me, even in jest, a deficient aesthetic. It owes something to Stevens's notion of making poems while sitting on a dump, using language to deny the refuse that you see; but Stevens did not linger long in that crude view.

When Levine shades off into the various forms of his sentimental endings (togetherness, doom, death, the sad brown backs of peonies, what have you) it is easy to lose faith in his good sense. The writer who thinks up these disastrous endings has never, it seems, met the writer who writes the beginnings—or indeed who writes whole poems. We are either on the loading docks at the Mavis Nu-Icy Bottling Company (or at the airport where the porter is mopping up)—or we are at these stagy dénouements.

The airport poem, which has a convincing atmosphere at the beginning, ends with a passenger, now returning home, dreaming

> of tears which must always fall
> because water and salt were given us
> at birth to make what we could of them,
> and being what we are we chose love
> and having found it we lost it over and over.

This is only a step away from Lois Wyse or Rod McKuen. It combines the false lachrymose, and the false vatic, and the false unctuous all at once, trading on vague echoes of religion ("were given us at birth") and philosophy ("being what we are"). I prefer any day, even when he is disavowing it, the Levine of a vivid America—

>   . . . the oily floors
>   of filling stations where our cars
>   surrendered their lives and we called
>   it quits and went on foot to phone
>   an indifferent brother for help.

I am not convinced that Levine's observations and reminiscences belong in lyric poems, since he seems so inept in what he thinks of as the obligatory hearts-and-flowers endings of "poems." Perhaps if he didn't think he was writing "poems" he could leave off his romantic organ tones and be truer to his stubborn earthiness. "All of me," he says with some truth, "[is] huddled in the one letter ["n"] that says / 'nothing' or 'nuts' or 'no one' / or 'nobody' gives a shit. But says it with style."

Levine's moody shrugs of disavowal mask a dismay at being an intellectual; he seems to find it a disloyalty to his origins. His definition of style, in the poem I have been quoting, betrays the problem of his unintegrated nature (poet and truculent boy) better than I could do:

>   . . . But says it
>   with style the way a studious boy learns
>   to talk while he smokes a cigarette or pick
>   his nose just when the cantor soars before
>   him into a heaven of meaningless words.

This—another failed ending—takes the easy way out by *calling* style picking your nose (in an affectation of indifference) while at the same time finding *real* style in the cantor's ascent (meaningless though it may be) into the heaven of words. The chip on Levine's shoulder has become the beam in the eye of his poetry. He believes, as a poet, only in what he can see and touch. That much is believably tendered; the rest—all those portions of the human world that we labeled philosophical, or phantasmagorical, or playful, or hypothetical, or contrafactual, or lawlessly paradoxical—escape him. They seem to escape Carter and Rich too, if we look at them whole. Probably they escape our solemnly sociological culture, for the most part; and a culture gets the poets whom it nurtures. The poets of a different persuasion—Merrill, Ammons, Nemerov, Ashbery, to name only four—are in the minority, and seem likely to remain so.

JOSEPH PARISI

One for the Rose

In showing the prosaic underside of the heroic and in celebrating
the unusual in the ordinary, the consistently strong poems of this
tenth collection reaffirm Levine's position as one of our most
vital poets. As usual, the style is plain, the movement smooth,
the rhythms sinewy, as these short lyrics proceed to their striking
(if occasionally overly self-conscious) closing lines. Here a man
can cry without embarrassment, releasing the little boy within; a
patient can lift himself from his hospital bed, remembering Keats
and peonies; a boy can buy a rose bush or fall off a roof, learning
a practical lesson or gaining imaginative insight. Tender lines to a
new mother recall the Platonic myth of preexistence, while the
extravagant shape of an old suit is made to measure the phases of
a lifetime. And throughout, the theme of one poem turns into
new expression for how we find love and seem to lose it "over
and over."

Booklist, January 1, 1982. Reprinted with permission.

DAVID WALKER

From *"One for the Rose/The Southern Cross"*

Levine's *One for the Rose* has been roundly panned by Helen
Vendler in the *New York Review of Books,* for reasons that seem to
me mostly specious. Vendler argues that Levine believes "real-
ism is the only credible base for verse," and that whenever he
departs from the realist mode—to the philosophical or fantastical
or playful—the results are disastrous. To the contrary, *One for the
Rose* seems to me most successful when it abandons the gritty
realism of his recent volumes and mines instead the mythic vein
represented in his earlier work by such poems as "Not This Pig,"
"They Feed They Lion," and "Angel Butcher."

Like most of *7 Years from Somewhere* (1979) and *The Names of
the Lost* (1976), a number of these poems begin in the careful,
drab detail of memory and move toward apotheosis. Poems that
begin like these are instantly recognizable as Levine's:

> I woke in a cold room
> near the port. I rose and dressed
> and went downstairs for coffee,
> but the cooks were arguing
> over *futbol* and didn't see me.
> So I walked the shadowed streets
> until I came to the old burned
> cathedral of Santa Maria del Mar.
>
> ("That Day")

> My oldest son comes to visit me
> in the hospital. He brings giant

Field 26 (1982). Reprinted with permission. Walker reviews new books by Levine
and Charles Wright.—ED.

peonies and the nurse puts them
in a glass vase, and they sag quietly
on the windowsill where they
seem afraid to gaze out at the city
smoking beneath. He asks when I
will be coming home. I don't know.
("Having Been Asked 'What is a Man?' I Answer") -

Or, to quote a short poem entire:

RAIN

Rain falling on the low-built houses
that climb the back of this mountain,
rain streaming down the pocked roads
and bringing with it the hard yellow earth
in little rivers that blacken my shoes,
speechless as ever, like shy animals.
I wait in the doorway of a tobacco shop
and the men go in and out cursing the season.
They light up before they step back into it,
shoulders hunched, heads down, starting
up the long climb to a house of wet cardboard
and makeshift paper windows. No, this
is not the island of Martinique or Manhattan
or the capitol of sweet airs or the dome
of heaven or hell, many colored, splendid.
This is an ordinary gray Friday after work
and before dark in a city of the known world.

The problem is not that the vision and sentiment expressed here
are suspect, but that they're so familiar. The poet's blue-collar
Detroit and dusty Spain, his sad losers and awkward adolescents,
are presented honestly and often movingly, but so have they
been in earlier volumes. And particularly given the single form
in which Levine presently writes, the unbroken skinny column,
the prospect of a whole book of these poems—even removed
from the format of the *New Yorker* (for which they sometimes
feel tailored)—would be fairly forbidding.

Happily, the new collection is leavened, given energy and

freshness, by a whole series of poems that draw less on the transcription and refraction of memory than on fabular, fictive, parabolic impulses. In "The Poem of Flight" Levine reinvents himself as the original pilot of the Wright brothers' plane. In "The Myth" he is an inexplicably atavistic suburban father,

> crashing through the berry bushes and nettles
> like a wild dog, baying at the moon
> on long summer nights until the neighbors
> turned up their stereos, sleeping when
> and where I chose under a blanket of stars
> and waking to mornings of peace among doves
> who mourned the lives of doves. I never wept
> because life was what it was. . . .

In "The Fox" he explores his kinship with a totem animal, and "On My Own" is a wonderful fable of metamorphosis and magical power reminiscent of Singer and Garcia Marquez. Other poems, like "One," seem obviously to draw on memory, but through a process of juxtaposition and mysterious association the self of the poem becomes mythic rather than simply autobiographical.

Most of these poems are too long to quote whole, and too intricately structured to allow a section to suffice. I'll quote one poem and let it stand for the rest:

THE FIRST TRUTH

> The second truth is that the rose blooms
> and the dark petals burn to dust or wind,
> and when nothing is left someone remembers
> it was once spring and hurries through the snow
> on the way home from a day's work, his
> quilted jacket bunched high about his neck
> against the steady December wind. The day
> ends before anyone is ready, even
> this single man who lives alone and feeds
> two stray cats and himself on large tins
> of exotic ocean fish drowned in mustard sauce
> or unpeeled potatoes boiled and left to cool.

He sings as he shaves, staring into his eyes
which to him are as mysterious as the eyes
of the two striped cats or the dark eyes
of the black woman who worked beside him
all that day and sighed just the once, after
she'd finished her small lunch of soda pop
and processed cheese and stood up to return
to her job. She wore a small wedding ring
and a gold cross on a gold chain. In the mirror
he sees his own silver chain disappear under
his shirt and the thick arms that want to crush
someone he has never known against his body
and stand in silence, warm against the wind,
which he knows is blowing because it blew
that morning on the way to work and that evening
on the way back. He stands, half-shaven, staring
into a face that is suddenly his own face
which has given him a name ever since he could speak.
He steps back as far as he can to see all of the man
he would give up if you knocked at his door.

This poem seems particularly interesting because, while it uses
characters of the sort we often see in Levine's work, its treatment
of them is resonant and unpredictable. The single man and his
shaving mirror, the black woman and her meager lunch, the
steady wind—all serve to demarcate a familiar urban landscape
and atmosphere. But the poem's meditative metamorphosis—
the way in which the opening generalization becomes a meta-
phor of the seasons, only gradually focusing dramatically and
gaining narrative interest, then widening at the end to include
the reader in a mysterious moment of vision—is imaginatively
exhilarating. And the means by which the two characters are
linked through the associations of cats and food and chains ele-
vates the poem's experience beyond that of portraiture, produc-
ing instead a potent revelation of knowledge and desire.

"The First Truth" also provides refutation of two of Vendler's
generalizations. The language of this poem reflects neither "stub-
born earthiness" nor "romantic organ tones," the only two
modes of which she apparently thinks Levine is capable. Re-
leased from the confines of realist scenarios, his imagination

finds verbal expression that is close to the bone yet suffused with a restrained lyricism. Phrases such as "his / quilted jacket bunched high about his neck" and "unpeeled potatoes boiled and left to cool" suggest how sensitive Levine is to sound—it's an authentic American music Williams would have admired. Nor is the charge that Levine is "simply a memoir-writer in prose who chops up his reminiscent paragraphs into short lines" borne out by this poem. That it might work in prose is irrelevant; what seems to me the real issue is what the line-breaks contribute. And in this case it's a gread deal: the lineation sets up complex patterns of rhythm, suspension, and revelation which add in scarcely definable but crucial ways to the effect of the poem. Perhaps a better experiment than Vendler's (rewriting the poem as prose) would be to relineate:

> The day ends before anyone is ready,
> even this single man who lives alone
> and feeds two stray cats and himself
> on large tins of exotic ocean fish
> drowned in mustard sauce. . . .

Surely most readers can sense the loss. *One for the Rose* is not an entirely successful volume, but in those poems in which his fictive imagination comes fully into play, Levine displaces romantic autobiography into mythic narratives of great economy and impact.

EMILY GROSHOLZ

From "Poetry Chronicle"

Philip Levine's poems in *One for the Rose* often begin in the midst of the ordinary: "This is an ordinary gray Friday after work / and before dark in a city of the known world." Not just anything, however, can count as ordinary, for it is an honorific term which Levine uses to bless things. Bus stations in Ohio are one of his paradigms, and so are small shops, bars, and hotels in midwestern cities crossed off with rows of small, shoddy trees and polluted rivers. His people are working people, his times of day the gray mornings before we go to work and the gray dusk we come back home in. The ordinary is what social and literary convention passes over as transient and meaningless; Levine criticizes these norms through a poetic act of redemption which remembers certain lost places and people, exhibits their significance, calls them by name.

His strategy of redemption is to move back and away from his specific ordinary, viewing it from a great height as someone lifting off in an airplane would, or from the distanced perspective of memory. Thus "Salt" begins with a woman weeping alone in an airport late at night, between a porter mopping the floor and an old cleaning lady emptying the ashtrays. Then up and out: we follow the airplane of the man who has left her, flying from Cleveland to Chicago over cloud banks and the Lakes, as he returns to his wife and children through a light drizzle, and dreams of "the rain that hangs / above the city swollen with red particles / of burned air" or of tears:

> tears which must always fall
> because water and salt were given us
> at birth to make what we could of them,

Reprinted by permission from *The Hudson Review* 35, no. 2 (Summer 1982). Copyright © 1982 by The Hudson Review, Inc.

and being what we are we chose love
and having found it we lost it over and over.

Or, again, from a room in the back of Peerless Cleaners,
where a little pants presser is telling a child about revolution and
the dignity of labor, Levine draws back thirty-eight years, over
the conflagration of World War II, the theaters of Europe and the
Pacific, and addresses his old instructor.

Come back, Cipriano Mera, step
out of the wind and dressed in the robe
of your pain tell me again that this
world will be ours. Enter my dreams
or my life. Cipriano, come back
out of the wind.

Encompassing his ordinary creatures in a wider vision, Levine
shows them riding upon the thousands of days of history, the
breast of earth which itself rides on the dark abyss of space. This
vision might lead to the wisdom of Silenus, for such expanses
engulf and dwarf the pinpoints of light. But Levine, looking
back on our small illuminated places, observes that we have
nothing except (of course, what else?) each other.

When Levine is moving out in a poem, so that we can see
there gold edges of our local cloud, the signs of this transforma-
tion are usually wind or water. For someone who believes that
the center of creation would like to listen to our music, but can't,
that god will not rise from the stone of his cathedrals, wind is a
natural replacement for spirit. Wind animates the forlorn geome-
try of earth, and lifts even the impacted deadlines of our cities.
And the sea is threshold and freedom for a city kid brought up
landlocked in the heart of America, "the sea / rocking the deep
cradle of all / of us and water and salt without end." The sea is
the tide in our veins, our blood which is mostly salt water, and
our tears. When the wind is tangled in the small, shoddy trees of
Ohio, it sounds like the sea.

PETER STITT

From "Poems in Open Forms"

The objection I had to Philip Levine's last two books (released at once in 1979) was that the poems were sentimental, too tied to the literal truth of the writer's life, and thus weakly written, almost garrulous. These reservations apply only in isolated cases in Levine's new book, *One for the Rose,* which seems to me a triumphant return to the high quality of his earlier work. The poems in this volume are tied together by a subtle underlying conception that determines both their form and their content. Levine surprises us in one poem, "Roofs," by delivering a truth which he applies seriously to both poetry and life. After trying to fly like Superman by jumping from the roof of a garage, the speaker says: "From this I learned / nothing so profound as Newton / might, but something about / how little truth there was / in fantasy." What is remarkable about this passage is that so many of these poems are fantasies—they place the speaker in a triumphant situation which he never could occupy in life. And that of course is the point: in actual life one must never be deluded by fantasy, but in poetry the imagination may be allowed to carry us away. Thus the poem ends on a vision from another kind of roof; back on top of the garage, the speaker notices "nothing in sight but blue sky / a little closer and more familiar, / always calling me back as though / I'd found by accident or as in / a dream my only proper element."

And it is this imaginative vision of something greater, more heroic, than ordinary life that makes Levine realize all the more strongly the very nature of human life. The profound and beautiful poem "Having Been Asked 'What Is a Man?' I Answer" ends with the speaker leaving the hospital:

The Georgia Review 36 (1982). Copyright 1982 by The University of Georgia. Reprinted by permission of *The Georgia Review* and the author.

> I will read Keats again, I will rise
> and go into the world, unwired and free,
> because I am no longer a movie,
> I have no beginning, no middle, no end,
> no film score underscoring each act,
> no costume department, no expert on color.
> I am merely a man dressing in the dark
> because that is what a man is—
> so many mouthfuls of laughter
> and so many more, all there can be
> behind the sad brown backs of peonies.

Such a vision of man, of course, turns us back on the circle by demonstrating the need for the imagination, the need for laughter—the need, that is, for poems of the sort that Levine writes when working at his very best.

In a poem called "My Name," Levine gives a brilliant definition of the way he writes when working at his characteristic best. The poem takes the name "Philip Levine" apart, saving the most important letter *n* for last. Finally the poet sees

> all of me huddled in one letter that says
> "nothing" or "nuts" or "no one" or "never"
> or "nobody gives a shit." But says it
> with style the way a studious boy learns
> to talk while he smokes a cigarette or pick
> his nose just when the cantor soars before
> him into a heaven of meaningless words.

The cantor's meaningless words, of course, represent the false kind of fantasy mentioned earlier, the kind that impels us to jump from garage roofs thinking we can fly. Levine's best poems are always spoken in great style by that boy who learned to pick his nose in the temple.

Another example is a fantasy of childhood called "On My Own," in which the speaker has to go to a new elementary school in mid-year:

The teachers were soft-spoken women
smelling like washed babies and the students
fierce as lost dogs, but they all hushed
in wonder when I named the 400 angels
of death, the planets sighted and unsighted,
the moment at which creation would turn
to burned feathers and blow every which way
in the winds of shock. I sat down
and the room grew quiet and warm.

The poem ends in the same wonderful vein, as this visionary child goes home from school:

If you had been there
in your yellow harness and bright hat
directing traffic you would never
have noticed me—my clothes shabby
and my eyes bright—; to you I'd have been
just an ordinary kid. Sure, now you
know, now it's obvious, what with the light
of the Lord streaming through the nine
windows of my soul and the music of rain
following in my wake and the ordinary air
on fire every blessed day I waken the world.

What this fantasy masks, of course, is a reality that all of us who went to elementary school know was quite different. The poem shows Levine's powerful imagination and his considerable lyrical gifts in full flower. *One for the Rose* is an unusually strong book; its open forms are as free as the imagination can make them, but again . . . we know the author is always in full control of his materials, never relinquishing his reins to them.

JOEL CONARROE

From "Poets of Innocence and Experience"

Philip Levine has . . . been publishing poetry of high quality for more than two decades, and . . . he too has not yet become a household word—not that many poets have. The Pulitzer Prize, for example, has eluded him, the American Academy of Arts and Letters has not elected him, and his work is not widely anthologized. He has, however, been twice honored by the National Book Critics Circle, and he won the American Book Award in 1980. He is, if not a major figure (are there any major living poets?), clearly an artist worth attending to.

Selected Poems contains representative work from ten collections, beginning with *On the Edge* in 1963 and ending with *One for the Rose* in 1981. Reading through the book consecutively is like stumbling through a forbidding woods finally to emerge in a sundappled field. Levine seems to have gone through the reverse of a midlife crisis; I would describe it as a renaissance except I'm not sure about the "re." Call it a midlife emergence. His early books are grim, documenting a sensibility accustomed to failure, loss, bigotry, and violence. Examples of the latter are especially chilling. Here from his first book are lines about Hiroshima:

> They spoke of the horse alive
> without skin, naked, hairless
> without eyes and ears, searching
> for the stableboy's caress.

Horrible as this is, it does not represent Levine at his darkest. He chose not to include a poem called "Gangrene," about the torture of three prisoners, one beaten on his genitals with a ruler, one

Washington Post Book World, August 5, 1984. Reprinted with permission.

wired for electric shocks, and the third forced to swallow his own vomit. It is the stuff of nightmares. In suggesting that the work of Levine's middle age (he is now fifty-six) presents a more hopeful view of things, I do not want to imply that he suddenly turned into Pollyanna. Far from it. The imagery is still dark, the world still full of pitfalls. He does, though, seem to have laid to rest some of the events that haunted him for years, including his father's death when he was five:

> The sun
> has cleared the trees, the wind
> risen, and we, father and child
> hand in hand, the living and
> the dead, are entering the world.

The closing lines from two recent poems help define his new sense of things, and of himself, revealing a singer who has found his proper pitch. First, from "Belief":

> Do you hear
> The waves breaking, even in the darkness,
> radiant and full? Close your eyes, close
> them and follow us toward the first light.

And from "The Voice":

> I embrace whatever pleases me,
> and the earth is my one home,
> as it always was, the earth
> and perhaps some day the sky too
> and all the climbing things between.

PHOEBE PETTINGELL

Voices for the Voiceless

Emerson, that most democratic of Americans, was moved by the symbols of work and aspiration laborers invent for parades and rallies. "The people fancy they hate poetry," he observed, "and they are all poets and mystics." Philip Levine has never lost sight of his own working-class background. No one better expresses how inarticulate and cut off from literature men and women can be: his subjects are trapped in dehumanizing jobs, unemployed, freaks, immigrants divorced from their native languages, or helpless and victimized children and animals. But their actions, indeed, their very presences sing to this poet. His *Selected Poems* provides a generous sampling of the diverse voices he has been fashioning for the voiceless over the last two decades.

The poems from Levine's first collection, *On the Edge* (1963), may shock readers who know him only through his more recent compassionate, free-flowing meditations. The book slammed us with youthful anger and defiance (though Levine was then in his mid-thirties, a late developer in the Whitmanian mode). Critics have often said he was hampered by the period's formal verse structures; I think the control they exerted contributed to the power of his rage against injustice and sterility. Rather than pen verses that are the frustrated lives of its citizens, Levine evokes a nation that "calls for its soul." At one point, he tries to imagine William Blake rousing America into apocalyptic poetry, then admits he can't. "When I opened [my eyes] there was only / the blank door and beyond it / the hall." The hero of the title poem is Edgar Allan Poe, who was more remarkable for his nightmare vision of the psyche than for his jangly verse. This Poe, born "On the Edge" in Michigan in 1928 (as was Levine), is not a poet; he is a spy, eavesdropper and judge:

Reprinted with permission of The New Leader, September 17, 1984. Copyright © the American Labor Conference on International Affairs, Inc.

I heard you lie, even to your daughter.
I did not write, for I am Edgar Poe,
Edgar the mad one, silly, drunk, unwise,
But Edgar waiting on the edge of laughter,
And there is nothing that he does not know
Whose page is blanker than the raining skies.

Leaving behind such slightly self-conscious symbolism, *Not This Pig* (1968) describes a broad spectrum of victims. A pig trotting to slaughter in "Animals Are Passing from Our Lives"; a Spanish Midget in a bar; a little girl revolted by an inedible sandwich; "Baby Villon," a universal street Arab—each enlarges Levine's sympathies, and ours, as he shows their resistance in the face of hopelessness. To him they are akin to the thief-child, "My imaginary brother, my cousin / Myself made otherwise by all his pain." In "Silent in America," he prays, with a note of desperation,

> Let me have
> the courage to live
> as fictions live, proud, careless,
> unwilling to die.

The poems of *Red Dust* (1971, reprinted in *Ashes* in 1979) employ the short syllabic lines Levine has made distinctive in examining the tension between America's dream of the good life and its natural violence. Although Levine is frequently compared to Whitman, he often demonstrates why boundless optimism is impossible for many of us. "I do not believe in sorrow," he asserts, because "it is not American." In a plane above California's Fresno valley, where towns "smoke like thin pipes of the Chinese," he tries to sustain that pipe dream, but "the cold underside of my arm . . . sweats with fear / as though it lay along the edge / of revelation." Flying over clouds of pollution, he experiences ambivalence:

> And so my mind closes around
> a square oil can crushed on the road
> one morning, startled it was not

the usual cat. If a crow
had come out of the air to choose
its entrails could I have laughed?
If eagles formed now in the
shocked vegetation of my sight
would they be friendly? I can hear
their wings lifting them down, the feathers
tipped with red dust, that dust which
even here I taste, having eaten it
all these years.

In the same year as *Red Dust* came *Pili's Wall,* an extended poem in the voice of a small Spanish girl who decorated stone surfaces with her drawings. Unlike the Michigan Edgar Poe, or the stoic pig, Pili is a creative artist. Like Levine, she speaks for those who cannot. Her own environment is hostile: "What can a child know, / says the moon / Look at her bones, / unbroken, and her teeth." The poem lets us envision the child's pictures as well as their message:

> Here is a face for you
> who will not show
> your face.
>   I cut a smile
> and give it to you, the rain
> gives you tears.

Finished, she endows it with defiance: "Spit your teeth / in the face of creation."

They Feed They Lion (1972) and *1933* (1974) mark Levine's transition from anger to elegy. His burning outrage bursts forth through the biblical cadences of Black speech in "They Feed They Lion," one of those unforgettable apocalypses reminiscent of Blake's "London," or Yeats's "The Second Coming." The poem develops into a kind of savage joy, invoking the racial tensions that boiled over into the 1967 Detroit riots. Levine is an anarchist, and he rejoices that "From 'Bow Down' come 'Rise Up.' "

Out of burlap sacks, out of bearing butter,
Out of black bean and wet slate bread,
Out of the acids of rage, the candor of tar,
Out of creosote, gasoline, drive shafts, wooden dollies,
They Lion grow.

Elsewhere, the volume jumps with the exuberance of "the true and earthy prayer of salami," and the funky "Angel Butcher"—a quite original transformation of Rilke's omnipresent poetic angels. But in "1933," the year Levine's father died, this energy has melted into an almost mystic acceptance.

The sun is gone, the moon is a slice of hope
the stars are burned eyes that see
the wind is the breath of the ocean
the death of the fish is the allegory
you slice it open and spill the entrails
you remove the spine
the architecture of the breast
you slap it home
the oils snap and sizzle.
you live in the world
you eat all the unknown deeps
the great sea oaks rise from the floor
the bears dip their paws in clear streams
they hug their great matted coats
and laugh in the voices of girls
a man drops slowly like brandy or glue

From that point on Levine seems less concerned with forming speeches for the voiceless that are defiant. In his next book he found it enough to remember *The Names of the Lost* (1976): not only his own private dead but also "The Rabbi of Auschwitz," and, most poignantly, the anarchist martyrs of the Spanish Civil War. Levine was a mere eight years old in 1936, yet he seems to have imbibed the passion of the Spanish cause from his Detroit neighborhood and he writes about it with the authority of an eyewitness as well as the love of a disciple. The historical focus is further developed in *Ashes* (1979) and *7 Years from Somewhere* (1979).

Levine evolves toward still another approach in *One For The Rose* (1981).

> No one believes
> that the lost breath of a man
> who died in 1821 is my breath
> and that I will live until
> I no longer want to, and then
> I will write my name
> in water, as he did, and pass
> this breath to anyone who can
> believe that life comes back
> again and again without end.

The dead man here is Keats, one of the volume's many manifestations of Levine's Keatsean persona. There is, in addition, a charming reincarnation of his defiant one as an "unseen fox / whose breath sears the thick bushes / and whose eyes burn like opals," who feels he "must proclaim / not ever ever ever / to mounted ladies and their gentlemen." "I Was Born in Lucerne" breaks with "all the chichés I could have lived with" (for example, a Detroit birthplace). The poet claims not to be bound to an urbanite's experiences because, in his Swiss incarnation, he has "stared into the burning eyes of earth / . . . seen the snow covering it all."

   Philip Levine's wonderful, fresh identities ring true. And his speaking over the years for those with scant chance to speak for themselves has made his own voice one of the most powerful and generous in poetry today.

JOSEPH PARISI

Selected Poems

From nine striking volumes, Levine has wisely chosen his strongest and most characteristic work, poems whose freshness of observation and immediacy of emotional impact have not diminished during the more than two decades of his career. With their grimy setting of Detroit, many of these stark lines make grim (though not preachy) statements about the cost in alienation exacted by industrial society, vividly portraying workers and other walking wounded who sometimes, somehow maintain the human spirit. Levine's power to transcribe the speech, the often black humor, the sense of resignation, despair, hope, and the sheer physicality of his people and their place commands attention, though his themes are relatively few and frequently recurring. Other poems, particularly those centered on his family, reveal the warmth and sensitivity beneath the acquired, somewhat defensive cover of hurt and bitter realism. Levine's energy and the strength of his individual voice charge these poems, whatever their subjects and settings, with an urgency that convinces his readers and makes them care.

Booklist, August, 1984. Reprinted with permission.

PETER STITT

From " 'My Fingers Clawing the Air': Versions of Paradise in Contemporary American Poetry"

In the concluding lines of his *Selected Poems*, Philip Levine defines his paradise and his hell, what he has been running from forever, searching for forever:

> What was I doing in Akron, Ohio
> waiting for a bus that groaned slowly
> between the sickened farms of 1951
> and finally entered the smeared air
> of hell on US 24 where the Rouge plant
> destroys the horizon? I could have been
> in Paris at the feet of Gertrude Stein,
> I could have been drifting among
> the reeds of a clear stream
> like the little Moses, to be found
> by a princess and named after a conglomerate
> or a Jewish hero. Instead I was born
> in the wrong year and in the wrong place,
> and I made my way so slowly and badly
> that I remember every single turn,
> and each one smells like an overblown rose,
> yellow, American, beautiful, and true.

The blue-collar past is there, the dirt, the emptiness, the grime, the sense of squandered chances; the humor; the glory of it anyway and after all.

The negative in Levine's poetry is represented by two things:

The Georgia Review 39 (1985). Copyright 1985 by The University of Georgia. Reprinted by permission of *The Georgia Review* and the author.

the hopelessness, the dead-endedness, of a working-class life, and the fact of death itself. He makes us feel what it is like to punch a clock dawn after dreary dawn. In the poem "Words" we read of the speaker's son "waking for work— / he is late and doesn't / have time for coffee / or *hello* . . . / . . . it's only /me and the gray day." Later:

> my son
> will come home, his
> hands swollen and cracked,
> his face gray with
> exhaustion. He will
> slump before his dinner
> and eat. He will say
> nothing of how much
> it costs to be 18
> and tear some small
> living for yourself
> with only your two hands.

The flatness of language and rhythm, the shortness of line— these things are appropriate to the subject matter here; Levine's truth is a stark one, as is his form.

Levine applies his flattest writing—flattest now in a spiritual rather than a formal sense—not to the working-class life, which at least has some positive aspects, but to the barren fact of death; "Letters for the Dead" contains these lines:

> And the children die
> the sacraments we waited for
> go gray
> little flat sacks of refuse
> until no one can look
> or look away
>
> the father, enormous
> bunched against the green wall
> says
> over and over
> *Can you believe we loved you*

All night
rain in the still river
off the loading docks at Wyandotte
locked wheels
blind eyes of cars
the scattered intestines of purses
a pale carp
warped on its side

they bump slowly underwater

Besides what they say about working and death, the last two
passages quoted also illustrate Levine's "middle" style. It is very
much a free-verse style, with varied line lengths and unpredict-
able rhythms—a style that relies primarily upon image and state-
ment to carry the poem forward.

"Letters for the Dead" is from the transitional volume *1933*,
published in 1974. Before that Levine's work embodies many
more formal elements, tending even toward high rhetorical flour-
ishing. "They Feed They Lion" is a poem justly famous for its
powerful form:

Out of burlap sacks, out of bearing butter,
Out of black bean and wet slate bread,
Out of acids of rage, the candor of tar,
Out of creosote, gasoline, drive shafts, wooden dollies,
They Lion grow.
. . . .
                    From my five arms and all my hands,
From all my white sins forgiven, they feed,
From my car passing under the stars,
They Lion, from my children inherit,
From the oak turned to a wall, they Lion,
From they sack and they belly opened
And all that was hidden burning on the oil-stained earth
They feed they Lion and he comes.

The heavy use of parallelism is complemented by the driving
rhythms, the intensely accurate images, the biting colloquial
language.

In his later poems, Levine seems to conflate the two earlier styles; his lines are expanded to become at once rhythmical, open, free-flowing, image-packed, colloquial and formal together. His sense of humor (so readily apparent in his collection of interviews, *Don't Ask*) comes even more to the foreground as well. "I Was Born in Lucerne," from Levine's most recent individual volume, *One for the Rose,* begins with other people insisting to the speaker that he was humbly born in Detroit: "I say, / No, in a small Italian hotel overlooking / the lake." The poem ends with this outburst from Fancypants:

> You wonder why I am
> impossible, why I stand in the bus station
> in Toldeo baying No! No! and hurling
> the luggage of strangers every which way,
> why I refuse to climb ladders or descend into
> cellars of coal dust and dead mice or eat
> like a good boy or change my dirty clothes
> no matter who complains. Look in my eyes!
> They have stared into the burning eyes of earth,
> molten metals, the first sun, a woman's face,
> they have seen the snow covering it all
> and a new day breaking over the mother sea.
> I breathed the truth. I was born in Lucerne.

The lines combine sincerity with parody, high humor with a sense of tragedy, classical rhetoric with the talk of the streets. Moreover, there is a kind of insistent seizure of paradise in this poem: the poet's good-humored, tongue-in-cheek violation of his own history reveals his transcendence of the spiritual nihilism that had nagged his work in earlier phases.

Philip Levine certainly must be ranked with the finest poets America has produced. He also belongs with those who are most thoroughly American, writing in the great tradition of William Carlos Williams—eschewing opera in favor of jazz, the drawing room in favor of the kitchen, the silk-covered cushion in favor of the bus-station bench. His *Selected Poems* is a monument for our age.

REG SANER

From "Studying Interior Architecture by Keyhole"

Ten years ago an angry colleague—demanding to know why our department was about to pay good money for a reading by Philip Levine—accosted me point blank to say, "You'll see! The man's a clown! He's the worst poet in America!"

Now, as for "clown," any of us can behave badly, foolishly. Perhaps Levine once had. I couldn't care less. But "worst poet" left me, leaves me still, in fog. On that count my colleague had momentarily become the most fatuous critic in North and South America.

Philip Levine's achievement is by now so much beyond question, that his *Selected Poems* make a book one must have. Eventually of course there will be a *Collected Poems,* but a poet's own selection proves readable, wieldy, un-tomelike.

I actually recall Levine's insisting he wasn't prolific. Over the past couple of decades, however, he has averaged a book every two years! His *Selected Poems* prune this abundance, with shrewd rigor, to just under one hundred pieces in a handsome volume, sewn.

Like two other poets with working-class sympathies, James Wright and Richard Hugo, Levine's childhood rubbed his nose in hard facts not limited to the depression years in Detroit. The secret of his considerable power—as with Hugo and Wright—stems from the intense conviction that he has seen what he has seen. He knows what he knows. And gives the feel of having more in common with Sisyphus than with Daedalus.

So the longer poems rarely get off to a jack-rabbit start. Their slow, prosaic openings—when they occur—are made up for by Levine's maverick gift for closures with that unpredictable right-

Denver Quarterly 20 (1985). Reprinted with permission.

ness of an "original." Then too there is his wily avoidance of literary and artistic references. From the poems you would not know Levine had ever been inside a library, seen a painting, attended a play, or heard a concert. He is truly a blue-collar fox. In the world of Philip Levine's poetry, dawn often breaks cold, grey, and cheerless, the darkest part of the day where daybreak means work, and where work is dirty, mechanically dangerous, degrading.

It is a world whose saving graces may arrive "late / and tired, beyond the false lights / of Pasadena / where the living are silent in America." It is a world where even grass is "holding on," where "salt" and "lies" become a fifth element. It is a world of assembly-line faces "too tired / of being each other / to try to be lovers." For example, Hamtramck, Michigan. There "In the darkness / of this world men / pull on heavy canvas gloves, / dip into rubber coats / and enter the fires."

The second stanza of "Fist" is an instance of this latter point. The poem's vision is quintessential Levine, and is brief enough to cite, but its form is atypical of his best work, which needs a full page, or several, to produce its effects:

Iron growing in the dark,
it dreams all night long
and will not work. A flower
that hates God, a child
tearing at itself, this one
closes on nothing.

Friday, late,
Detroit Transmission. If I live
forever, the first clouded light
of dawn will flood me
in the cold streams
north of Pontiac.

It opens and is no longer.
Bud of anger, kinked
tendril of my life, here
in the forged morning
fill with anything—water,
light, blood—but fill.

To be at all effective Levine's main rhetorical mode of straight-ahead "honesty" relies, more than in so compressed an example, on inconspicuous diction and normal syntax. Except in poems like the now classic "They Feed They Lion," where rhythm is everything, Levine's rhythms rarely draw attention to themselves. These deliberate limits run the risk of flatness. How could they not? But the spectacle of arm wrestling often features the scant "action" of great muscular tension. At best Levine's "plain" style feels tense in this way, as if overcoming strong resistance.

No wonder in such a dour world the word "nothing" occurs unusually often, along with repetitions of "no one," "not," "didn't," "couldn't," and "won't." No wonder Levine's perhaps strongest evocation is titled "To My God in His Sickness."

Yet amid this dim physical grit of lockups, Detroit grease shops, and a society tending to pit all against all, even feeble gestures toward humane illumination of that dimness acquire radiance through contrast, like chicory blossoms poking up from asphalt. A beautiful turning point comes in "Lost and Found," which opens with "a light wind beyond the window, / and the trees swimming / in the golden morning air. / Last night for hours I thought / of a boy lost in a huge city . . ." and though it is vandalism to quote piecemeal, here are the concluding lines:

> . . . Now he
> is home, the one I searched for.
> He is beside me as he always
> was, a light spirit that brings
> me luck and listens when I speak.
> The day is here, and it will last
> forever or until the sun fails
> and the birds are once again
> hidden and moaning, but for now
> the lost are found. The sun
> has cleared the trees, the wind
> risen, and we, father and child
> hand in hand, the living and
> the dead, are entering the world.

Escape artists know it's easier to get free of a hundred feet of rope than ten feet carefully tied. Similarly, Levine's strategy in poem after poem is to emphasize loaded odds, to show how "the way things are" conspires against us in withholding almost everything of true worth—and then to show that value can be wrested from it, however Pyrrhic the victory. Form and rhythm tease into existence the desires they intend to satisfy. All art does so. Thus his procedure is no mere stratagem. Their tone says, "These poems have been paid for." And you believe it. He knows what he knows. That is the art of Philip Levine.

DAVE SMITH

From "Short Reviews"

Philip Levine's *Selected Poems* shows two distinct movements. The first is the auditioning of form—image, litany, narrative—to replace the fifties prosodic decorum in which he began. He settled on lyrical syllabics. The second movement is the deep discovery of his subject, immigrant Detroit, the American orphan-story, a discovery which entailed creating a voice. This is a character we can call Philip Levine, the tough, wise-ass, big-hearted anarchist who hates privilege, cultivates surly macho, and rejects academia. It's instructive to remember that Levine took an M.F.A. from Iowa at age twenty-nine and has professed continuously for twenty-nine years. His originality has been, notwithstanding, to find a subject near the American heart and from it create a fresh poetry committed to freedom of the individual spirit. Levine's truth is America's pain.

Levine's *On the Edge* (1963) and *Not This Pig* (1968) wed a heritage of learned poetry to the immigrant experience of betrayed dreams. He wrote "what is there to choose / but failure" because that is what Detroit's consumer rapacity, using people like machines, seemed to offer. He has dropped most of these poems from *Selected Poems,* retaining those distinguished by an anger and a fabular imagination that cuts through the staid verse—"On the Edge," "Blasting from Heaven," "Animals Are Passing from Our Lives"—and keeping a handful of poems which show him searching for new form. Interesting now mostly as a prototype, "Silent in America" shows "Fresno's / dumb bard" saying of his art: "my / jaws ache for release, for / words that will say / anything." Most of the words here belong to Berryman, Lowell, Dylan Thomas, Whitman, Eliot, and Shakespeare. Yet in the brotherly spirit of "Baby Villon" and in

"Short Reviews" first appeared in *Poetry* (October, 1985), copyright 1985 by The Modern Poetry Association. Reprinted by permission of the Editor of *Poetry.*

the experiments of *Red Dust* (1971), Levine began to fuse subject and form. He developed what I would call the heroic lyric, a form suitable to eulogize the lost in nearly religious chanting. Levine's heroes, like his poetry, began in literature, with Poe, Whitman, and Baudelaire, but they became Poles, Jews, Southern emigrants—especially blacks and women. He loved the shop laborers, abused and powerless but comradely, bound into a bandit society of hard work, fidelity, courage, street smarts, and tribal love. When Levine mixed voices of gospel rhythms, Biblical cadences, and street lingo with the shape of fairy tale archetypes, he created his breakthrough book, *They Feed They Lion* (1972). The title poem revealed Levine's unmistakable signature:

> Out of the gray hills
> Of industrial barns, out of rain, out of bus ride,
> West Virginia to Kiss My Ass, out of buried aunties,
> Mothers hardening like pounded stumps, out of stumps,
> Out of the bones' need to sharpen and the muscles' to stretch,
> They Lion grow.

In the last year of the Vietnam War, Levine's boiling anger spoke for the speechless in America. It still does.

If readers fixed Levine as the angry poet in the transmission shop, he was on the move. *1933* (1974), named after the year of his father's death and, in his imagination, the year of his orphaning, showed subtle changes. In elegies to his family he muted the anger and pushed backward to a view of a more tranquil, hopeful time. His poem became a moral tale of the dispossessed coming to consciousness. Levine, like Augie March, was engaging an urban spiritual autobiography, something new in American letters. But like Melville he was diving into the darkness, in "Belle Isle, 1949," in order to rise "into the final moonless atmosphere / that was this world. . . ."

In his subsequent books, *The Names of the Lost* (1976), *Ashes* (1979), *7 Years from Somewhere* (1979), and *One for the Rose* (1980), Levine has seldom departed from the syllabic columns of his heroic lyric. Fusing elegy and narrative, his themes are homelessness, cruelty, the will to live, and the beauty of the natural world. This last has, I think, yielded some of his most impressive work, for he has a pastoral talent that makes him eloquent in defense of "the small tough patches of grass / that fight for water and air. . . ." Of course these poems become effective moral fables that extend Levine's ground sense of tribal identity and national betrayal, but it is their curious sweetness which charms in the *Selected Poems*. Nevertheless, one learns here that the heart of Levine's force is rage to live. He can be preachy, hectoring, rigid, glib, habitual, and blustering; but he is a true poet whose fundamental conviction, the individual human worth, is indispensable. His righteous anger becomes our passion in *Selected Poems,* a conscience really, and nowhere more wonderfully than in "The Fox." Here the poet speaks as a fox shunted from a park path by "ladies and gentlemen on horseback." The definition of his life as song itself, all that we can own, seems the appropriate image, with appropriate ferocity, for this poet-orphan:

> feeling the steady measured beat
> of his fox heart like a wordless
> delicate song, and the quick forepaws
> choosing the way unerringly
> and the thick furred body following
> while the tail flows upward,
> too beautiful a plume for anyone
> except a creature who must proclaim
> not ever ever ever
> to mounted ladies and their gentlemen.

If you don't own Philip Levine's *Selected Poems,* you don't care much about our poetry.

In *Sweet Will*'s sixteen new poems, Philip Levine is once more on the road, seeking home, remembering rites of passage. But the scenes are softer, the social indictments less specific, the prophesy of a redressed future gone. Levine has come to a new poetry of resignation and the sweetness of pity for what cannot be changed. He believes that "the last darkness" will be followed by "new soft rays of the sunlight," and in "An Ending" he tells us:

The voice I hear now is
my own night voice, going out
and coming back in an old chant
that calms me, that calms
—for all I know—the waves
still lost out there.

In its elegiac tone and reminiscences, *Sweet Will* resembles
1933, yet the book is very much about Levine himself, a spiritual
autobiography beginning with various voyages from Detroit
and ending in a hymn to Europe's dead. That visit and this book
reveal fundamental truths to Levine:

how life goes on, how seasons pass,
the children grow, and the earth gives
back what it took. My shoes darken.

("Jewish Graveyards, Italy")

Perhaps the heart of Levine's pilgrimage poems is the 501-line
tour de force called "A Poem with No Ending." Levine com-
ments on his poetry in it: "Mine never end, they run on / book
after book, complaining / to the moon that heaven is wrong / or
dull, no place at all to be." Here in ten achronological narrations
from memory, Levine tells the story of searching "for someone
other / than myself." The poem has its share of violations of the
peaceful life, but it is startling to discover how domestic, under-
stated, ordinary, and serene this poem is—from a near-magical
birth to an idyll on Belle Isle to a holiday with family on a
Spanish beach. Yet this now is the center of Philip Levine's emo-
tional circuitry—from promises broken, home lost, inevitable
mortality and pain to the chronicle of the spirit's love of the
bountiful world.

Several of the poems in *Sweet Will* are flatter than Levine's
best work, as if lacking in energy. Some seem too long ("A Poem
with No Ending") and at least one is unbelievable ("Those Were
the Days"). But this does not account for the feel of something
missing. It is, I think, the scalding strength of his anger, a hard
thing to sustain at age fifty-seven, that has made his poetry
tough and passionate. I suspect that readers will have to get used
to a different Levine now, but it is one who has always been

close. Levine, I think, will tinker more with his form (as this book shows him experimenting) to make it less stylized talk. *Sweet Will,* then, is a transitional collection. Its best work is equal to Levine's splendid poems of the seventies—"Salts and Oils," "The Present," "An Ending," "An Ordinary Morning," and "Jewish Graveyards, Italy." They are the poems of an emergent tenderness and faith in "a world / that runs on and on at its own sweet will." Linking himself to the Wordsworth who loved this world uncommonly in uncommon poetry, Philip Levine has lifted his moral tale to the level of joyful celebration. As he says:

> I am beginning
> once more to rise into the shape
> of someone I can be, a man
> no different from my father
> but slower and wiser. What could be
> better than to waken as a man?

("A Poem with No Ending")

WILLIAM PITT ROOT

Songs of the Working Class

Philip Levine's epigraph for his first new collection since *One for the Rose* in 1981 and *Selected Poems* in 1984 comes, interestingly, from Wordsworth. The excerpt concludes, "Ne'er saw I, never felt, a calm so deep! / The river glideth at his own sweet will . . ." and one supposes here is the source of the book's title, *Sweet Will*.

But the reader soon finds the title has another root, in the episode about Stash, with whom Levine worked over three decades ago at Detroit Transmission, night shift. It seems Stash would drink too much each Friday and pass out on the oily concrete floor and that it was unwise to disturb him. "Just let him get up at his / own sweet will or he'll hit you," the young Levine is advised by the old black coworker.

When Stash arises, he wipes away his blood with "a crumpled handkerchief," climbs onto the wooden soda-pop case at his punch press and hollers "at all / of us over the oceanic roar of work, / addressing us by our names and nations— / 'Nigger, Kike, Hunky, River Rat,' / but he gave it a tune, an old tune, / like 'America the Beautiful.' " And of course we are in the presence of the Phil Levine who, as a poet, does for midcentury blue-collar workers what Walker Evans, the photographer, did for the Okies and drifters of the Dust Bowl Depression era, isolating the passing moments and installing them in a context so vivid and true that the images created are often memorable, occasionally unforgettable.

For Evans, as for Levine, the process is a deceptively simple surrender to the power of subject matter, a faith that the straightforward method will work the most magic and the least distortion.

The comparison is an invited one. Levine has chosen for his

St. Petersburg Times, November 3, 1985. Reprinted with permission.

cover photograph Walker Evans's "Joe's Auto Yard, Pennsylvania, 1936," depicting dozens of old wrecks by a dirt road. Beyond, a pasture climbs to a horizon relieved by a few bare winter trees. The image is stark, unpretentious, and gradually becomes touching. The same can be said of many of Levine's new poems.

The Wordsworth epigraph is a reminder that it was, after all, Wordsworth, Sweet William, who called for renewed attention to the concerns and language of working people and plain speech. Few poets since have taken that aspect of Wordsworth's call more literally or faithfully than Levine, who is now in his third decade of drawing upon his memories of a period when he worked what he once called "a succession of stupid jobs," work he describes in "A Poem with No Ending" as "jobs that gave us / just enough and took all we had."

Sweet Will continues in Levine's blue-collar reminiscent vein, telling in his familiar style—nearly always in three-beat lines that look like unjustified newspaper columns and often sound like a sharp journalist's prose, as well—of on-the-job experiences which, surprisingly, remain interesting, largely because they are told in lively earnest.

The characters tend to be portrayed as hard-handed, tough-minded, somewhat unimaginative men who acquire sympathetic dimensions when viewed through the poet's admiring lens. These are men who bear their hardships because they believe they must. Their character is forged and tempered in a time and place largely innocent of politics or any sense of alternatives. Levine's poems are "sad tales of men / who let the earth break them back, / each one, to dirty blood or bloody dirt."

Levine's own persona is more often that of a witness than a participant, a witness eager to testify on behalf of plaintiffs in the courts of heaven, be they ancestors, coworkers or people anywhere oppressed by forces beyond their control. His nostalgia—or his admiration for those formed in a more stable moral and cultural time than ours, which is riddled with ambiguities and consequently with the temptation to despair—is shared by many of his readers, who find in this man's poetry concerns that include but extend themes common to country-western songs. I mean solid working-class sentiments, as innocent of condescension as of too easy glorification.

In the long center-piece, "A Poem with No Ending," Levine

says quietly, "I tramped / the streets no longer looking for / the face I sought in childhood, / for now that face was mine, and I / was old enough to know / that my son would not suddenly / turn a corner and be mine / as I was my father's son." Levine's sensibility is, perhaps, derived from a past now gone from us, but the indefatigable compassion he reveals so consistently is timeless, which beats the pants off being relevant, contemporary, postmodern and so on. "I began this poem in the present / because nothing is past," he says at one point, and "What could be / better than to awaken as a man?" at another. Only a grouch would quibble.

The appeal of Levine's work to young writers is considerable and, I believe, generally healthy. Along with such poets as Richard Hugo, John Logan, James Wright, Randall Jarrell, and, more recently, Galway Kinnell, Levine writes unapologetically, unpretentiously, often movingly, of how it feels to be an adult, a man alive in the passing stream of his own existence, aware of his fellow humans and their dilemmas, largely indifferent to the influences of literary ideas but exquisitely responsive to the nuances of experience itself. His careful renderings of events and people are exemplary, but the tendency to a prosaic flatness is less so. In his long poem, he says, "This is the first night of my life / I know we are music." Levine is capable of more music than we hear in *Sweet Will*. Not only in previous books, but in this one he can rise to the lyric bait, as he does in the short piece, "The White Iris." Granted that this is a book dedicated to "a calm so deep," still I miss the drums and thunder of such poems as "They Feed They Lion."

And that may be my problem. Concluding "Last Words," Levine writes of another kind of music and rhythm as he describes

<blockquote>
how
a wind rides up the hillside
steadily toward you until it surges
into your ears like breath coming
and going, released from its bondage
to blood or speech and denying nothing.
</blockquote>

PETER STITT

From "The Typical Poem"

Philip Levine's faith is placed not in God and Christ but in the earth and nature. The title of his latest book comes from a Wordsworth passage ending: "The river glideth at his own sweet will." Levine presents himself as a naturalist here, but not in a philosophically negative sense. For him, the physical world has not only the indifference found by Stephen Crane but an inherent and inevitable beauty as well. And that is as much of abstract understanding as we get in this book, which offers for an ars poetica these lines from "Jewish Graveyards, Italy":

> I move from one cluster of stones
> to another studying the names
> and dates that tell me nothing I
> hadn't guessed. In sunlight, in moonlight,
> or in rain, it's always the same,
> whatever truth falls from the sky
> as slowly as dust settling in
> morning light or cold mist rising
> from a river, takes the shape
> I give it, and I can't give it any.

Though this writer cannot give shape to *truth,* he can give shape to reality, the look and feel of the actual world. Thus his poems are basically written in a syllabic free verse and attain their meaning through a manipulation of imagery.

Because of its meditative nature, *Sweet Will* is something of a departure for Philip Levine—who is better known for his narrative zing and lyric intensity. The best poem in this volume is a fifteen-page meditation called "A Poem with No Ending." Levine announces his method and some of his meaning at the very

First published in *The Kenyon Review,* n.s. 8, no. 4 (Fall 1986). Copyright © by Kenyon College. Reprinted with permission of the author and the publisher.

beginning: "So many poems begin where they / should end, and never end. / Mine never end, they run on / book after book, complaining / to the moon that heaven is wrong / or dull, no place at all to be. / I believe all this." It is telling that the belief announced here should be a negative one; very often Levine approaches a subject from its other side, telling us not the *is* that interests him but the *is not* that doesn't. From this we understand the *is*—as when he begins a passage later in this poem by saying, "No, that wasn't childhood, that / was something else, something that. . . ."

Near its beginning, "A Poem with No Ending" announces through imagery its negative pole, which may be defined as essentially the harsh world of mankind. The poet speaks of "the last spring / before war turned toward our house / and entered before dawn, a pale / stranger that hovered over each bed / and touched the soft, unguarded faces / leaving bruises so faint / years would pass before they darkened / and finally burned." War—and by extension the other cruelties of a deprived, depression-era, working-class upbringing—is a nasty, psychic seed planted early to bear fruit much later.

It is also through imagery that, in ensuing sections of the poem, Levine indicates the more positive faith that draws him on—for example the natural music that underlies human existence:

> There is a song, bird song or wind song,
> or the song old rooms sing when no one
> is awake to hear. For a moment I
> almost catch the melody we make
> with bare walls, old iron sagging beds
> and scarred floors. There is one
> deep full note for each of us.
> This is the first night of my life
> I know we are music.

The poem as a whole ends on a similarly affirmative natural image: "I see beyond / the dark the distant sky breaking / into color and each wave taking / shape and rising landward." This is the quietest book Philip Levine has ever written, but, though the river that glides through it is still on the surface, the sweetness of its will runs deep indeed.

MARK JARMAN

From "The Trace of a Story Line"

One of the most intriguing parables of the Synoptic Gospels is the parable of the sower; Mark 4:3–9 might be said to be the simplest and most direct version of this story.

> Listen! A sower went out to sow and as he sowed, some seed fell along the path, and the birds came and devoured it. Other seed fell on rocky ground where it had not much soil, and immediately it sprang up, since it had no depth of soil; and when the sun rose it was scorched, and since it had no root it withered away. Other seed fell among thorns and the thorns grew up and choked it, and it yielded no grain. And other seeds fell into good soil and brought forth grain, growing up and increasing and yielding thirtyfold and sixtyfold and a hunderedfold.

Completing his parable Jesus admonishes his listeners, "He who has ears to hear, let him hear." Pressed to explain the parable, he makes it clear that what the sower sows is the word, God's Word. His listeners are likened to kinds of soil. According to *The Interpreter's Bible,* the parable is, like all of Jesus's parables, "an earthly story with a heavenly meaning." But it is also another kind of story, one that exists apart from the meaning that Jesus gave it. It is an everyday fact, or was an everyday fact in a world where seeds were sown before the ground was plowed. In this regard it is straight out of the Palestine Farmer's Almanac. Another interesting exegesis in *The Interpreter's Bible,* however, is that Jesus is speaking autobiographically. The sower's experience has also been his experience as a preacher.

Ohio Review 37 (1986). Reprinted with permission. In this essay Jarman examines the narrative focus in Levine's *Sweet Will* and in Charles Wright's *The Other Side of the River.*—ED.

What I want to examine is how the story to which a meaning might be attached is presented as meaningful in itself, how the earthly story has been created without a heavenly meaning, although there is often in both poets a yearning for some meaning other than the natural fact of experience. In Philip Levine and particularly in his twelfth volume of poetry we have a poet whose natural impulse is toward the significant anecdote, even the extended narrative, and a belief in the redemptive power of nature. For Levine it is that world poised in Romantic opposition to the city where so much of his poetry is also set. Levine's poems have always been full of names, some attached to people and some anonymous in their chaste separation from an imaginable body, and *Sweet Will* is no exception. When name and place come together, story occurs. Why this happens is one question I would like to answer. The other is what is the nature of meaning when the metaphorical form of a story is negated? Levine and Wright are also poets who return again and again to the denial, to insistence on the absence of anyone who might understand or care or remember, even to the insistence that they themselves do not always comprehend what they have written, either now or any longer. They invoke nothingness and its synonyms so often in their poetry that absence takes on an actual presence, like the holy spirit in a tongue of flame.

It may have come earlier, but sometime during the composition of *One for the Rose,* the 1981 volume that preceded his *Selected Poems,* Philip Levine decided that he did not have to be Philip Levine anymore. That is to say, he seemed to conclude that identity, that frozen form, could be changed by narrative. Thus, in *One for the Rose,* there is the poem "I Was Born in Lucerne," which begins "Everyone says otherwise" but insists to the end "I breathed the truth. I was born in Lucerne." Directly before it in the book comes the poem "My Name" in which the letters of Levine's name are invested with separate meanings, especially the *n,* "one letter that says / 'nothing' or 'nuts' or 'no one' or 'never' / or 'nobody gives a shit.' But says it / with style. . . ." Of course, Levine has never ceased being Levine; he has simply fleshed himself out further, more exotically, more imaginatively, and *Sweet Will* continues this elaboration. To do this, as he always has, Levine uses narrative like a great talker and liar.

There are sixteen poems in *Sweet Will* and narrative is central to each. This is partly due to temperament; just as Wright might be said temperamentally to prefer the epiphany, the moment of radiant illumination, to the mundane and pedestrian build-up. Where Wright is a mental traveler or represents himself as such, Levine depicts himself physically in motion—walking, driving, riding, and in one case sailing—toward the moment of utterance. The volume opens with "Voyages," which appears to tell about life on Lake Erie aboard one of "the old lake boats" whose Captain drank; one of the stupid jobs, perhaps, that Levine's biographical note often refers to. "Enormous in his long coat / Sinbad would take the helm and shout out / orders swiped from pirate movies." Among the realistic details the name *Sinbad* calls the story itself into question. The answer shuttles back and forth between levels of irony and fantasy. "Salts and Oils," next in the book, offers a similar double exposure as it catalogues a series of adventures and meals, beginning, "In Havana in 1948 I ate fried dog / believing it was Peking duck. Later, / in Tampa I bunked with an insane sailor / who kept a .38 Smith and Wesson in his shorts." The poem unfolds as quickly as imagination can carry it, so masterful has Levine become with his Scheherazaderie, that it ends both convincingly and outlandishly.

> One quiet morning
> at the end of my thirteenth year a little bird
> with a dark head and tattered tail feathers
> had come to the bedroom window and commanded
> me to pass through the winding miles
> of narrow dark corridors and passageways
> of my growing body the filth and glory
> of the palatable world.

The most highly charged and beautiful word in the language is the word *once*. The problem for any storyteller is how, having uttered that word, to end. Levine states in the book's central poem, "Poem with No Ending," that his poems "never end, they run on / book after book, complaining / to the moon that heaven is wrong / or dull, no place at all to be." Yes, indeed, but in the sleight-of-hand of the narrative line, Levine shows very well not only how to end but what we expect by an end, and what we hope for when we see that the beginning is not satisfactory. Having, in the first two poems, played with cause and effect, with sequence and apparent fact, in the third poem, "Those Were the Days," Levine presents himself in a world that the readers of the never-ending poems of Philip Levine know immediately to be out-of-character.

> The sun came up before breakfast,
> perfectly round and yellow, and we
> dressed in the soft light and shook out
> our long blond curls and waited
> for Maid to brush them flat and place
> the part just where it belonged.
> We came down the carpeted stairs
> one step at a time, in single file,
> gleaming in our sailor suits, two
> four year olds with unscratched knees
> and scrubbed teeth. Breakfast came
> on silver dishes with silver covers
> and was set in table center, and Mother
> handed out the portions of eggs
> and bacon, toast and juice.

One expects the end at any moment in this poem, and it comes in the form of a poetic turn, a volta, that is a transformation.

> My brother flung
> his fork on the polished wooden floor
> and cried out, "My eggs are cold, cold!"
> and turned his plate over. I laughed
> out loud, and Mother slapped my face
> and when I cleared my eyes the table
> was bare of even a simple white cloth,
> and the steaming plates had vanished.

This is the broken spell of many another myth and fairy tale, with parallels in the punishment of Tantalus, in Keats's "La Belle Dame Sans Merci," and even in Christina Rossetti's "The Goblin Market." These parallels exist because metamorphoses are pleasurable to Levine (and he makes them so to us), and like all such archetypal tales they exist beyond any attempt to edify them, to apply meaning to them. The magical realm vanishes, as we knew it would have to since this is Philip Levine's poem; then,

> My brother said, "It's time," and we
> struggled into our galoshes and snapped
> them up, slumped into our pea coats,
> one year older now and on our way
> to the top through the freezing rains
> of the end of November, lunch boxes
> under our arms, tight fists pocketed,
> out the door and down the front stoop,
> heads bent low, tacking into the wind.

The ending of "Those Were the Days" also marks the ending for this sort of playfulness in this sad and haunted book. There were more poems of this sort in *One for the Rose*. *Sweet Will* is haunted by presences from the past, the father lost in 1933, the poet's brother, and the poet himself as a young man. There are places, too, California, Detroit, and Europe, with some references to Spain but also settings in Italy. If there is a singular purpose to the book, and I think there is, it is to discover what has made Levine the poet we recognize.

After the first three poems Levine's use of narrative becomes more an isolated instance, stripped to the mystery of fact, so that in "Look" a son and mother on different shifts at a factory are imagined greeting each other as they pass on the street. In "The Present," a poem in five parts, memories of work as a teenager include the poet's brother, the kindness of a fellow worker named Baharozian, and a man's fall from a high pallet where he slept in a warehouse. The title poem returns to the subjects and even the apparent form of poems in *Not This Pig* and *They Feed They Lion*. It sharply emphasizes the difference between past and present. It is in "Poem with No Ending" that we see Levine testing the unadorned power of narrative. Two of the stories he tells stand out for comment. One in part six of the poem is again a story about work, this time as a mover some thirty years before.

In another house an old man summoned
me to a high room. There before us
was a massive steamer trunk full
of books he could take back home
to Germany now he could return.
Tolstoi, Balzac, Goethe, all
in the original. Oh yes, I knew
the names, and he called down
to his wife, how wonderful!
This boy knows the names. He brought
the top down carefully, turned the key,
and stepped back, waiting for me
to carry it down three flights
by myself and offered me money
when I couldn't budge it, as though
I'd been pretending. This boy,
this American, in his pressed
work clothes, surely he could do it,
surely there was a way, if only
I would try. I left him shaking
his great head and passed his wife
on the stairs, a little brown mouse
of a woman laughing at such folly.

There are words here, like "this American" and "such folly," that
invite us to hunt for symbols, but there is also at the core a
simple irreducible fact that has been placed in parallel correspon-
dence to other similarly mysterious events whose meaning
might be called hermetic. Two sections later there is an account
of how walking "in the high mountains of the West" the poet
and his youngest son had "descended / slowly for a mile or more
/ through a meadow of wildflowers / still blooming in July."
They wander on and the father listens to the son talk of animals
"with the gift of speech." They enter a thick forest and the father
realizes that he has lost the way. They rest in a clearing. Finally
the father hits on an idea.

I bet him he couldn't lead us back
the way we'd come through the dark
bear woods and across the great plain

and up and down these hills.
A dollar? he said. Yes. And talking
all the way, he took the lead,
switching a fallen branch before him
to dub this little tree as friend
or a tall weed as enemy, stopping once
to uproot a purple wildflower for me.

Despite the dangerous sweetness of this episode, the faith the
father puts in his little boy is similar to the faith the narrator must
put in his tale. He must believe it will lead him back, that its
passage will be self-evident between *once* and *the end*.

Because Levine has made that journey so often and so success-
fully it may be the reason why in "Last Words" he tries to imag-
ine a death he escaped, and in so doing imagine death itself. This
is a pursuit of Wright's too, and for Wright it has to do with a
palpable desire for transcendence. This may also be Levine's aim,
but there is something else closer to what I hope to conclude
about both poets' use of narrative. Imagining himself to have
been struck down somehow beside a country road he writes,

I did not rise.
A wind or a stray animal or a group
of kids dragged me to the side
of the road and turned me over
so that my open eyes could flood heaven.
My clothes went skittering down
the road without me, ballooning
out into any shape, giddy
with release. My coins, my rings,
the keys to my house shattered
like ice and fell into the mountain
thorns and grasses, little bright points
that make you think there is magic
in everything you see. No, it can't
be, you say, for someone is speaking
calmly to you in a voice you know.

We do know that voice, and because we do and because we insist
on the nonfictional authenticity of the poem's speaker we might

legitimately withhold belief when he immerses himself in the imagination of his death. The reader that Levine imagines negates this story, terminates it, just as the poem's title is negated (it is not the last poem of the volume), and by doing so invests it with meaning or, at least, makes meaning possible.

The negation Levine imagines and puts in the mouth of his reader here is an act he himself engages in in almost every poem. Such negation can be interpreted tonally. In "Salts and Oils," after detailing his adventures in post–World War II America, Levine admits,

> These were not
> the labors of Hercules, these were not
> of meat or moment to anyone but me
> or destined for story or to learn from
> or to make me fit to take the hand
> of a toad or a toad princess or to stand
> in line for food stamps.

The self-deprecating irony of this is clear, but some of these demurrals are refuted in part by the sometimes magical or fanciful events of the poem, including the already quoted passage that begins "One quiet morning." Levine concludes that we have been told all this finally because "it pleases me." Once again, there is self-deprecation in that remark and sleight-of-hand, too.

This handling of illusion, as I have implied, occurs in the metamorphosis of the story in "Those Were the Days." The ludicrous luxury Levine imagines for his brother and himself, four-year-olds with unscratched knees, is negated by age and by the change of situation. The impossibility of the former story is made clear by the contrasting one whose terms are believable because we know the world of Levine's poems and because the hardship, coming at us brutally and suddenly, startles us into belief. The point is that in poising these opposites against each other, Levine makes them clearer formally.

In a way Levine's use of negation implies its opposite always, as in "Look."

> They will pass, mother and son,
> on the steet, and he will hold

her straight, taut body for
a moment and smell the grease
in her hair and touch her lips
with his, and today he will not
wonder why the tears start and
stall in her eyes and in his.
Today for the first time in
his life he will let his hands
stray across her padded back
and shoulders, feeling them
give and then hold, and he will
not say one word, not *mother*
or *Ruth* or *goodbye*.

And to the reader, the one he exhorts to look at these two actors
in the poet's memory, altogether alive there in the illusion of
narrative, he says "Go ahead and look! . . . No one's blaming
you." That is a "no one" fully as real as any "someone" or as the
"I" of the poet himself. What such negation does, however, is to
isolate the moment, slash and burn everything around it, so that
it has or attains a kind of chastity, even purity, as fact. It could be
that this is a chastening of the sentimental, Levine's way of keep-
ing himself and the reader honest.

As I indicated before, the difference between the past and the
present is clearly distinguished in the book's title poem. This
poem could be seen as a paradigm of the way Levine's other
poetic talents—for physical detail, for setting, for realism of char-
acter, for native dignity—affect his use of narrative.

The man who stood beside me
34 years ago this night fell
on to the concrete, oily floor
of Detroit Transmission, and we
stepped carefully over him until
he wakened and went back to his press.

One of the older workers assures the young Levine that the man
will get up "at his own sweet will." The man's story takes six
stanzas to tell, and in the telling much more is told. When Stash
rises again he addresses his fellow workers,

"Nigger, Kike, Hunky, River Rat,"
but he gave it a tune, an old tune,
like "America the Beautiful." And he danced
a little two-step and smiled showing
the four stained teeth left in the front
and took another suck of cherry brandy.

The poem's last four stanzas insist on the pastness of all this through the use of negation, which is insisted on as truth. "In truth it was no longer Friday. . . . In truth all those people are dead. . . . And in truth I'm not worth a thing. . . . Not worth a thing!" In truth the world that "runs on and on at its own sweet will" is demarcated by two great negations, eternal periods of darkness, and in one way or another every story is an imitation of this span.

This may seem to be a cause for despair. It may even be the reason that Levine, who is not a desperate poet, so often responds to his own storytelling by negating it, as if by implying that it never happened he could keep it from happening, like his imagined death in "Last Words." To avoid the suggestion that either Levine or Wright is anywhere so superficial, however, I would regard Levine's "The House," which precedes "Last Words," as the epitome of his skepticism at its deepest. Although he can imagine a wedding taking place "in the stuffy front room" of the house and the arrangements infusing the gray place with a sparkling anticipation, in fact, "no one is going in or out"; the poem that is only a house or the house that is a poem first has a locked door and is vacant. Nothingness and all it implies have for Levine, and for Wright, too, as much substance as their opposite. I think this is made clear throughout Levine's work in poem after poem. The most recent expression of it is in "rain," which is the third and last section of "Jewish Graveyards, Italy," the last poem of the book.

I can
stand under an umbrella, a man
in a romance I never finished
come to tell the rain a secret
the living don't want and the dead know:
how life goes on, how seasons pass,

the children grow, and the earth gives
back what it took. My shoes darken.
I move from one cluster of stones
to another studying the names
and dates that tell me nothing I
hadn't guessed.

This passage includes the tonal adjustments the poet makes to avoid sentimentality, but the larger issue is very much present. Here nothing is what exists outside the poem, and its representative to the poem is narrative as Levine uses it.

Much of what I have tried to express in this essay is better put by the critic Harriet Davidson. What Davidson points out is that in Eliot's *The Waste Land* there are a number of narrative segments that no metaphorical analysis of the poem has ever really explained. She argues that they are in fact mimetic of temporality and as such "opaque to interpretation" much as are the events, the disunified moments, of our lives. Within Eliot's poem they are a relief from the barren symbolic landscapes of the lyric passages, yet they also represent a grim alternative to a potentially beautiful nature, for they insist on life's finitude. Finally, paraphrasing Heidegger, Davidson states, "In order to have possibility, we must have finitude." I believe this is what Charles Wright and Philip Levine, very similar and distinctly different poets, understand about narrative, too. Their similarity and difference is underscored by the use of the river, an ancient symbol of time, in the titles of their books. Levine draws his from Wordsworth's sonnet of 1802, "Composed upon Westminster Bridge," to depict time's movement through the present. Wright's title [*The Other Side of the River*] shows him concerned with what is beyond time or rather with what faces it from the other side of our own regard. All that we can see and tell about is our portion of the river. Wright and Levine know that this is what narrative means. It is partly for this that they are valuable poets. They would not have asked for an explanation of the parable of the sower, aware as they are in their own poetry that the meaning of a story is manifold and one.

ROGER JONES

Sweet Will

At sixteen poems, *Sweet Will* is Philip Levine's shortest collection to date and brings together many of the various styles Levine has used in past collections, from the straightforward realism of *One for the Rose* to the fierce surrealism of *1933* and *They Feed They Lion* to the compelling but sometimes obscure dramatic stances of *The Names of the Lost*. Though we have become familiar with Levine's style now—the long, single, sleevelike strophes, the meticulous detail, the powerful controlling voice— we lose sight of the fact that Levine is also one of our most restless technicians, particularly in his quest for new thematic directions. For example, whereas in *One for the Rose* and *7 Years from Somewhere* Levine brought his poems to thunderous endings, in these new poems the strategy is just the opposite: he seems to have elected this time to work with the unresolved ending. In fact, in many of the poems one gets the feeling that the poem could continue indefinitely (and one poem is, in fact, titled "A Poem with No Ending"). This lack of a resounding finish allows Levine to open the poem and move freely through the intricate details of his own vast memory and imagination, and to avoid the necessity of one eye always being cocked toward the needs of structure. There is, of course, a sense of structure to these poems. But they no longer strain toward some overall moral kernel; Levine seems more content to follow Williams's lead and allow the world to be itself—even the world within memory.

The most persistent theme in *Sweet Will* is that of travel, which also becomes a metaphor for time and endurance. The people in these poems have gone great distances, seen and experienced

Reprinted from *Prairie Schooner,* by permission of University of Nebraska. Copyright 1987 University of Nebraska Press.

many things. In "Voyages," for example (the opening poem), the speaker's memory of travel takes on mythic dimensions:

> Once we set sail here
> for Bob-Lo, the Brewery Isles, Cleveland.
> We would have gone as far as Niagara
> or headed out to open sea if the Captain
> said so, but the Captain drank. Blood-eyed
> in the morning, coffee shaking in his hand,
> he'd plead to be put ashore or drowned,
> but no one heard. Enormous in his long coat,
> Sinbad would take the helm and shout out
> orders swiped from pirate movies.

The speaker relates the various legs of his journeys across America, and remembers how they all ended:

> I settled down, just as you did, took
> a degree in library sciences,
> and got my present position with
> the county. I'm supposed to believe
> something ended. . . .
>   I'm supposed to represent
> a yearning, but I like it the way it is.
> Not once has the ocean wind changed
> and brought us a taste of salt . . .
>   Not once
> have I wakened cold and scared
> out of a dreamless sleep
> into a dreamless life and cried
> and cried out for what I left behind.

The ending emphasizes the speaker's refusal to sentimentalize, unlike some of Levine's past characters who have sentimentalized despite their tenacious defiance. We are forced to return, when we finish the poem frustrated by Levine's refusal to do the work for us, to re-read. The book is prefaced by a quotation from Wordsworth, whose *Prelude* often employed a similar tactic.

Two long poems—"The Present" and "A Poem with No

Ending"—serve as the collection's nucleus. The former poem is a collection of vignettes describing the speaker's past jobs at an ice factory and bottling plant. He describes those characters who epitomized the spirit of each place (and we always must recall how Levine sees both political and moral heroism in blue-collar hardiness)—one an old man who, the speaker tells us, is "twenty years / younger than I am now putting this down / in permanent ink on a yellow legal pad / during a crisp morning in October," and another who

> . . . told us a fat tit
> would stop a toothache, two a headache.
> He told it to anyone who asked, and grinned—
> the small eyes watering at the corners—
> as Alcibiades might have grinned
> when at last he learned that love leads
> even the body beloved to a moment
> in the present when desire calms, the skin
> glows, the soul takes the light of day,
> even a working day in 1944.

The past, however, dissolves matter-of-factly into the present, and the speaker faces it without undue philosophizing:

> I began this poem in the present
> because nothing is past. The ice factory,
> the bottling plant, the cindered yard
> all gave way to a low brick building
> a block wide and windowless where they
> designed gun mounts for personnel carriers
> that never made it to Korea. . . .
> Seventeen winters have melted into an earth
> of stone, bottle caps, and old iron to carry
> off the remains of Froggy Frenchman
> without a blessing or a stone to bear it.

Similarly, "A Poem with No Ending" strings together memories and experiences, though the sequences here are only loosely associated around the themes of travel, time, and endurance. In one sequence, for example, the speaker returns to an old house, where he is turned away by the present tenant. He recalls "The back of a closet that burst into sky," but concludes "that wasn't childhood, that / was something else, something / that ended in a single day and left / no residue of happiness I could reach again." In the opening sequence, the speaker recalls how

> the rains swelled
> the streets, how at night I mumbled
> a prayer because the weight
> of snow was too great to bear
> as I heard it softly packing
> down the roof. . . .
> That is the poem I called "Boyhood"
> and placed between the smeared pages
> of your morning paper. White itself,
> it fell on the white tablecloth
> and meant so little you turned
> it over and wrote a column
> of figures you never added up.

Though profuse, the various memories Levine records in "A Poem with No Ending" make a rich tapestry of experience, which, though seemingly without easy philosophical meaning, nonetheless matter. For as the speaker asks at one point, "What could be / better than to waken as a man?"

Philip Levine remains a vigorous, keenly attentive recorder of life and people. *Sweet Will* swarms with such life, strikes out in defiant new directions, and shows why Levine is quite simply one of the best poets we have.

CHRISTOPHER BUCKLEY

The Extension of Method and Vision
in Philip Levine's *Sweet Will*

For more than twenty years now Philip Levine's poetry has
shown a marked originality and singularity of style, voice, and
vision. The Levine poem is recognizable for its tight line, its
fiery turns of imagery augmenting a narrative base, as well as for
its telling detail, acerbic diction, and commanding rhythms issu-
ing from an anaphoric use of a contemporary rhetoric. But
mostly, Levine's poems are known for their willingness to en-
gage the smug and ungenerous powers of the world and make
anger and moral indignation stand up for the disenfranchised.
Levine's poems have consistently offered a power and fierce
beauty which speak ultimately for love and humanity, and which
fly in the face of much of the temporal order.

But with the publication of his *Selected Poems* additional quali-
ties about Levine's work became more apparent. Most obvi-
ously, there were few important American poets who had writ-
ten, consecutively, as many first-rate books of poems. Even if
one were to overlook his strong first three books—*On the Edge,
Not This Pig, Red Dust*—it is really something to consider the
singular and powerful achievement of each of the next six books
from Atheneum which preceded *Selected Poems: They Feed They
Lion; 1933; The Names of the Lost; Ashes; 7 Years from Somewhere;
One for the Rose*. Second, and perhaps more important, one real-
ized that there is an augmentation to his themes, an elevation or
enlarging of concerns. Particularly, the last three books demon-
strated this expanded vision. While the middle books were cer-
tainly less defiant and more accepting than the first four books, a
reader had to notice that a majority of the latter poems, espe-
cially the longer ones, were less reflexive to incident and cause,

Crazyhorse 34 (1988). Reprinted with permission.

that they were more meditative, even metaphysical. His most recent books largely took on a focus and resolution that extended beyond autobiography and incident, beyond poignant witnessing alone, even, certainly, beyond death and the physical world.

And so it is with *Sweet Will,* Levine's first book since *Selected Poems,* for in its arrangement of sections, in its progression of individual subjects and themes, the focus of the book displays the very movement of Levine's work over the years. The poems build from an autobiographical and narrative base to subjects outside the historical self; from adamant and defiant to reflective and meditative; from the physical world to those concerns that suggest possibilities beyond corporeal life.

Of the book's three sections the first contains the most narrative, autobiographical elements. However, these bits of history, these stories and elegies do not work in a strict narrative fashion beginning to end; rather, they are "used" for effect. That is, they serve no linear end in and of themselves, but instead are mitigated by comment and speculation and even by the blatant altering of narrative facts, disruption of chronological time, and conscious intrusion of the writer into the theme and construction of the poem.

In the first poem, "Voyages," Levine begins as we have come to expect—quick, precise, spare details, a catalog rendering the scene, giving us a texture, a sense of decay, of the past, all of which lead to the specifics of the narrative situation. The poem is spoken in first person, intimately involved in what will unfold.

> Pond snipe, bleached pine, rue weed, wart—
> I walk by sedge and brown river rot
> to where the old lake boats went daily out.
> All the ships are gone, the gray wharf fallen
> in upon itself. Even the channel's
> grown over. Once we set sail here
> for Bob-Lo, the Brewery Isles, Cleveland.

And while the poem proceeds to tell the story of a time apparently early in Levine's life when he worked on freight ships on Lake Erie, the speaker becomes an Everyman by the poem's end. The poem then is about the wreckage of the past; it is about surviving our poor beginnings, coming to terms with life although we set out on something as grand as a "voyage," getting from place to place. Here then is the last third of the poem.

> I settled down, just as you did, took
> a degree in library sciences,
> and got my present position with
> the county. I'm supposed to believe
> something ended. I'm supposed to be
> dried up. I'm supposed to represent
> a yearning, but I like it the way it is.
> Not once has the ocean wind changed
> and brought the taste of salt
> over the coastal hills and through
> the orchards to my back yard. Not once
> have I wakened cold and scared
> out of a dreamless sleep
> into a dreamless life and cried
> and cried out for what I left behind.

Levine did not take a degree in library science and work for the county into his old age. "Voyages," then, is not as much witnessing and autobiography as it is imagination and exaggeration for the sake of making a larger point about what life becomes if we take it into our own two hands and do not succumb to the prescribed conditions—what it's like to get surely and finally beyond one's beginnings and accept that. This first poem is a prime example of the direction in which Levine is headed in extending his methods and themes beyond his beginnings.

The poems "Salts and Oils" and "Those Were the Days" continue much in the same mode. The poems are personal, but inflated and exaggerated far beyond what we know of Levine—they *create* a persona who is imbued with the fire of determination, that individual spirit taking hold of the world despite hardship or even privilege. This focus remains the same although the stories differ and introduce a good deal of fiction into the poems.

One of the most moving poems in the first section, "Look," is a poem narrated in the third person, and although it is probably safe to say Levine draws on his own experience here, the details do not point to a specific person, time, and history. The truth, the emotional truth, is not wrung out of the historical character/family as in *1933* or *Names of the Lost,* but is brought to the surface of the poem through the profoundly human but somewhat anonymous situation. The scene is offered up purely and simply for its poignancy and resonance; it issues initially from the bonds of family facing the depressed economic conditions of their lives—the brother has gone off to work early, and the speaker meets his mother on the street as she returns from the night shift.

> They will pass, mother and son,
> on the street, and he will hold
> her straight, taut body for
> a moment and smell the grease
> in her hair and touch her lips
> with his, and today he will not
> wonder why the tears start and
> stall in her eyes and in his.
> Today for the first time in
> his life he will let his hands
> stray across her padded back
> and shoulders, feeling them
> give and then hold, and he will
> not say one word, not *mother*
> or *Ruth* or *goodbye.*

Levine then steps back, outside the scene, and focuses on the pity of mortality, the pity of lives that passed so. He even addresses the reader, lets the scene become emblematic so that we all feel the spiritual loss in such a life, the oversights of such a world, and the tenacity of all those who simply will to stay alive.

> . . . Do you see them there
> stopped in each other's arms,
> these two who love each other?
> Go ahead and look! You wanted
> to live as much as they did,
> you asked the day to start,
> and the day started, but not
> because you asked. Forward
> or back, they've got no place
> to go. No one's blaming you.

In the five-section poem "The Present" Levine continues his manipulation of time, and again the urgency is in the vision and not simply in the particulars of the working life he describes. For although the scenes in the poem go back to the forties in Detroit, Levine is always pulling the situation forward into the present. In the second section Levine the writer enters:

> The old man who sleeps among the cases
> of empty bottles in a little nest of rags
> and newspapers at the back of the plant
> is not an old man. He is twenty years
> younger than I am now putting this down
> in permanent ink on a yellow legal pad
> during a crisp morning in October.

The focus is on concept, the power of memory which allows the emotion and suffering of the past to remain present. Levine, the poet, consciously intrudes into the story, tells us he is putting it down in "permanent" ink, lets us know it is all carried with us, always. It is not simply the past and therefore finished and unimportant. Rather, it is all relevant, all living in the present.

Again in the fourth and fifth sections Levine enters the poem formally to reinforce this concept.

> I began this poem in the present
> because nothing is past. The ice factory,
> the bottling plant, the cindered yard . . .

And this is a risky move, entering and commenting on your own poem, but it works well, for the weaving of the detail—concrete, biting, specific—holds down the voice, keeps it from becoming lofty. And the tone is right. "This still matters," it says. But to emphasize the subjects and themes of the poem over the style, Levine never gives his intrusions much length; he quickly moves back to the past with talk of the work, of the "personnel carriers / that never made it to Korea." He thinks back to his brother going to work, to the Frenchman injured at work who by now has returned, elementally, to earth. And so he thinks of death, and so he then thinks of life, his life which contains this past as he enters the poem at the end, formally, and concludes it on the concrete imagery of the present moment, the light falling on the basics that sustain us.

> . . . This morning I
> rose later than usual in a great house
> full of sunlight, but I believe it came
> down step by step on each wet sheet
> of wooden siding before it crawled
> from the ceiling and touched my pillow
> to waken me . . . From across the lots
> the wind brings voices I can't make out,
> scraps of song or sea sounds, daylight
> breaking into dust, the perfume of waiting
> rain, of onions and potatoes frying.

One element of style and vision which should be noted in this poem and in the book as a whole is its expansiveness, that ease and accuracy with which Levine unites apparently disparate elements, personal and historical details. For instance, Levine makes a connection in human terms between "Teddy the Polack" in the soda pop factory and Alcibiades.

> Teddy the Polack told us a fat tit
> would stop a toothache, two a headache.
> He told it to anyone who asked, and grinned—
> the small eyes watering at the corners—
> as Alcibiades might have grinned
> when at last he learned that love leads
> even the body of the beloved to a moment
> in the present when desire calms, the skin
> glows, the soul takes the light of day,
> even a working day in 1944.

The first section concludes with the title poem "Sweet Will" and the setting is familiar to us from many earlier poems— Detroit Transmission, the blue-collar factories of Levine's working youth. Although the material is familiar, Levine does a little something different with the poignant detail of the factory episode. He moves from detail and incident to metaphysical speculation. Instead of allowing the story of "Stash" to be only the story

of all those beaten and dehumanized by work, instead of allow-
ing the immediate force of the witnessing to be the only force,
Levine steps back, takes the long look over thirty-four years and
speculates on the worth of it all. He looks hard into the face of an
existential, uncaring, and inscrutable force and sings a little
praise to the indomitable spirit that survives it.

> In truth all these people are dead,
> they have gone up to heaven singing
> "Time on My Hands" or "Begin the Beguine,"
> and the Cadillacs have all gone back
> to earth, and nothing that we made
> that night is worth more than me.
>
> And in truth I'm not worth a thing
> what with my feet and my two bad eyes
> and my one long nose and my breath
> of old lies and my sad tales of men
> who let the earth break them back,
> each one, to dirty blood or bloody dirt.
>
> Not worth a thing! Just like it was said
> at my magic birth when the stars
> collided and fire fell from great space
> into great space, and people rose one
> by one from cold beds to tend a world
> that runs on and on at its own sweet will.

So while in detail, specific place, and incident this first section
is closest to earlier Levine work, he certainly is directing the sum
of those details (not all of which are as elegiacal and autobio-
graphical as earlier work) toward a larger concept and focus. The
people and places, the characters and stories in the poems now
serve a controlling vision and emotion rather than having, as
often before, the emotion and speculative understanding serve
the actual people and events. The scope, then, is enlarged, What
are the possible outcomes of our choices—what if lives were
lived otherwise or our beliefs changed? What if we are not as
instrumental to the workings of the planet as we once felt or still
feel we are? Or what if we *will* to see outside the usual arrange-

ment and focus and structures of our life? These concerns appear once more in the second section of the book, the fine long poem "A Poem with No Ending."

In "A Poem with No Ending" the consciousness of the poet is paramount. Levine steps in right away and comments on the work, the artifice of craft and, by extension, his life. The title suggests not only a lack of predictable and neat resolution, but the apparent finality of life and its events, its chronological significance, are also called into question.

> So many poems begin where they
> should end, and never end.
> Mine never end, they run on
> book after book, complaining
> to the moon that heaven is wrong
> or dull, no place at all to be.

A conflict is established. While acknowledging such traditional metaphysical structures as "heaven," he tells us that it is "dull." And the image of death is inherent in the life and elements of earth, no matter our efforts as boys or men to have it not be so, to hold off aging.

> If you knew how I came to be
> seven years old and how thick
> and blond my hair was, falling
> about my shoulders like the leaves . . .
> if you could see me pulling
> wagon loads of stones across
> the tufted fields and placing
> them to build myself and my brother
> a humped mound of earth where
> flowers might rise as from a grave,
> you might understand the last spring
> before the war turned toward our house
> and entered before dawn, a pale
> stranger that hovered over each bed
> and touched the soft, unguarded faces
> leaving bruises so faint

years would pass before they darkened
and finally burned. . . .

The poem in its many unnumbered sections is narrative in voice, but it lacks a strict linear progression. It begins with boyhood and soon jumps to a grown man speaking of his return to see what remains of that time and place, and there was happiness neither then nor now.

I passed the old house and saw
even from the front that four trees
were gone, and beside the drive
a wire cage held nothing . . .
No, that wasn't childhood, that
was something else, something
that ended in a single day and left
no residue of happiness I could
reach again if I took the first turn
to the left and eyes closed walked
a hundred and one steps and spoke
the right words.

And in the fourth section, he suggests there is a larger way in which we can view existence: even if it is impersonal and seemingly undirected, life continues. He goes back to his grandfather, to what the mind and heart still know of that time. Nothing will be better, different or improved, but the love is still there and the toughness and stoicism that save one from the elements. Even the little fictions that ease us from the mundane facts of our lives are still there.

The tiny stories my grandpa
told in which dogs walked upright
and the dead laughed. I was born
of these and his pocket of keys,
his dresser drawer of black socks
and white shirts, his homilies
of blood and water, all he never
gave me and all he did. Small
and dying he opened his eyes
to a certain day, to

stale water and old shoes,
and he never prayed. I could say
that was the finished poem and gather
my few things into a dark suitcase
and go quietly into the streets and wait.

And in the fifth section of the poem, he goes further back, and
the voice takes on the texture and presence of a shade, but so
naturally and gracefully the reader is kept moving right along
from the actual darkness to a more metaphysical one.

I hear the shouts
of children at play. Sunday afternoon
in August of '36, and the darkness
falls between us on the little island
where we came year after year
to celebrate the week. First I can't
see you, my brother, but I can hear
your labored breathing beside me,
and then my legs vanish, and then
my hands, and I am only a presence
in long grass. Then I am grass
blowing in a field all night, giving
and taking so many green gifts
of the earth and touching everything.

And while Levine becomes one with natural elements so as to
drift back in time and see the particulars of his life, the poem
does not ask for cheap grace or simple-minded transcendence.
By again entering the poem and talking of craft Levine shows us
how the will and vision can stop time, hold and cherish it. But
Levine concludes the section acknowledging the limits of craft
and how at best, perhaps, it is a little buffer against mortality, for
what you discover in this rumination is not necessarily what you
wanted or willed.

In this place and at this time,
which is not time, I could take
the long road back and find it all.
I could even find myself. (Writing
this, I know it's not true.)

And so it continues down the marvelous length of the poem—the past entering in again with its weight and insistence, the dead with their lives still demanding life from the speaker, still living in Levine, and then Levine stepping in with comments on his own construction. Death weighs in as the champion, but Levine is in there sparring with the continuum of living memory that has a vital if disjointed emotional sense of its own; and by the fact that all of this is surviving and ordered to some degree in the heart, it has a spiritual sense or reality as well suggesting perhaps it does not end finally and for all time.

The twelfth and last section juxtaposes life and death, light and darkness, death in the passage of time and the life and continuum of the sea. The simple and emblematic setting for this is probably the beach of Castelldefels outside of Barcelona where Levine spent time in the late sixties and seventies. With his family, he is waiting for the local *tranvia,* the commuter train, into the city. The method here is subtle and exact; Levine begins speaking in the past tense, and once he had us there ends it in the present tense. Coming back from the sea, the images begin to hint mortality; the dark is certainly dominant over the light.

> When my eyes stopped watering
> sky and sea were one black cloth
> broken by no light, and we walked
> back to the little unlighted station
> where the dark-eyed children dozed
> on benches beside their mothers.

Coming into the main station at Barcelona, there is a long series of tunnels through which local and through trains must pass. Levine recounts this simple and probably routine trip in such exact but emblematic detail that it seems as though the people may really be entering the city of the dead.

> The cars were crowded. The train
> stopped at each sea town to pick up
> the last stragglers, and we stood
> pressed together, groaning, as we
> jarred and jolted over the old track
> and finally entered the black tunnel
> that led to the center of the city.

And now a little pragmatic existentialism enters as the poet looks out for some sign or answer, but the most salient image in these lines is the comparison of the memory to the sea, implicit in that it is not only the random association of time and memory, but its life-source. Moreover, though there then seems to be little life, the old cycles of life begin again.

> . . . I
> see in the ocean of my memory
> the shore birds going out and nothing
> coming back. No light enters
> the little room, but I can hear
> the unsteady tapping of an old man
> going home and the young starting
> out for work. It's Monday morning
> now, and their harsh voices rise . . .

The old adage about nothing ever being truly destroyed answers the apparent contradiction of ideas presented in the title and in the conclusion of the poem. Of course the poem ends, and it does so by resolving that very conflict of our notion of endings. Levine neither takes the metaphysical A Train to the skies, nor does he subscribe to the notion of life and its meanings as contained in some linear progression that ends identifiably. And so the style and strategy of the poem perfectly reflect this notion in that it does not offer one story from A to Z, but rather allows the emotional and associational currents to move an idea and vision forward, almost symphonically—theme, variation, recapitulation. In the final lines Levine suggests that death is not *the* closure but that at least in the life of the earth, in the survival of will, there is continuance:

> . . . I see beyond
> the dark the distant sky breaking
> into color and each wave taking
> shape and rising landward.

The third section of the book opens with a poem entitled "An Ending," which carries on the conflict of mortality and belief in life continuing. Levine is less positive here and asserts that despite our myths and beliefs, no one comes back from death. The poetic vision jump-cuts again through time from perhaps a beach outside Barcelona to a beach in Florida.

> . . . the calm warm sea of Florida
> 30 years ago, and my brother
> and I staring out in the hope
> that someone known and loved
> would return out of air and water
> and no more, a miracle a kid
> could half-believe, could see
> as something everyday and possible.

But the elements of the earth do not return a dead father and belief sours, turns to loneliness and questioning. The answer is up for grabs:

> . . . and I
> stand in a stillness that will last
> forever or until the first light
> breaks beyond these waters. . . .

There is a little of the old anger here, not with any specific situation or fate, but with the large questions called down from the sky—is our kinship with the earth or with the spirit? The masterful touch in this poem, as in the entire book, is that Levine manages these weighty considerations without pretension or abstraction, and by couching them in the environment and in elemental images, in relevant narrative vignettes, he makes these questions reasonable, accessible, immediate and believable.

Levine concludes the third section and the book with one of the strongest, most natural, and seamless poems of meditation he has written, "Jewish Graveyards, Italy." It is divided into three sections with subtitles—*Dust, Shade, Rain.* It is a classical meditation; it examines specifically, and with concentration, a single environment, one predisposed to significance and the questioning of the meaning of human life and death. And Levine takes up these questions but by no means are his thinking and conclusions traditional or predictable. The poem is something like a secular hymn.

In *Dust,* he is in the graveyard at summer and he is attended by "crickets, salamanders, ants / The large swart flies. . . ." In a place of death and peace the poet is still surrounded by the small and vital lives of nature; the world still intrudes. And he will not let himself fall into a romantic disposition; he will not be moved beyond the hard facts of existence. And yet that existence has some light, some power that reaches out to him beyond the simple facts of death, though they are everywhere:

> Full, majestic, vanished names
> that fill my mouth and go out
> into the densely yellowed air
> of this great valley and dissolve
> as even the sea dissolves beating
> on a stone shore or as love does
> when the beloved turns to stone
> or dust or water. The old man
> rocks and whistles by turns
> into the long afternoon, and I
> bow again to what I don't know.

The poet recognizes something, some power, some fact beyond the dusts of mortality, and yet, as always in this book, he is unsure as to what it is exactly, if it *is* exactly, given the obvious persistence of lives ending.

In *Shade* even the mythopoeic presence of Death loses its inflated significance.

> As for death, I saw only a huge symbolic spider
> that refused to scuttle
> into a bin of firewood when I snapped my hankie.

And although Levine admits the presence of a "soul" it seems to be a coefficient of youth.

> . . . The raw azures and corals
> of the soul raged across
> the great, black pastures of my childhood
> at their pleasure.

But now, thinking perhaps of Keats in a similar place, reflecting as a grown man, he does not find the same force or resolve he knew as a child; he does not find evidence of the afterlife, neat and foreseeable.

> That was prayer. But now when I open them
> I don't find the grave
> of the unknown English poet the world scorned
> or his friend who lived,
> I don't hear the music of a farther life beyond
> this life. I hear traffic
> not far off. I see small wild daisies climbing
> the weeds that sprout
> from the grave of Sofia Finzi Hersch, who died
> in New Jersey and rests . . .

Rain is the last section and the poet and the graveyard give way here to ideas, not lofty or formal ideas, but rather ones struggled with on a realistic plane. Aside from the life-giving image of renewal in this section's title, Levine looks straight ahead at existence here, at the conflicts and partial resolutions which rise naturally and necessarily from the setting. There is almost a truce arrived at with the earth, its life and death which are visited on our desires, our will to hold on to life and have it add up to something larger than a return to chemical elements. There seems to be some truth beyond this life, but it is oblivious to us—we can shape this life, Levine seems to be saying, but we can do little to shape its resolution. We may as well then believe what we believe and exercise our wills, for life and the earth are luminous in every aspect of living.

> . . . In sunlight, in moonlight,
> or in rain, it's always the same,
> whatever truth falls from the sky
> as slowly as dust settling in
> morning light or cold mist rising
> from a river, takes the shape
> I give it, and I can't give it any.
> A wind will come up if I stand
> here long enough and blow the clouds
> into smoking shapes of water
> and earth. Before the last darkness

rises from the wet wild grasses,
new soft rays of last sunlight
will fall through, promising nothing.
They overflow the luminous thorns
of the roses, they catch fire
for a moment on the young leaves.

Though a little slimmer than previous volumes, *Sweet Will* is nonetheless a "big" book of poems, expansive poems that take in many experiences and many ideas—the sweet mixed in among the bitter, and certainly the confounding among the clear, the basic yet important human ideas. The extension of Levine's methods, from the earlier narrative and singular focus to the rich, inclusive, and symphonic mode of recent work, grandly accommodates a larger and more reflective and inquisitive vision—a vision that will admit the contradictions of time and our physical circumstance, but one which relies on the spirit and the will to pull the past and present into focus, where they continue.

RAY OLSON

A Walk with Tom Jefferson

More of same from Levine, and that's a very good thing. Again
his concern is the persistence of the human spirit despite the buf-
fetings of time and industrial society and the existential fact of
individual loneliness. His settings for these alternately autobio-
graphical and reportorial poems continue to be the Detroit of his
youth and the New York City and California of his maturity. The
precision and clarity of his observations of nature and the every-
day, as in "The Rat of Faith," "28," "Making It Work," and several
others that are not per se reflections upon nature, are positively
oriental: not for nothing does Levine dedicate the suite of alter-
nating urban and country thoughts, "Winter Words," to the Chi-
nese master, Tu Fu. But it's Levine's compassion for the common
person and consideration of common experience that make his
work so compelling, especially in the powerful title poem, a por-
trait of a retired black auto worker of indomitable faith. Another
fine book from a preeminently democratic poet.

Booklist, May, 1988. Reprinted with permission.

PHOEBE PETTINGELL

Voices of Democracy

Thomas Jefferson, our preeminent American democrat, once wrote that "those who labor in the earth are the chosen people of God, if ever he had a chosen people, whose breasts he has made his peculiar deposit for substantial and genuine virtue." These words might stand as the epigraph for the title poem from Philip Levine's thirteenth collection, *A Walk with Tom Jefferson*. Its hero—christened in a hopeful spirit with the name of our third president—is an elderly black man who as a child moved north to Detroit from a hardscrabble farm in Alabama.

Levine has already established himself as the bard of Detroit, his native city. The neighborhood he grew up in and its myriad little houses used to exemplify the melting pot in which European immigrants were supposed to take advantage of equal opportunity to prosper, to assimilate the American Way. But "after the town exploded / in '67 these houses / were plundered for whatever / they had. Some burned / to the ground, some / hung open, doorless, wide-eyed / until hauled off / by the otherwise unemployable / citizens of the county / to make room for the triumphant / return of Mad Anthony Wayne, / Père Marquette, Cadillac, / the badger, the wolverine, / the meadow lark, the benign / long toothed bi-ped / with nothing on his mind."

The eighteenth-century Jefferson held that revolution must periodically renew Liberty. Levine makes no such claim for the Detroit riots. Despite his ironic fantasy of burnt-out urban neighborhoods reverting to primeval forest, prepared to receive fresh explorers of our continent, he really perceives the vacant lots as a monument to failed promises—the junkyard of our civilization. The poet and his Tom stroll through panoramas of "ice boxes yawning / at the sky / their breath still fouled with years / of eating

Reprinted with permission of The New Leader, June 13, 1988. Copyright © the American Labor Conference on International Affairs, Inc.

245

garlic sausage / and refried beans, / the shattered ribcages / of beds that couldn't hold / our ordinary serviceable dreams. . . ." Levine's persona associates this desolation with the meaningless assembly-line jobs he and his coworkers once performed for the local auto manufacturers. Cogs in the machine themselves, they never were told what part it was they were supposed to be making. Yet he has not succumbed to cynicism: "Tom Jefferson / is a believer. / You can't plant winter vegetables / if you aren't, / you can't plant anything, except / maybe radishes." Just as our pioneer forebears ploughed farms out of wilderness, this old man cultivates a fecund garden in the urban jungle, having perserved his sharecropper's heritage—a green thumb.

"There is a natural aristocracy among men," Thomas Jefferson insisted. "The grounds of this are virtue and talents." The modern Tom is nature's noble man. Neither a lifetime of dehumanizing work interspersed with unemployment nor the death of his only child during the Korean War have embittered him. While Tom served in the Seabees during World War II, his son had planted and harvested their garden. When the young man went into the Army, Tom resumed planting:

> A father puts down a spade, his son
>   takes it up,
> "That's Biblical," he says,
>   "the son goes off,
> the father takes up the spade
> again, that's Biblical."

The sentiment is not exhausted resignation, but a wise acceptance born of working "this poor earth good for so much giving and taking."

From the first, Levine has written poetry that speaks for the inarticulate victims and survivors of a harsh society; a little tenement girl who becomes a grafitti artist, martyred anarchists of the Spanish Civil War, American blacks who affirm that "from 'Bow Down' come 'Rise Up.' " This newest book carries on that emphasis. He writes of "the old woman named Ida Bellow," murdered for five dollars in front of her eighteen-month-old granddaughter who "can't tell because she can't speak"; of a schoolboy terrorized by monstrous dogs, "fanged masters of the avenues." To my mind, however, Tom Jefferson is Levine's most heroic individualist to date. Undefeated by a life of privation, injustice, and grief, he still combines the "fierce spirit of independence and originality of his namesake" with the spiritual humility of another famous Tom, the protagonist of Harriet Beecher Stowe's manifesto for the freedom of all human beings.

Levine's poetic ramble takes place in late autumn, a dying time for plants whose withered brownness mirrors the city's decay. "But Tom believes / the roots need cold, / the earth needs / to turn to ice and snow so a new fire / can start up in the heart of all that grows. / He doesn't say that. / He doesn't say the heart / of ice is fire waiting, / he doesn't say the new seed / nestles in the old, / waiting, frozen, for the land to thaw / . . . he doesn't / say all this is a lost land, / it's Biblical." No, it is up to the poet to speak these words, to retrieve them out of the eloquent silence of the downtrodden.

In one of his best-known poems, William Wordsworth described how he had once walked across a moor to try to dispel the depression he felt at having to pursue his calling in a society that often destroys poets by its indifference. There he met a "leech gatherer," an old Scot who stood barelegged in pools hoping to attract those nasty animals, then used for bloodletting. The steadfastness of this poor man's sacrificial vocation inspired Wordsworth. Levine's Tom Jefferson exhibits that same strain of "Resolution and Independence." Through his endurance, we too become believers.

MARIANNE BORUCH

From "Comment: Blessed Knock"

This sense of witness, though more impassioned, is Philip Levine's habit of art, more triggered—and sometimes broken—by the weight of the world, both its abandoned and brimming places outside the self. *A Walk with Tom Jefferson* is his twelfth book, and with it Levine comes closer to the kind of Whitmanesque transcendence he seems to have sought for years. . . . he is an urban poet, and, as Lowell in an interview with V. S. Naipaul urged poets to be, Levine is "removed . . . and gregarious" in that stance. "You won't have anything to write about if you don't see people," Lowell warned, emphasizing "human richness" in poetry, a point he made in an earlier interview with Frederick Seidel. This human gift, characteristic of Levine's work, takes on extraordinary life in this collection, especially in the long title poem which concerns not *the* Tom Jefferson but another, someone equally insightful, an old black man living and gardening richly against the burned out squalor of Detroit "between the freeway / and the . . / ballpark."

The poet begins with narrative precision, pinning down the place, its decades of urgent immigrants, its weather, its broken lots and buildings, its perennial elegance anyway—iris "no one puts in," the "sticky sap rising / in the maples . . . / even over the wet stink / of burned houses." Beauty in relief, *as relief*: Levine cuts it in warily, with muscle, the speaker coming into the poem early to recall an August evening at the stadium, "the last / inning 50,000 / pulling at the night / air for one last scream. / They can drain the stars / of light. No one / owns any of this."

Ownership. This is what Levine always gets us back to, how much we own of ourselves against the monstrous and tedious demands of a life, an American life; how much is left us after the buying and selling, making and destroying in jobs and ambitions

American Poetry Review, July–August, 1988. Reprinted with permission.

blackened with greed. His work from the first has circled the survivor, and Tom Jefferson is that man, without illusions. From Alabama, Jefferson says, " 'we all come for $5 / a day and we got this! / His arms spread wide," the poet tells us, "to / include block after block / of . . . old couches and settees / burst open . . . / . . . beds that couldn't hold / our most ordinary, serviceable dreams, / blue mattresses stained / in earnest, the cracked / toilet seats of genius. . . ." On and on slips Levine into a chant of the lost, the wasted, the abandoned, a whole city-state of foul and broken objects, twentieth-century life. No ideas but in these things, perhaps, and, oddly, in the accumulation a lyric transformation takes hold, increased, articulated by Tom Jefferson's own litany on the terror between husband and wife, father and son, poor black and poor white. "That's Biblical," he says again and again, citing David and Saul, Philistine and Israelite, matters of land and blood. Always, in backdrop, is the real garden he keeps, with its metaphorical reassurance, and both living details of autumn ("little pyres pluming / the afternoon . . .") and stubborn ingenuity (Jefferson's "chromed / shopping cart under the porch").

By now, we are well into myth, where even a "bottle cap" or a ". . . wad / of tinfoil / from an empty pack of Luckys" speaks of the "vanished human hand." The depth of reverie propels the speaker into personal memory, nights years ago at the Cadillac plant where another kid turned and asked "what was / we making out of / this here metal." And the poet doesn't know. But "whatever it was we / made, we made out of earth. Amazing earth, / amazed perhaps / by all it's given us. . . ." This is the sort of "exultant movement, the blazing out" that Lowell praised in Theodore Roethke's work; Levine's great care ensures and sustains that moment until it passes through us, a physical agony and release, until America, what we can see of it, is altered.

MARK JARMAN

From "The Pragmatic Imagination and the Secret of Poetry"

The great American contribution to the history of thought is pragmatism, attributed mainly to C. S. Peirce and William James and described wittily by José Ortega y Gasset in *What Is Philosophy?*:

> With that amiable cynicism which is characteristic of the Yankees, characteristic of every new people . . . pragmatism in North America dared to proclaim this thesis—"There is no other truth than success in dealing with things."

Two major American poets, Wallace Stevens and Robert Frost, can be linked directly to James's thought; the former was his student and the latter called James "(the) teacher who influenced me most (whom) I never had." And since Ortega's words seem almost to paraphrase William Carlos Williams's most famous credo—"No ideas but in things"—we really must add him to the list as well. Pragmatism's insistence that philosophy must deal with the empirical world is fundamental to the work of these three modernists and creates there a tension between things as they are—as they appear to the senses—and as they might be. That is to say, against the restraints of pragmatism the poet must pose his own imagination; to make statements about being, he must risk creating a metaphysics. Robert Frost called this trying to say a few things the world can't deny. He meant taking the risk of deducing—from things and their relationships—truths about be-

Gettysburg Review 1 (1988). Reprinted with permission. In this essay Jarman reviews *Zone Journals* by Charles Wright and *Flesh & Blood* by C. K. Williams as well as Levine's *A Walk with Tom Jefferson.*—ED.

ing, or beliefs that might, as the preacher says in "The Black Cottage," cease "to be true" but "will turn true again, for so it goes." Pragmatism, bred in the bone of modern American poetry, makes us suspect metaphysics while trusting the imagination. We look to the imagination to express a unified ontological view of the world, while at the same time we see the world as fragmented, incapable of manifesting a metaphysical reality. Thus the poet, encouraged by pragmatism to trust the imagination, takes a risk in trying to say something the world can't deny. I call it a risk because, in simple American terms, we may not buy it; readers, faced with the metaphysical statement, may not believe it.

And so I bring together recent books by three poets—Charles Wright, C. K. Williams, and Philip Levine—who attempt to resolve the conflict between pragmatism and metaphysics. Their means of expression are very different, ranging from Wright's mystical, koanlike statements, to Williams's baffled and angry questions about mortality, to Levine's classically simple but elegant affirmation through negation. All three seem to want to come to terms with another assertion by Ortega, also found in *What Is Philosophy?*:

> Life is not a mystery, but quite the opposite; it is the clearest and most present thing there is, and being so, being purely transparent, we find difficulty in studying it closely. The eye goes beyond it, toward wisdoms that are still problematical, and it is an effort for us to stop it at these immediate evidences.

From these words one can understand Ortega's admiration for pragmatism and the discomfort a poet might have at being told that "life is not a mystery." And yet, I think this view is fundamentally shared by these three poets; it is the pragmatic ground of their imaginations.

> *Truth? A pebble of quartz? For once, then, something.*
> —Robert Frost

Philip Levine has mastered the undeniable statement, the formulation of a fundamental truth about reality. He makes what Ortega y Gasset claims is the only valid response to reality:

Since there is no way to escape the essential condition of living, and as living is reality, the best and most discreet course is to emphasize it, to underline it with irony. . . .

"Picture Postcard from the Other World," the penultimate poem in *A Walk with Tom Jefferson,* ends by describing what might be pictured on the postcard:

> It could be
> another planet just after its birth
> except that at the center the colors
> are earth colors. It could be the cloud
> that formed above the rivers of our blood,
> the one that brought rain to a dry time
> or took wine from a hungry one. It could
> be my way of telling you that I too
> burned and froze by turns and the face I
> came to was more dirt than flame, it
> could be the face I put on everything,
> or it could be my way of saying
> nothing and saying it perfectly.

This passage plays with a conditional list of possibilities, all of which are themes and motifs of Levine's poetry, in this book and in his previous books. Like Williams and Wright, Levine has a clear idea of the transcendent, but a much surer sense of its earthly limitations—that the other planet has at its center "earth colors," that the "face I / came to was more dirt than flame." The play of elemental opposition that has always been important to his poetry is here; the cloud "that formed above the rivers of our blood" brings rain and takes wine; it is possible both to burn and freeze. But the most telling lines are the last two, which underline the entire list with an Ortega-like irony:

> or it could be my way of saying
> nothing and saying it perfectly.

That use of the conditional tense is one aspect of Levine's style that has been imitated over the years, and the imitations suggest why it is compelling; it blankets reality with possibilities. For this to work one must share Levine's conviction, tempered by his inimitable humor, that to say nothing is, in fact, to say something, to deny is the only way to affirm. But only Philip Levine can make this work; it is his poetic signature.

Which leads me to the question of authority. To say "only Levine" might imply "not Wright and not Williams." But that is not my point. What I am speaking of is a coming into being, a full maturity that is something a poet may or may not seek. To my mind, Wright and Williams are engaged in the process of becoming, reforming their already identifiable styles into new shapes and thus shifting the lines of their own personalities, their authorial presence in the poem. Levine has imagined himself completely in this book; we recognize him and believe him because his imagination of himself equals his imagination of the world; he underlines both with irony when he suggests the possibility of saying nothing and saying it perfectly, because he has also presented a unified and undeniable picture of reality.

Actually, *A Walk with Tom Jefferson* does not make as much use of negation as do Levine's previous books, especially *Sweet Will*. The new volume contains nineteen poems, two of them quite long, "28" and the title poem; the latter makes up all of the fourth and last part of the book. What the book shares with Wright's and Williams's books is an abundance of detail, a proliferation of imagery, a faith in the world. Levine ranges more widely than he ever has before: from autobiographical reminiscences of his early manhood to speculations on the nature of the soul; from fictional suites about imagined characters to a theory of prosody; from a hilarious diatribe against dogs to the relaxed glories of the title poem. Based like many of his poems on a Wordsworthian concern for the life of another, set in a defeated urban milieu where it is still possible to have a relationship to the earth, "A Walk with Tom Jefferson" probes deeply and comes up with that "something" that Frost thought he glimpsed at the bottom of the well.

Perhaps because of his roots in Detroit and the succession of stupid jobs mentioned in his bookjacket biography, but certainly because he has written about factory work, work in which things are often made for purposes obscure to the maker, Levine seeks the irreducible thing at the heart of experience or of the human soul—sometimes the soul itself. In "Buying and Selling," the first poem in the book, it is "untouched drive shafts, universal joints / perfect bearings so steeped in Cosmoline"

> They could endure a century and still retain
> their purity of functional design, they
> could outlast everything until like us
> their usefulness became legend and they
> were transformed into sculpture.

In "The Whole Soul" Levine asks of that essential human quality: "Is it long as a noodle / or fat as an egg? Is it / lumpy like a potato or / ringed like an oak or an / onion and like the onion / the same as you go toward the core?" Once he hits on the idea of "the core" he is able to state, in the form of a question of course, what is fundamentally true about the body's utility as a vehicle for the soul:

>   . . . for it is not
> the human core and the rest
> meant either to keep it
> warm or cold depending
> on the season or just who
> you're talking to, the rest
> a means of getting it from
> one place to another, for it
> must go on two legs down
> the stairs and out the front
> door, it must greet the sun . . .

Like C. K. Williams, Levine is most exacerbated by mortality and its fact leads him to some of his strongest statements. In "28" he speaks of "Nothing . . . that waiting blaze / of final cold, a whiteness like no other." In "Bitterness," hearing of the death of "a love of my young manhood," he faces it with the original Levine negation:

>   I did not
> go out into the streets to
> walk among the cold, sullen
> poor of Harlem, I did not

> turn toward the filthy window
> to question a distant pale sky.
> I did not do anything.

This is the classical simplicity, the elegance I spoke of in regard to Levine's negations. He has made the undeniable statement about the fundamental nature of reality by refusing to present himself in any sort of romantic or heroic posture against death. However, the setting of the poem is actually a February morning in his garden in California, where he thinks back to hearing the news in New York; he is digging through clay to plant a fruit tree that "will give flower and fruit longer / than I care to think about." Even this is a response to mortality, this time as a denial or a recognition of denial. But it summons from the reader a long thought, and I would say a distinctly metaphysical thought, in practical American terms, terms of bitterness at the fact of death, the fact that ends all the aspirations that make up the American soul.

Of course, there are other defeats for these aspirations besides death, and Levine is one of our most eloquent poets of failure. "A Walk with Tom Jefferson" does share Frost's and Wordsworth's attention to the milieu of other persons, in this case a defeated neighborhood in Detroit, "A little world, with only / three seasons, or so we said— / one to get tired, one to get / old, one to die," a block of seven rundown houses near the baseball stadium, where he walks with Tom Jefferson, namesake of the "father of democracy," an enlightened man like the other, though descended from men the other might have owned. They talk of many things, but mostly what drew men and women like Tom up from the rural South, and how in the "chalky soil" of their gardens they keep that past alive. The poem covers so much it is risky to say what it is "about," but it seems to be a long meditation on the "amazing earth" and on the fact that in the brutal factories of Detroit, the product was made of earth's raw materials:

> Whatever it was we
> made, we made of earth. Amazing earth,
> amazed perhaps
> by all it's given us . . .

The poem digs through memories elicited by the conversation with Tom Jefferson down to the poet's own past in Detroit, working for "Chevy Gear & Axle," and to the question "What were we making out / of this poor earth good / for so much giving and taking?" If Levine has a faith, it is that the earth gives with exemplary selflessness, because it cannot help but give. Our failure is that what we make of it often does not equal that gift. Looking deeply into the past, Levine discovers, at least possibly, that "we actually made / gears and axles / for the millions of Chevies / long dead or still to die":

> It said that, "Chevrolet
> Gear & Axle"
> right on the checks they paid
> us with, so I can
> half-believe that's what we
> were making way back then.

There is pathos in this, but truth too, the workable truth of a practical vision that cuts through metaphysics and responds with that mixture of humor and sadness that we call irony. Truth is what we make it—gears and axles, ball bearings, fruit trees, the human soul. Through his negations, Levine, in Ortega y Gasset's terms, stops the eye at these immediate evidences and affirms existence.

ROBERT SCHULTZ

From "Passionate Virtuosity"

When Walt Whitman addresses his reader in "Crossing Brooklyn Ferry" and speaks of the subtle tie "which fuses me into you now, and pours my meaning into you," he names the desire of any poet to fill the reader, if only for the duration of the poem, with his or her imaginative experience. Not every poet would put it the way Whitman does. His aggressive images of fusing and pouring, with their sexual urgency, can be replaced by the more tactful "Success in Circuit" of Emily Dickinson's famous stanza:

> Tell all the Truth but tell it slant—
> Success in Circuit lies
> Too bright for our infirm Delight
> The Truth's superb surprise. . . .

But whatever the approach toward the reader or the metaphor used to describe it, the poet's success lies in surprising us into the presence of his or her truth. It is a difficult and unlikely achievement, but when we sense ourselves transported, when we have willingly assented to the poem's terms, we have known the poet's authority.

If it is difficult for the writer to achieve such authority, it is equally difficult for us to say how it has been achieved. Responding to aptness of cadence and sureness of line in one poet, we feel confident the secret must reside in technical mastery. Then we read another and are convinced that everything depends upon emotional sincerity. And then, of course, we want it all. As the novelist John Barth has written: "Technique in art . . . has about the same value as technique in lovemaking. That is to say, heart-

Reprinted by permission from *The Hudson Review* 42, no. 1 (Spring 1989). Copyright © 1989 by The Hudson Review, Inc.

felt ineptitude has its appeal and so does heartless skill, but what you want is passionate virtuosity."

To read Philip Levine's twelfth book of poetry, *A Walk with Tom Jefferson,* is to read the work of a poet who long ago developed the technical mastery to say exactly what he wants to. His is not a poetry of formal symmetries or conspicuous finish, but in nearly every poem of this new book he evokes atmosphere, emotion, and landscape with vividness and precision. In "Winter Words," his favorite bird, the sparrow, is an emblem of his affiliation with the common, the powerless, and the numerous, but it is also convincingly present, an actual bird in an empty parking lot "who picks about the gravel, and . . . invites / me in with a twist of his head, a knock / of his beak." The vigor of this emblematic sparrow is undeniable, communicated by the verbs "twist" and "knock" and by the echoing plosives in "knock" and "beak" at the ends of parallel anapestic phrases.

Levine's art, however, is the kind which hides itself, anxious that manner not distract from its urgent matter, and so this poet's authority is chiefly emotional and moral. As readers of his previous volumes know, Levine is at his strongest when he represents the lives of those who work and persevere in the bleak precincts of desperation. In the present volume, the long title poem presses upon us the ruined landscape of a Detroit neighborhood burned during the 1967 race riots.

> . . . block after block
> of dumping grounds,
>   old couches and settees
> burst open, the white innards
>   gone gray . . .
> the shattered rib cages
>   of beds that couldn't hold
> our ordinary serviceable dreams,
>   blue mattresses stained
> in earnest. . . .

"We all come for $5 / a day and we got this!" says Tom Jefferson, a black man working and gardening to survive among the remnants.

Levine's solidarity with the troubled, with the working

poor, and with those our society has abandoned is the source of his poetry's dignity and moral authority. But this same commitment—in those few poems in which it seems merely willed, programmatic, or factional—can diminish the power of his work to move us. In "Picture Postcard from the Other World" he professes a *taste* for the melancholic, trivializing the complaints against loneliness and disillusionment elsewhere in the poem. And in "Dog Poem"—a hilarious *tour de force*—one nevertheless wonders whether the poem's humor overcomes the self-pity it is founded upon. Some of the same problems arise in "I Sing the Body Electric," which invites comparison with the Whitman poem of the same title. In it the poet declares his vocation. The morning is cold and windy—March in Hartford, Connecticut—and the poet has flown from California to give a reading of his work:

> I have crossed
> a continent to bring these citizens
> the poems of the snowy mountains,
> of the forges of hopelessness,
> of the survivors of wars they
> never heard of and won't believe.

It is an admirable purpose, but the poem is marred by self-pity (a waitress serves him "hot tea in a cracked cup" so that it spills on his newspaper) and by a bitterness toward the presumed fortunate who are represented by "the cats peering smugly from the homes / of strangers." In Whitman's poem evil is identified in terms of mistaken ideas and actions (the selling of a slave, the corruption of a body) while the poet's embrace of the human remains generous, hopeful, universal. Levine's poetry is diminished when it identifies evil in terms of groups, leaving the work factional in a way that Whitman's never was.

It could be argued that Whitman wrote at a point in our history when it was perhaps easier to believe in the promise of an expanding American vigor and democracy. Belief, in fact, is an important theme in Levine's book. In poem after poem it glimmers, lost, dreamed of, but unreachable. He writes in "Winter Words," in a section set at night in an apartment above 119th Street in New York: "I can almost believe / the sleeping world is the reflection / of heaven." And in the nearly allegorical poem "The Rat of Faith," the poet resists his instinct to shoot a rat feasting in his orange tree. He lets it live and reports that "Night after night / I wake from dreams of a city / like no other, the bright city / of beauty I thought I'd lost / when I lost my faith that one day / we would come into our lives." Finally, in the title poem, he presents a character who believes as he, himself, cannot. Levine's black, twentieth-century Tom Jefferson, enduring winter in a burned-out neighborhood, trusts that the bulb must freeze in order to sprout at springtime: "Tom believes / the roots need cold, / the earth needs to turn / to ice and snow so a new fire / can start up in the heart / of all that grows." This belief is presented as heroic, but Levine's own seasons are autumn and winter, not springtime, and his tone is elegiac for a society he believes has gone irretrievably wrong. He honors endurance, which is, he says, "the only choice we have."

PAUL MARIANI

Keeping the Covenant:
A Look at Philip Levine's *A Walk with Tom Jefferson*

A Walk with Tom Jefferson is an exceptional book by an exceptional poet. Moreover it signals Philip Levine's determination to continue in the direction taken in his previous book, *Sweet Will,* toward a more meditative, all-inclusive voice in a line which goes back to Wordsworth and Keats. Keats in particular has been a presence to reckon with in Levine, whether by direct quotation, allusion, or by the frequency with which Keats is mentioned in Levine's collected and uncollected interviews and by the fact that he edited a selection of the poet's work for Ecco Press several years ago.

But this assertion of influence needs an explanation. It is as if Levine, like Berryman and Hopkins before him, had found in the letters of Keats a program for the writing of poetry that Keats, except in fragments, did not live long enough to write himself. It is because many of us would not have expected to find the inheritor of a Keatsian poetic in a working-class American poet (and that one from Detroit) that critics—who should have known better—have not looked to Levine. But what underwrites Levine's best poems is in fact a mystical vision grounded in the harsh facts of reality or, conversely, the quotidian transformed by the imagination and done—as Berryman once wrote of Levine—with the delicious tang of Jewish humor.

To speak simply, scrupulously avoiding for the moment any reference to Whitman, Williams, Stevens, and the Spanish surrealists, it is also my sense that Levine has come latterly to Wordsworth via his long meditation on Keats, Wordsworth being present in the very title of Levine's *Sweet Will,* in the opening poem

Kenyon Review, n.s. 11, no. 4 (Fall 1989). Reprinted with permission.

of *Tom Jefferson*—"Buying and Selling," which recalls the "getting and spending" of "The World Is Too Much with Us," and—as I hope to show—in Levine's brilliant recasting of "Michael" in his own long poem, "A Walk with Tom Jefferson."

Consider for a moment Levine's development since putting together his very fine *Selected Poems* in 1984. Throughout that collection of ninety-seven poems written over a quarter century, we keep finding very strong poems, many frequently anthologized. Among the strongest assembled in his *Selected* one might name "The Midget," "Animals Are Passing from Our Lives," "Baby Villon," "Salami," "Zaydee," "At the Fillmore," "On the Murder of Lieutenant José del Castillo by the Falangist Bravo Martinez, July 12, 1936," "Starlight," "Lost and Found," "You Can Have It," "To Cipriano, in the Wind," "The Suit," "One for the Rose." And, as even his few detractors have recognized, there is the amazing rhetorical push, the constant element of surprise and the cumulative splendor and rage of "They Feed They Lion," a rhetoric which offers empowerment to the poor and the illiterate. That poem is a miracle of rhetoric that closes with these blazing lines (lines that bring to my mind the presence of the prophetic Blake of *The Four Zoas*):

> From my five arms and all my hands,
> From all my white sins forgiven, they feed,
> From my car passing under the stars,
> They Lion, from my children inherit,
> From the oak turned to a wall, they Lion,
> From they sack and they belly opened
> And all that was hidden burning on the oil-stained earth
> They feed they Lion and he comes.

If the lines are atypical (atypical in the Jarrellian sense in which one is successfully struck by lightning while standing in an open field) it might be worth noting the "typical" nature of Levine's lines, which, while he has not been afraid to experiment (consider, for example, the short, Creeley-like lines of *Pili's Wall* [1971], or the early rhymed Wyatt-like quatrains of "For Fran"), frequently polarize themselves between Williams's run-on false tercets, quatrains, and quintains and the Romantic blank verse line, with Levine tending toward the latter in his more recent work. In truth, he seems to have shaped the blank verse line as distinctively for his own purposes as either Frost or Stevens did earlier in this century. And that, of course, will bring us back to a consideration of his allegiance to and differences from his Romantic predecessors.

"Buying and Selling," the opening poem in *A Walk with Tom Jefferson,* is a seventy-two-line autobiographical narrative in which Levine recalls with humor and sadness his delayed *bildungsroman,* as he returns us to himself at thirty. The year is 1958, and in the opening line of the poem the poet is doing what poets do. That is, he is singing, as the winds blow through this latter-day Aeolian harp making his way to the far western edge of the country, traveling over the Bay Bridge in his Ford. The poet is on his way, not—it seems—to the singing of poems, but "to a life of buying / untouched drive shafts, universal joints, / perfect bearings so steeped in Cosmoline / they could endure a century and still retain / their purity of functional design."

Like Hart Crane passing over another bridge at the other end of the country thirty years ago, whoring his imagination by trying to make a living in advertising, Levine too plays with the counter demands placed on all American poets who try to determine what value we shall place on things and on the language. "What does it cost to love the locust tree in bloom," Williams had asked in *Paterson,* before he gave us the answer: "Not less than everything." Levine, who has had to make his way, as he tells us, with more than his share "of stupid jobs," knows more than most what it costs to make one's way in America, where many whom he has given voice to in his poems never made it out of the factories and warehouses of the bleak, postwar Czechoslovakian cities we call South Philly, Detroit, Lowell, and Syracuse.

Humor can help to deflect the boredom and the agony and Levine is a master of the comic. But he is also a master of rage and a master of the visionary, all of which he employs in his poems. Consider how he intimates the presence of Dante and Virgil into these lines, played against the actual work he is doing of buying and selling auto and truck parts for his brother back east:

> At Benicia
> or the Oakland Naval Yard or Alameda
> I left the brilliant Western sun behind
> to enter the wilderness of warehouses
> with one sullen enlisted man as guide.

Benicia and Alameda have enough of the sound of Stevens's Haddam and Farmington, next door to the heavenly Jerusalem of eighteenth-century rural America. But the Oakland Naval Yard? And the poet's modern-day guide through the modern labyrinth: "one sullen enlisted man." That certainly undercuts the ancient myth of the sacred guide to the mysteries of the underworld as well as that other myth of the westward odyssey that drove three centuries of Americans first toward the Alleghenies and then all the way to the Pacific.

Consider also Levine's masterful use of catalogue in this as in many of his masterful poems, how with five or six counters he can evoke an entire world (in this he works skillfully with and against Whitman's catalogues in a way only Williams and—among his contemporaries—the early Kinnell appear to have equalled). Here is one of those catalogues:

> There under the blinking artificial light
> I was allowed to unwrap a single sample,
> to hack or saw my way with delicacy
> through layer after layer of cardboard,
> metallic paper, cloth webbing, wax
> as hard as wood until the dulled steel
> was revealed beneath.

But against this mechanical world with its arcane symbols, "functions / and values known only to the old moguls / of the great international junk companies," the poet counters with his own functions and values *unknown* to those moguls. He has tried to accommodate himself to the values of his society and be a good citizen, but in truth, another order of reality beckons: the order of poetry and the life of the spirit. In fact, the only reason he is here in Oakland is to try to put bread on his family's table. Still, like many of us, he cannot help weeping—and laughing—at the vision of his younger self weeping "publicly in the Dexter- /

Davison branch of the public library / over the death of Keats in the Colvin / biography," when he had prayed—like Keats—"to be among the immortals." He thinks back to other jobs he held, selling "copper kitchenware, / Fuller brushes, American encyclopedias" from "door to unanswered door in the down / and out neighborhoods of Detroit," and then back to this job at thirty, bidding and buying, slipping a few bucks to the forklift operators to buy their honesty, even as he knows that honesty is one of those things that cannot be bought. But even the golden sun of California, like any other sun, must finally relinquish its place, and finally night falls over the poem as well. Levine remembers standing there at the now-shut entrance to the warehouse, watching the last trucks leave, and—in the dying expansiveness of the final lines of the poem, he inhales a sadness

> stronger than my Lucky Strike, stronger
> than the sadness of these hills and valleys
> with their secret ponds and streams unknown
> even to children, or the sadness of children
> themselves, who having been abandoned believe
> their parents will return before dark.

In the closing of the huge doors of the now-deserted warehouse, Levine signifies, perhaps, the bankruptcy and emptiness of an American dream based on materialism. Like Williams, Levine too wonders what of value will be left after the great American warehouse has been emptied by the great moguls, not only those in "Chicago, Philadelphia, Brooklyn," but others in Saudi Arabia and Japan. The secret ponds and streams of this land will still be there, but the tragedy is that they will be unknown even to the children—those who deserve, yes, deserve—to be filled with wonder at the daily miracle of life.

If we ask who has abandoned whom, we the land or the land us, we are still left with the feeling that the skies are darker now and that, for whatever reasons, we cant' help feeling lost. Except that the poem helps return us to the beauty of our lost dreams and our lost selves. The poem also helps us count the real costs of our self-alienation and, by implication, what it would cost to restore ourselves. That means learning how to put together again—re-member—what we were and what we might become, which we do by remembering and by singing. Levine knows that the best may already be behind us, that the best was in the struggle itself, in the high hopes we treasured even when we thought we'd failed because we did not understand the value of what we had. In spite of the costs, in spite of so much that has gone, Levine's poetry, with its unflinching fidelity to the past, is there to remind us of the good of what we had.

I wish I could talk about some of the other poems in this volume that deserve attention—in particular "For the Country," "These Streets," "Dog Poem," "Picture Postcard from the Other World," and especially "28," with its brilliant cameo of a young Levine at Stanford learning from the critic and poet, Yvor Winters, then in late middle age, the man Levine refers to in the poem only by his unlikely first name, Arthur. Here is part of "Arthur's" portrait in Levine's supple and elastic blank verse lines:

> At 56, more scared of me than I of him,
> his right forefinger raised to keep the beat,
> he gravelled out his two great gifts of truth:
> "I'd rather die than reread the last novels
> of Henry James," and "Philip, we must never lie
> or we shall lose our souls." All one winter afternoon
> he chanted in Breton French the coarse poems of Tristan
>   Corbière,
> his voice reaching into unforeseen sweetness, both hands
> rising toward the ceiling, the tears held back so long
> still held back, for he was dying and he was ready.

There are beauties there well worth mentioning, not the least of which is capturing this finical and brilliant critic and scourge of Modernism in lines that pay a tender yet just tribute to Levine's dead mentor.

But I want what space I have to talk about the extraordinary title poem that takes up the entire last quarter of this volume. Levine has given us extended meditations before. "Pili's Wall" was a relatively earlier one, and "A Poem with No Ending" in *Sweet Will* runs to fifteen pages and over five hundred lines, or about the same length as the "Tom Jefferson" piece. But "A Poem with No Ending" uses a strategy of temporal collage—pieces, memories, landscapes—set beside each other, the whole held together by the poet's voice. It's a wonderful strategy as Levine uses it—and he works it brilliantly in many of his poems, this cutting back and forth from a fixed time frame set somewhere in Levine's past, so that by the time the poem is finished Levine has managed to intersect many places and many moments: the California Sierras, the Catalonian landscape of Barcelona and the Llobregat River, as well as Detroit, Manhattan, pre-Castro Havana, Los Angeles, San Francisco.

But "A Walk with Tom Jefferson" is different. Here a single landscape is revisited—a racially mixed section of Detroit near the Detroit Tigers' stadium, which has somehow managed to survive the devastating riots of 1967. The first thing to note—and we are meant to note—is that *this* Tom Jefferson ("Same name as the other one") is not the president of the United States but rather an old black man who came up from the South with his father in the late 1920s to find work in one of Henry Ford's plants at the rate—good in those days—of five dollars a day. Tom eventually married, witnessed the Detroit race riots of 1943, served with the Navy Seabees during World War II, saw his eighteen-year-old son go off to Korea, saw the war take his boy, and now lives out his life with his wife in a landscape where most of the homes were looted, destroyed, or burnt to the ground twenty years ago.

The poem's ironies begin with the opening lines—"Between the freeway / and the grey conning towers / of the ballpark": freedom, incarceration, both in the shadow of the great American pastime, baseball, and a neighborhood that is and is not there: "miles / of mostly vacant lots, once / a neighborhood of small / two-storey wooden houses," a neighborhood not unlike the one Levine himself grew up in back in the thirties and forties. And, in fact, this Tom Jefferson is another of those dark or dwarf twins which, Joyce Carol Oates has noted, pervade the world of Phil Levine, himself a twin. The other irony, of course, is that Tom Jefferson recalls his white namesake, the author of the Declaration of Independence, that brother to dragons who kept slaves himself. But, Levine wonders, isn't it *this* Tom Jefferson who has really kept the biblical covenant evoked in the documents which founded and shaped this country?

One hundred and thirty years after *Song of Myself* and how tired the American urban landscape is, even more tired than the one Williams evoked fifty years ago in "Morning," as he watched an old Italian woman scour an empty lot looking among the shards of cement and plaster and weeds for something of value. In this section of Detroit, Levine notes, "No one puts in irises" anymore, "and yet before March passes / the hard green blades push / their way through / where firm lawns once were." Those and the locust and maple and beech trees, still returning to life even amidst this terrible desolation, perhaps returning us now to a world that predates our problematic puritan presence here, before there was any city on a hill. The only way to make anything here now (if by anything we mean money) is during baseball season, when cardboard signs reading "Park Here" on these burned-out lots will get you three bucks a night.

It's wonderful how Levine captures Tom Jefferson, an amalgam of black men he has known, with honesty, dignity, anger, and humor. Joe Louis grew up around here, Tom Jefferson remembers, remembering too part of the folklore that has helped sustain him for the past half-century: Joe Louis, who knocked out Max Schmeling—the black man who knocked out Hitler's darling—thus helping all Americans prepare for entry into war. And of course there is the promise of the soil, the promise that spring and seed and new growth bring us each year, the promise that Tom brought up with him from Alabama, the roots and hardy runners of his burnt summer squash signs that he has dug into the chalky soil of this dumping ground and will not let go.

The place itself—nearly abandoned—has already begun to revert to a wilderness, heralding the "triumphant / return of Mad Anthony Wayne, / Père Marquette, / Cadillac, / the badger, the wolverine, / the meadow lark." In truth the place is a dumping ground, more reminiscent of what Galway Kinnell found in the empty New York lots along "the Avenue Bearing the Initial of Christ into the New World" rather than Stevens's more exotic catalogue in "The Man on the Dump," except that this dumping ground bristles with Levine's sardonic humor:

> the shattered rib cages
>   of beds that couldn't hold
>   our ordinary serviceable dreams,
>   blue mattresses stained
>   in earnest, the cracked
>   toilet seats of genius. . . .

And of course there are Levine's fabled, surrealistic cats and dogs, the ones you hear about in places running back to seed: unleashed seven-foot Great Danes, rabid dog packs, something called Dogman running on all fours with the packs, "house cats grown to the size / of cougars," the bones of drunks and children discovered with the spring rains. Against that landscape one finds—as in Williams's *Paterson,* with its Lambert's Castle—the presence of the rich and privileged looking down on our degradation, in this instance Ford's new Renaissance Center and the old Rouge River plant (which "adorns" the book's cover) and whose phenomenal and exploitative successes made the center possible.

Halfway through the poem Levine begins to employ the refrain of Tom's words, "That's Biblical." That refrain, a riff played with subtle variations, evokes not only Ecclesiastes's "There is a time," but the covenant of Wordsworth's "Michael," including— of course—such New World poets as Levine, Wright, Kinnell, Williams, and Whitman (among others), who have sworn their covenant with the land. For the covenant is *with* the land, not in tearing its entrails from it and transforming them into the molten fire of the Rouge Auto Plant (so many cars that have already returned to the earth), not in buying and selling—though even here the earth seems to forgive us—but rather in growing, in staying *on* the land, in staying rooted, in listening and in remaining faithful to the ancient rhythms of the seasons, with their healing consolations.

But this is no easy romantic vision. Levine knows—as Tom Jefferson knows—what the costs have been to their sense of community. Take for example the race riots of 1943, when blacks were lynched and beaten to death on the streets supposedly protected by the National Guard and were then asked to make "airfields / the way they needed us / making Fords before the war." It's crazy, Tom knows, crazy the way they segregated troops during the war he fought in, before his son went to fight and die in Korea. Saul and David. David and Absalom. The ancient patterns of son and father repeat themselves, even as Tom Jefferson has seen the best of it—the hope of a better life, the hope at least that his son would have a better life—disappear in death and absence and the cold wind sighing off the Detroit River. One way or the other, Tom has learned, it's "Biblical" after all.

In "Michael," Wordsworth had also evoked an obliterated landscape and the cottage once called by neighbors "the Evening Star," long since plowed under by those who came after and took possession of the land. Like Tom, Michael too had had but the one boy, Luke, who had gone off to the city at eighteen, run into dissolute ways, and then fled overseas, never to return home. But Michael, nearing death, his heart broken, remains true to his covenant to love his son, to love his land forever. The sign of that covenant is the old sheepfold, made of stones thrown up freely by the stream and left unfinished at Michael's death. Still, it is a reminder to any who have read Wordsworth's poem that Michael and his wife remained faithful to a way of life.

The parallels with Levine's poem should be obvious to any who can read, though the poem's ironies are what lend a bitter dignity and pathos to Levine's way of seeing what Tom, older, might call life, or the way things are. The bitterest irony, perhaps, in Levine's poem is the realization that neither Tom nor his son have broken the covenant on which this country was founded: whether it be the agrarian pastoral vision of contact with the soil, or the gospel of hard work, or even the promise of defending one's own and other's liberties with one's life. In the long run, Tom seems to understand, the Constitution gains its authority not from the founding fathers only, but from an older bedrock of authority. As Tom says over and over until the saying assumes a certain weariness and fatalism, one way or another, it's all "Biblical." It's not the Tom Jeffersons of Detroit who have temporized the covenant, Levine knows, but those who have followed in that other Jefferson's footsteps.

Toward the close of the poem, Tom "parks his chromed / shopping cart under the porch," utters a final word of hope— "tomorrow" (a word made problematic by Levine's earlier use of it in "Waking in March")—and goes inside. Levine himself, however, is left outside, musing over this "lost land," this "holy land," which has been used over and over again. There are no arrowheads here, only the anonymity of a polished bottle cap or the tinfoil from an empty pack of Luckies left over from his world. Those, and memories.

The poem closes with those memories as Levine, who "left" this world thirty-five years before, remembers the new Sherman tanks built from the earth's bowels passing "two to a flat-bed car, / on their way to a war, / their long guns / frowning," and remembers too working at the Chevy Gear & Axle presses years later (the place itself like so much else gone back to earth now) as he made . . . what? Two twenty-five an hour? Gears and axles? Or prepared to make this poem, something that would last a good deal longer than those cars, most of which have gone back to the "poor earth good / for so much giving and taking." Instead, as if to redeem that time, he has spent the past thirty years giving us his wonderful, health-giving poems. That, "A Walk with Tom Jefferson" says in its very making, has been Levine's covenant with the dispossessed, the barely legible names of the worthy, by whom we mean the real salt of the earth.

LINDA GREGERSON

From "Short Reviews"

New York, Detroit, Fresno, Medford: from a shifting home front, the poet at sixty files his report on "God's Concern / for America." The evidence is not such as to make the poet sanguine. The walls that keep the darkness out are everywhere paper-thin. The news from above is mostly of ourselves: the autumnal sunset brilliant with pollutants, "all the earth we've pumped / into the sky," makes a pageant of doom from the by-products of human hope and industry ("A Walk with Tom Jefferson"). In Fresno, just this side of the fault line, the poet dreams the end of the world ("Waking in March"). The news arrives, bad joke that it is, from the glow above Los Angeles, and the poet can do no more than "go from bed / to bed bowing to the small damp heads / of my sons. . . ." Outside the dream, the children have long since left home, but every parent knows those rounds by heart, knows the fault line panic opens beside the beds and their sweet burdens. The children have fallen asleep imagining that it is safe to do so; the parent, standing for safety, knows that safety is illusion. Who's in charge here? "If I told you that the old woman / named Ida Bellow was shot to death / for no more than $5 and that a baby / of eighteen months saw it all from / where she wakened on the same bed / but can't tell because she can't speak / you'd say I was making it up" ("These Streets").

While America goes to the dogs, the poet with America stuck in his throat rehearses the lessons of his American masters, of Stevens and Whitman ("I Sing the Body Electric"), of Williams ("A Theory of Prosody"), of the carping Yvor Winters ("28"). Levine writes, as the good ones do, to save his life. He also writes a revisionist esthetic of Decline and Fall, retrieving poetry from frontier bravado ("Rexroth / reminiscing on a Berkeley

"Short Reviews" first appeared in *Poetry* (December, 1989), copyright 1989 by The Modern Poetry Association. Reprinted by permission of the Editor of *Poetry*.

FM station in the voice / God uses to lecture Jesus Christ"). To Whitman's triumphant corporal embrace, to Stevens's pungent oranges and extended wings, Levine replies with the echoing actuarials of Hartford on a Sunday morning ("In my black rain coat I go back / out into the gray morning and dare / the cars on North Indemnity Boulevard / to hit me, but no one wants trouble / at this hour"). To Williams's manifesto on the modernist poetic line ("As the cat / climbed over / the top of // the jamcloset . . ."), Levine replies with feline Nellie, who "would sit behind me / as I wrote" and paw at the hand that extended a line too far. "The first / time she drew blood I learned / it was poetic to end / a line anywhere to keep her / quiet." To Winters, for whom meter was morality and syntax a hedge against chaos, Levine replies with loopy numerology: the poet at fifty-six traces the numbered highways of America, the enumerated rehearsals of oblivion (fourteen hours of fevered sleep, three close encounters with death), and the domestic plenum (two opposing families of five) back to himself at twenty-eight, just half the age of the century, half the age of his newfound mentor (Winter in Los Altos), half the age of the older self who writes this poem. Winters titled his collected prose *In Defense of Reason*. Levine's bittersweet critique of reason records the patent incapacity of form to structure meaning, all the while making meaning of vaporous coincidence.

Escaping the dead end of swing-shift Detroit for sumptuous California, the artist as a young man delivered himself into the hands of one who, all but forgotten among younger writers now, was a name to conjure with in the middle decades of this century: a poet who came to believe that free verse led to madness, a critic who represented the far right fringe of the canon police, a teacher, bless him, who fostered most passionately those protégés most certain to defect. While Winters presided in the hills of Los Altos and the gentlemen's club of Stanford, the young Levine kept house with two kids and a pregnant wife in East Palo Alto, Stanford's shadow ghetto, an unincorporated stretch of cinderblock and prefab for the un- and the underemployed. For the apprentice poet, California's royal way—El Camino Real—was a divider strip between the good life and real life, a place for poaching lilacs. The poaching has stood him in good stead, evolving a poetry whose range of consciousness and conscience, whose capacity for anger and debunking and sweet recuperation lends heart to the embattled republic, or to those of its citizens with leisure to read.

In the title poem of his new book, Levine takes a mentor of another sort. Brought up from Alabama on the dream of five dollars a day, Tom Jefferson, grown old now, tends a garden in the gutted Promised Land, "Between the freeway / and the gray conning towers / of the ballpark" in post-industrial Detroit. Having lost his youth to the auto plant and his son to Korea, Tom Jefferson quotes scripture and pushes a shopping cart through abandoned lots. Tom Jefferson "is a believer. / You can't plant winter vegetables / if you aren't. . . ." Tom Jefferson takes his name from the slave-holding theorist of liberty and "property," revised to the pursuit of happiness. Walking with Tom Jefferson, Levine recalls his own first part in capitalism's long last coma:

> when I worked nights
>   on the milling machines
> at Cadillac transmission,
>   another kid just up
> from West Virginia asked me
>   what was we making,
> and I answered, I'm making
>   2.25 an hour,
> don't know what you're
>   making, and he had
> to correct me, gently, what was
>   we making out of
> this here metal, and I didn't know.

What he ultimately made, of course, was work of another sort. The thirteen bound volumes of that work to date, remarkable intersections of private memory and political fable, will not, unaided, cure what ails us. But in an age more notable for over-flowing landfills than for neighborhood renewal, it is much to make poems that heal the breach between ignorance and under-standing, labor and wage.

PART TWO　*Essays*

DAVID ST. JOHN

Where the Angels Come toward Us:
The Poetry of Philip Levine

The publication of Philip Levine's most recent collection of po-
etry, *Sweet Will* (Atheneum), following by only a year his su-
perbly edited *Selected Poems* (Atheneum), presents an excellent
opportunity to consider the twenty years of work these two
volumes represent.

Throughout his career, Philip Levine has looked for an Ameri-
can voice, a voice that could stand comfortably in the tradition of
Whitman and William Carlos Williams. Levine's primary im-
pulse is narrative, and his poems are often narratives of human
struggle—of the particularly American struggle of the immi-
grant, and of the universal struggle of individuals ignored and
unheard by their societies. Levine's poetry gives voice to these
"voiceless" men and women who he feels have been too rarely
recognized and honored in our literature.

Philip Levine's poetry, known for being urban and "angry," is
also filled with great naturalistic beauty and great tenderness. His
poems present a poetic voice that is both as colloquial and unliter-
ary as daily speech and as American as jazz. Levine has always
desired a relatively "invisible" and unadorned style, one that
could allow the voices of his speakers and the details of their
stories to fully command the reader's attention. Yet the technical
achievements and the formal underpinning of his poetry are too
often neglected. The *Selected Poems* makes clear that the metrical
and rhymed poetry of Levine's early books, as well as his superb
syllabic verse, remains some of the most highly crafted and
imaginatively powerful poetry of the time.

For Levine, poetry is almost always the poetry of witness.

Antioch Review 44 (1986). Reprinted with permission.

Here is his requiem for the silent fifties, and the title poem of his first collection, "On the Edge":

> My name is Edgar Poe and I was born
> In 1928 in Michigan.
> Nobody gave a damn. The gruel I ate
> Kept me alive, nothing kept me warm,
> But I grew up, almost to five foot ten,
> And nothing in the world can change my weight.
>
> I have been watching you these many years,
> There in the office, pencil poised and ready,
> Or on the highway when you went ahead.
> I did not write; I watched you watch the stars
> Believing that the wheel of fate was steady;
> I saw you rise from love and go to bed;
>
> I heard you lie, even to your daughter.
> I did not write, for I am Edgar Poe,
> Edgar the mad one, silly, drunk, unwise,
> But Edgar waiting on the edge of laughter,
> And there is nothing that he does not know
> Whose page is blanker than the raining skies.

The poem's speaker, with his refrain, "I did not write," was born—like Levine—in 1928, in Michigan. His name recalls, with a wry wit, one of America's more famous outsiders. Here are the elements of what will remain at the core of many of Levine's poems: a disenfranchised voice, often American, solitary yet resilient, self-ironic, accusing, compassionate, steadily proclaiming his or her role as observer from the harsh recesses of the working world. Since any real "power" to this voice, even in a democracy that promises the equal importance of *all* of its citizens' voices, has been neutralized, the speaker has seized instead the voice of this poem. In this way, in spite of the speaker's insistence upon his own silence, we find, in fact, that this silence has been *spoken*. That is, it has been written, and it is a silence that becomes both testimony and inscription.

"The Horse," another of the poems drawn from *On the Edge,*

illustrates the moral outrage that will steadily inform Levine's work. This poem, dedicated to a survivor of Hiroshima, establishes two of Levine's recurring concerns—the earth's constant ravishing and destruction by man, and the capacity of the natural world to regenerate and renew itself. It is this same power of resurrection, earthly resurrection, that Levine finds and champions in the oppressed men and women who people many of his poems, one of the most memorable of these victorious losers being the boxer of the poem "A New Day":

> The headlights fading out at dawn,
> A stranger at the shore, the shore
> Not wakening to the great sea
> Out of sleep, and night, and no sun
> Rising where it rose before.
>
> The old champion in a sweat suit
> Tells me this is Chicago, this—
> He does not say—is not the sea
> But the chopped grey lake you get to
> After travelling all night
>
> From Dubuque, Cairo, or Wyandotte.
> He takes off at a slow trot
> And the fat slides under his shirt.
> I recall the Friday night
> In a beer garden in Detroit
>
> I saw him flatten Ezzard Charles
> On TV, and weep, and raise
> Both gloved hands in a slow salute
> To a God. I could tell him that.
> I could tell him that those good days
>
> Were no more and no less than these.
> I could tell him that I thought
> By now I must have reached the sea
> We read about, or that last night
> I saw a man break down and cry

Out of luck and out of gas
In Bruce's Crossing. We collect
Here at the shore, the two of us,
To make a pact, a people come
For a new world and a new home

And what we get is what we bring:
A grey light coming on at dawn,
No fresh start and no bird song
And no sea and no shore
That someone hasn't seen before.

The delicate and powerful syllabics of "The Horse" and the
iambic tetrameter lines (with gorgeous variations) of "A New
Day" provide supple examples of Levine's technical grace and of
the coupling of formal exactitude with unfamiliar subjects that is
one of his many gifts. Even with its wink at Keats, "A New
Day" remains unforced and unliterary.

It was in his second book, *Not This Pig,* that Levine first
brought to maturity the line that would serve as the basis for his
narrative ambitions in the poems to come. One of the several
poems of seven-syllable lines in this volume, "The Cemetery at
Academy, California," best represents this solidifying of voice in
Levine's poetry. Here is the central stanza of that poem:

I came here with a young girl
once who perched barefoot on her
family marker. "I will go
there," she said, "next to my sister."
It was early morning and
cold, and I wandered over
the pale clodded ground looking
for something rich or touching.
"It's all wildflowers in the spring,"
she had said, but in July
there were only the curled cut
flowers and the headstones blanked out
on the sun side, and the long
shadows deep as oil. I walked
to the sagging wire fence

that marked the margin of the
place and saw where the same ground,
festered here and there with reedy
grass, rose to a small knoll
and beyond where a windmill
held itself against the breeze.
I could hear her singing on
the stone under the great oak,
but when I got there she was
silent and I wasn't sure
and was ashamed to ask her,
ashamed that I had come here
where her people turned the earth.

Levine loves to braid strands of narrative, visual, and medita-
tive detail into a unified poetic whole. He often uses details of the
present to stitch together fragments of memory, pieces of the
past (both public and private histories), to give texture and relief
to the surface fabric of a poem. This technique, which helps lend
narrative unity and historical resonance to his poems, is one
Levine will echo and refine throughout his career.

"Not This Pig," with its superb air of defiance, is often seen as
the poem most clearly embodying the strengths of Levine's
work of this period; yet I think a far more representative poem,
one more indicative of the directions he would take, is the deli-
cate and moving "Heaven." The poem reflects Levine's ever-
present questioning of individual and society, the relationship
between conscience and law. The poem has a basis in Levine's
own refusal to serve in the Korean War, but its central figure is
not Levine; he is *anyone* with beliefs:

If you were twenty-seven
and had done time for beating
your ex-wife and had
no dreams you remembered
in the morning, you might
lie on your bed and listen
to a mad canary sing
and think it all right to be
there every Saturday

ignoring your neighbors, the streets,
the signs that said join,
and the need to be helping.
You might build, as he did,
a network of golden ladders
so that the bird could roam
on all levels of the room;
you might paint the ceiling blue,
the floor green, and shade
the place you called the sun
so that things came softly to order
when the light came on.
He and the bird lived
in the fine weather of heaven;
they never aged, they
never tired or wanted
all through that war,
but when it was over
and the nation had been saved,
he knew they'd be hunted.
He knew, as you would too,
that he'd be laid off
for not being braver,
and it would do no good
to show how he had taken
clothespins and cardboard
and made each step safe.
It would do no good
to have been one of the few
that climbed higher and higher
even in time of war,
for now there would be the poor
asking for their share,
and hurt men in uniforms,
and no one to believe
that heaven was really here.

One of the valid conventional wisdoms about Philip Levine is
that he is one of the few urban—as opposed to suburban—
American poets. He is, certainly, our most gripping poet of the

city. Perhaps this is because he sees the used and abused city, the working city, not the city of galleries, museums, and restaurants. He sees and records the workings of the ravaged and exhausted city; he witnesses the blood and courage of those who live and work within it.

Perhaps the most compelling aspect of Levine's poetry is the place that anger is granted in his work. One of the few sources of power left to many of his speakers is to touch their own frustration and rage, and it is that current that electrifies their presence in these poems. The daily injustices that build into a larger sense of outrage accrue in Levine's poems much as they do in his speakers' lives—slowly and inexorably. It is an especially clarifying anger that we find at work throughout Levine's poetry, an anger that grants us the perspective of the real, and not a literary, world. It is an anger that we experience as a relief, the same relief we feel when the lens of a movie projector finally comes into focus; it is the clarity of truth that provides our sense of relief. No other American poet so clearly acknowledges the place and necessity of anger—in our lives and in our country—and it gives Levine's poetry an energy and an unkempt integrity that is unique.

In Levine's search for an authentic American voice, we can see the influence of daily speech, as well as the echo of black speech. It's not simply Levine's empathy with the oppressed and victimized that gives rise to a poem like "They Feed They Lion." It is also his desire to unleash the full power that he sees latent in American speech, in *all* of America's voices. We can hear it crashing forward in this poem, along with echoes of Whitman, Yeats, and Christopher Smart:

> Out of burlap sacks, out of bearing butter,
> Out of black bean and wet slate bread,
> Out of the acids of rage, the candor of tar,
> Out of creosote, gasoline, drive shafts, wooden dollies,
> They Lion grow.
> > Out of the gray hills
> Of industrial barns, out of rain, out of bus ride,
> West Virginia to Kiss My Ass, out of buried aunties,
> Mothers hardening like pounded stumps, out of stumps,
> Out of the bones' need to sharpen and the muscles' to stretch,
> They Lion grow.

One facet of Levine's special genius is that those "literary" influences are always an internal fuel for his poems, never an exterior decoration. "They Feed They Lion" concludes with this extraordinary verbal surge:

> From the sweet glues of the trotters
> Come the sweet kinks of the fist, from the full flower
> Of the hams the thorax of caves,
> From "Bow Down" come "Rise Up,"
> Come they Lion from the reeds of shovels,
> The grained arm that pulls the hands,
> They Lion grow.
> From my five arms and all my hands,
> From all my white sins forgiven, they feed,
> From my car passing under the stars,
> They Lion, from my children inherit,
> From the oak turned to a wall, they Lion,
> From they sack and they belly opened
> And all that was hidden burning on the oil-stained earth
> They feed they Lion and he comes.

Just as Philip Levine chooses to give voice to those who have no power to do so themselves, he likewise looks in his poems for the chance to give voice to the natural world, taking—like Francis Ponge—*the side of things,* the side of nature and its elements. And Levine is in many ways an old-fashioned troubadour, a singer of tales of love and heroism. Though it comes colored by the music of his world, what Levine has to offer is as elemental as breath. It is the simple insistence of breath, of the will to live—and the force of all living things in nature—that Levine exalts again and again. At the conclusion of his exquisite love poem, "Breath," he says:

> Today
> in this high clear room
> of the world, I squat
> to the life of rocks
> jewelled in the stream
> or whispering

like shards. What fears
are still held locked
in the veins till the last
fire, and who will calm
us then under a gold sky
that will be all of earth?
Two miles below on the burning
summer plains, you go
about your life one
more day. I give you
almond blossoms
for your hair, your hair
that will be white, I give
the world my worn-out breath
on an old tune, I give
it all I have
and take it back again.

The startling and memorable poems of *They Feed They Lion*
first brought Levine to national prominence, yet it's his next
book, *1933*, that most clearly reflects the realm of loss that
touches all of his work. The title refers to a year of great
personal loss (the death of his father) as well as to a world on the
verge of radical change. It is a world seen from the perspective of
innocence, the perspective of a child. The poems form a loose
family album of portraits of people and events culled from mem-
ory and given a unified shape. The spirit—the emblem of the
sparrow that inhabits these and other of Levine's poems—bears
witness to these losses and to this changing world of industrial
explosion, an ending depression, and a growing war. Each day
brings only the barest hope, but hope exists. It is in this book
that Levine, in confronting the vanished past and his father's
death, first confronts the image of his own mortality. And it is,
he says in one of his interviews, his "urge to memorialize details"
that helps him to stay the loss of places and people.

In the poem "Goodbye," about the funeral of a child (seem-
ingly a relative, perhaps a cousin, of Levine's), the poet sees in
his own reckoning with this death (a feared, mirror-death for the
child-speaker) that it is this occasion that enacts a shift from

childhood to young adulthood. The sparrow—both messenger and angel—is seen here as the embodied spirit of the lost child. Notice the double meaning of the conclusion of "Goodbye":

> In the first light
> a sparrow settled outside
> my window, and a breeze woke
> from the breathing river,
> I opened my eyes
> and the gauze curtains
> were streaming.
> "Come here," the sparrow said.
> I went. In the alley below
> a horse cart piled with bags,
> bundles, great tubs of fat,
> brass lamps the children broke.
> I saw the sheenie-man pissing
> into a little paper fire
> in the snow, and laughed.
> The bird smiled. When I unlatched
> the window the bird looked back
> three times over each shoulder
> then shook his head.
> He was never coming back inside,
> and rose in a shower
> of white dust above
> the blazing roofs
> and telephone poles.
>
> It meant a child
> would have to leave the world.

Almost all of the poems in this volume become entries and notations of homecoming and return. The title poem, "1933," seems to me one of Levine's finest. Surreal, gnarled, emotionally charged, and—in some ways—collapsing under the pressure of its own intensity, the poem rises to an elegiac beauty that allows the poet an essential recovery of his childhood. It is also a profound declaration of loss. The poem brings together again the son and the lost father (as will the later poems "Starlight" and

"The Face") in the most elemental of meetings. The voiceless father, whose voice arises in his son, the poet, and the details of their mutual loss will continue to thread their way through other of Levine's poems. It is the poem "1933" that freed Levine to write two of his most astonishing poems, also poems of sons and fathers, "New Season" and "My Son and I."

The poem "New Season" represents the culmination of Levine's work to this stage. It is personal and yet public; it concerns both the private matters of his life (the daily events in the life of one of his sons and the occasion of his mother's seventieth birthday) and the public past (the Detroit race riots that occurred when Levine was fifteen). In spite of its length, let me quote in full "New Season" in order to show the "braided" narrative movement the poem employs, a movement that occurs in many of Levine's best poems:

> My son and I go walking in the garden.
> It is April 12, Friday, 1974.
> Teddy points to the slender trunk
> of the plum and recalls the digging
> last fall through three feet
> of hard pan and opens his palms
> in the brute light of noon, the heels
> glazed with callus, the long fingers
> thicker than mine and studded with
> silver rings. My mother is 70 today.
> He flicks two snails off a leaf
> and smashes them underfoot
> on the red brick path. Saturday,
> my wife stood here, her cheek cut
> by a scar of dirt, dirt on her bare
> shoulders, on the brown belly,
> damp and sour in the creases
> of her elbows. She held up a parsnip
> squat, misshapen, a tooth pulled
> from the earth, and laughed
> her great white laugh. Teddy talks
> of the wars of the young, Larry V.
> and Ricky's brother in the movies,
> on Belmont, at McDonald's,

ready to fight for nothing, hard,
redded or on air, "low riders,
grease, what'd you say about my mama!"
Home late, one in the back seat,
his fingers broken, eyes welling
with pain, the eyes and jawbones
swollen and rough. 70 today, the woman
who took my hand and walked me
past the corridor of willows
to the dark pond where the one swan
drifted. I start to tell him
and stop, the story of my 15th spring.
That a sailor had thrown a black baby
off the Belle Isle Bridge was
the first lie we heard, and the city
was at war for real. We would waken
the next morning to find Sherman tanks
at the curb and soldiers camped
on the lawns. Damato said he was
"goin downtown bury a hatchet
in a nigger's head." Women
took coffee and milk to the soldiers
and it was one long block party
till the trucks and tanks loaded up
and stumbled off. No one saw
Damato for a week, and when I did
he was slow, head down, his right arm
blooming in a great white bandage.
He said nothing. On mornings I rise
early, I watch my son in the bathroom,
shirtless, thick-armed and hard,
working with brush and comb
at his full blond hair that suddenly
curled like mine and won't
come straight. 7 years passed
before Della Daubien told me
how three white girls from the shop
sat on her on the Woodward streetcar
so the gangs couldn't find her
and pull her off like they did

the black janitor and beat
an eye blind. She would never
forget, she said, and her old face
glows before me in shame
and terror. Tonight, after dinner,
after the long, halting call
to my mother, I'll come out here
to the yard rinsed in moonlight
that blurs it all. She will not
become the small openings
in my brain again through which the wind
rages, though she was the ocean
that ebbed in my blood, the storm clouds
that battered my lungs, though I hide
in the crotch of the orange tree
and weep where the future grows
like a scar, she will not come again
in the brilliant day. My cat Nellie,
15 now, follows me, safe
in the dark from mockingbird
and jay, her fur frost tipped
in the pure air, and together we hear
the wounding of the rose, the willow
on fire—to the dark pond
where the one swan drifted, the woman
is 70 now—the willow is burning,
the rhododendrons shrivel
like paper under water, all
the small secret mouths are feeding
on the green heart of the plum.

This melding of the narrative line with present and recollec-
tive detail is a crucial feature of Levine's later poetry. The narra-
tive voice, with its measured intelligence and quiet confidence,
shares a kinship with the voice of "The Cemetery at Academy,
California" and other earlier poems. It has been a natural progres-
sion from the seven-syllable syllabic line to the primarily three-
beat "free verse" line that characterizes these later poems. The
conversational ease of this voice is always remarkable, and Le-
vine seems closest here to one of his ambitions—to bring for-

ward a body of poetry that is accessible to *all* readers. It's instructive to look again at what Levine himself has to say about the development of this aspect of his poetry, in particular about his use of the three-beat line. In a passage from an interview with David Remnick, he says: "I think I developed that line from my favorite line, which is Yeats's trimeter line. I think it comes from an attempt to find a free verse equivalent. He can use it in a songlike way or mold it into long paragraphs of terrific rhythmic power. I was very early awed by the way he could keep the form and let the syntax fall across it in constantly varying ways, the way certain sixteenth-century poets could with pentameter. The short line appeals to me because I think it's easier to make long statements that accumulate great power in short lines. You can flow line after line, and the breaks become less significant because there are so many of them, and they build to great power."

It is equally important to consider the issue of Philip Levine's political beliefs, which he calls "anarchist" and which are, in fact, quite simple: he believes an individual human being is of more value than any government; he believes human freedom and dignity are the world's most precious resources (as opposed to, say, gold and oil); he believes that faith in the individual and the truthful (poetic) use of language are both political acts. In the preface to his book of interviews, *Don't Ask* (University of Michigan Press), Levine writes: "When I refer to myself as an anarchist I do not mean to invoke the image of a terrorist or even a man who would burn the deed to his house because 'property is theft,' which I happen to believe is true. I don't believe in the validity of governments, laws, charters, all that hide us from our essential oneness. 'We are put on earth a little space,' Blake wrote, 'That we may learn to bear the beams of love.' And so in my poems I memorialize those men and women who struggled to bear that love. I don't believe in victory in my lifetime, I'm not sure I believe in victory at all, but I do believe in the struggle and preserving the names and natures of those who fought, for their sakes, for my sake, and for those who come after." And in an interview with Arthur Smith, he adds: "I think the writing of a poem is a political act. We now exist in the kind of a world that Orwell was predicting, and the simple insistence upon accurate language has become a political act. Nothing is more obvious than what our politicians are doing to our language, so that if poets insist on the truth, or on an accurate rendition, or on a faithful use of language, if they for instance insist on an accurate depiction of people's lives as they are actually lived—this is a political act."

Philip Levine has always written poetry that is also more overtly political, and much of the best of it in his *Selected Poems* is drawn from the volumes *The Names of the Lost* and *7 Years from Somewhere*: "Gift for a Believer"; "On the Murder of Lieutenant José del Castillo by the Falangist Bravo Martinez, July 12, 1936"; "On a Drawing by Flavio"; "Francisco, I'll Bring You Red Carnations"; and two exceptionally powerful poems of domestic politics, "Ask the Roses" and "To My God in His Sickness." In these poems, as always in his work, Levine is giving voice to those without, as he returns "names" and presence to those whose names have been taken from them or erased by history. There is often a barely restrained passion in these poems; for those who prize decorum above all else in their poetry, Levine's poems will seem ill-mannered in their fierce convictions and desires. Like few other American poets, Levine forces us to consider our own moral values and, more generally, the place of moral values in any body of poetry. Levine's ethics are often the true refrain of his poems.

Levine managed, in his book *One for the Rose,* to disconcert some of his readers and to delight the rest with the kaleidoscope of voices and the fragments of self given full stage there. There is an imaginative range to these poems that remains pleasing and surprising even after many readings, and a mad, rakish quality that is invigorating. Levine's humor is at its most relaxed and open; the characters in these poems are full of extravagant and playful gestures, impossible histories, and biting commentaries. A sampling of these exuberant speakers includes: the world's first pilot, "The Conductor of Nothing," who rides trains endlessly back and forth across the country; a man who believes he once lived as a fox (and behaves accordingly); and a foundling who may well be the embodiment of the Second Coming! They are the most appealing gallery of rogues and impostors and saints of any book of American poetry in recent years. Still, perhaps the most powerful works of this period are the more typically "Levine" poems, "Having Been Asked 'What Is a Man?' I Answer" and "To Cipriano, in the Wind." Both of these poems address the nature of human dignity. The former considers courage in the face of serious illness; the latter celebrates the fierce beliefs of a man from Levine's past:

> Where did your words go,
> Cipriano, spoken to me 38 years
> ago in the back of Peerless Cleaners,
> where raised on a little wooden platform
> you bowed to the hissing press
> and under the glaring bulb the scars
> across your shoulders—"a gift
> of my country"—gleamed like old wood.
> "*Dignidad*," you said into my boy's
> wide eyes, "without is no riches."
> And Ferrente, the dapper Sicilian
> coatmaker, laughed. What could
> a pants presser know of dignity?

In Levine's most recent collection, *Sweet Will,* he uses as an epigraph to the book a passage from Wordsworth that concludes, "Ne'er saw I, never felt, a calm so deep! / The river glideth at his own sweet will. . . ." *Sweet Will* has been seen by some reviewers as a transitional volume, a book that takes up past concerns of Levine's poetry. Yet *Sweet Will* strikes me as an especially autobiographical collection, more nakedly so than any other of Levine's books. Like the river in the passage from Wordsworth, Levine glides ever forward, carrying with him his own past. The poems here carry with them the great freedom of voice won by the work of *One for the Rose.* It's my own feeling that *Sweet Will* is both a reckoning with past themes and concerns and also a sequence of highly personal and revealing annotations to those *Selected Poems.* Levine addresses his own past in the most direct manner of his career. Once again, he examines the current of politics in his poetry as it's expressed in the context of the crushing American workplace and in the history of European anarchism. But he announces most explicitly what he considers the real continuity of purpose in all of his poetic works—that he is, first and foremost, a storyteller, a moral storyteller. The poem that serves as a centerpiece for *Sweet Will,* "A Poem with No Ending," begins, "So many poems begin where they / should end, and never end. / Mine never end, they run on / book after book, complaining / to the moon that heaven is wrong / or dull, no place at all to be. / I believe all this." And it's true that all of Levine's work can be seen as being of a piece; like "To Cipriano, in the Wind," all of his poetry seems, whether public or private, to revolve around the questions of human freedom and human dignity. A poem that exhibits this force in Levine's poetry as dramatically as any is the title poem of this volume, "Sweet Will." A paradigm of the complex braiding of concerns that occurs in all of Levine's work, this poem is another of the defiant celebrations of the individual that distinguish his poetry. "Sweet Will":

> The man who stood beside me
> 34 years ago this night fell
> on to the concrete, oily floor
> of Detroit Transmission, and we
> stepped carefully over him until
> he wakened and went back to his press.

> It was Friday night, and the others
> told me that every Friday he drank
> more than he could hold and fell
> and he wasn't any dumber for it
> so just let him get up at his
> own sweet will or he'll hit you.

> "At his own sweet will," was just
> what the old black man said to me,
> and he smiled the smile of one
> who is still surprised that dawn
> graying the cracked and broken windows
> could start us all to singing in the cold.

> Stash rose and wiped the back of his head
> with a crumpled handkerchief and looked
> at his own blood as though it were
> dirt and puzzled as to how
> it got there and then wiped the ends
> of his fingers carefully one at a time

the way the mother wipes the fingers
of a sleeping child, and climbed back
on his wooden soda-pop case to
his punch press and hollered at all
of us over the oceanic roar of work,
addressing us by our names and nations—

"Nigger, Kike, Hunky, River Rat,"
but he gave it a tune, an old tune,
like "America the Beautiful." And he danced
a little two-step and smiled showing
the four stained teeth left in the front
and took another suck of cherry brandy.

In truth it was no longer Friday,
for night had turned to day as it
often does for those who are patient,
so it was Saturday in the year of '48
in the very heart of the city of man
where your Cadillac cars get manufactured.

In truth all those people are dead,
they have gone up to heaven singing,
"Time on My Hands" or "Begin the Beguine,"
and the Cadillacs have all gone back
to earth, and nothing that we made
that night is worth more than me.

And in truth I'm not worth a thing
what with my feet and my two bad eyes
and my one long nose and my breath
of old lies and my sad tales of men
who let the earth break them back,
each one, to dirty blood or bloody dirt.

Not worth a thing! Just like it was said
at my magic birth when the stars
collided and fire fell from great space
into great space, and people rose one
by one from cold beds to tend a world
that runs on and on at its own sweet will.

This poem, like the body of Philip Levine's poetry, makes one simple demand of us—that we read it by the light of human compassion. Quietly, dramatically, with growing power and beauty, the poetry of Philip Levine has become both the pulse and conscience of American poetry. He is one of our few essential poets, and in his eloquent voice he reminds us of the courage required to sing the most worthy songs.

ROBERT HEDIN

In Search of a New World: The Anarchist Dream in the Poetry of Philip Levine

Alienated, disillusioned, and victimized are terms that immediately come to mind when considering the people of Philip Levine's poetry. Whether in his native Detroit or in his adopted Spanish city, Barcelona, Levine memorializes people who have been "born in the wrong year and in the wrong place," the principal victims of an unforgiving, uncompromising system that is based, above all else, on human exploitation. Indeed, in over twenty years of writing, he has continually revealed a genuine affection and commitment to a people for whom society shows neither love nor obligation. For them, the American dream has gone to pieces, and every facet of their lives remains unfulfilled. If Levine's people have an anthem, it can be heard in "Saturday Sweeping," in the depraved words, "I don't get enough," that blare out from a radio.

Yet, no matter how grim their lives may be, his people refuse to surrender. Like Baby Villon, the tiny, punch-drunk Algerian prizefighter in the concluding poem to *Not This Pig,* they continue fighting, unwilling to accept that what their lives keep telling them may be true—that neither hard work nor prayer will bring about something better. Sustained by the hope that one day they will receive their just rewards, they believe that individual dignity must be preserved, no matter what the cost. As Cipriano, the old pants press operator in "To Cipriano, in the Wind," says: *Dignidad . . .* without is no riches."

Reprinted by permission of McFarland & Company, Inc., Publishers, Jefferson, N.C., from Vol. 4, no. 1 of *American Poetry: A Tri-Quarterly,* © 1986 Lee Bartlett and Peter White.

Of all his characters, clearly the most recurring and significant are the Spanish Civil War anarchists, primarily Buenaventura Durruti and Francisco Ascaso, whose struggles against an unjust social order Levine honors, if not nobilitates, throughout his work. More than any other, Durruti, to whom Levine dedicates *The Names of the Lost,* carries a utopian dream of the state, a "new world" as he calls it, freed of history and time wherein all tyranny is abolished and the individual is allowed to express the innate goodness and boundlessness of the self. In an interview published in the *Montreal Star* on October 30, 1936, a month before his death near the Model Prison in Barcelona, Durruti was quoted as saying: "We are going to inherit the earth. The *bourgeoisie* may blast and ruin this world before they leave the stage of history. But we carry a new world in our hearts." This vision, echoing the Old Testament prophecy that says the meek shall inherit the earth, is one to which Levine alludes in nearly all his major political poetry.

In "Gift for a Believer," for example, a poem addressed to Flavio Constantini, an Italian anarchist painter, Durruti is envisioned on his deathbed, whispering

> to an old woman that he would
> never forget the sons and daughters
> who died believing they carried
> a new world there in their hearts.

Essentially, the poem deals with the restoration of Durruti's vision. It is one, Levine tells us throughout the poem, that has never been fully extinguished, but has been forgotten or shunted aside, frustrated over the years by reality. Indeed, the word "forgotten" and its declensions are employed no less than six times over the course of this relatively short poem. At the end, when Levine employs images of newly born lambs, an appropriate symbol suggesting the rebirth of purity and innocence, and his wife's almost magical ability to make bread from the earth ("My wife kneels / to the cold earth and we have bread. / I see and don't believe."), the poem successfully links the resurrection of Durruti's new world hopes with nature's regenerative cycles. The poem concludes on still another symbol of renewal, this being rain

that runs like a pure thread
through all my dreams
and empties into tears, water
to wash our eyes, our mothers' last wine,
two palm-fulls the sky gave us,
what the roots crave, rain.

Because the concluding image of roots is as much organic as it is
spiritual, Levine is able to bring his poem to its rightful point of
departure, informing Costantini, his anarchist brother, that
Durruti's vision is not dead but, like the roots, craving revival.

Likewise, in "Francisco, I'll Bring You Red Carnations," Le-
vine pays homage to his fallen heroes buried in the cemetery of
Barcelona, a setting he employs in "Montjuich" and "For the
Fallen" and where, with each visit, his anarchist dream to break
"the unbreakable walls of the state" is restored. There, among
the 871,251 dead, he finds the same perpetuation of classes, the
same divisions of prosperity and squalor, as he finds in the cities
of the living. Even in death, the poor are crammed into "tene-
ments a dozen high"; the wealthy are entombed in nothing less
than palaces. "So nothing has changed," Levine writes, "except
for the single unswerving fact: they are all dead." There, too, he
informs his martyred hero, Francisco Ascaso, of the events that
have transpired since the Spanish Civil War:

Your Barcelona is gone,
the old town swallowed
in industrial filth and
the burning mists of gasoline.
Only the police remain, armed
and arrogant, smiling masters
of the boulevards, the police
and your dream of the city
of God, where every man
and every woman gives
and receives the gifts of work
and care, and that dream
goes on in spite of slums,
in spite of death clouds,
the roar of trucks, the harbor

staining the mother sea,
it goes on in spite of all
that mocks it.

Like many of Levine's urban settings, Barcelona is depicted as a city fallen out of grace, its old town polluted and slum-ridden. Only two things remain from the days of the Spanish Civil War: the police who enforce the unjust laws and Ascaso's dream of the "city of God" that "goes on in spite of all that mocks it." In the end, in an obvious reference to Buenaventura Durruti, Levine writes:

> We have it here
> growing in our hearts, as
> your comrade said, and when
> we give it up with our last
> breaths someone will gasp
> it home to their lives.

Though the vision is depicted as an enduring one, its presence as natural as the heart's daily rhythms, it nevertheless remains a private hope. As in "Gift for a Believer," it survives on an individual basis, passed among those who are sympathetic to the anarchist cause.

How Levine envisions this new world is never fully made clear, at least for any sustained number of lines. However, all his heroes diametrically oppose any system of governing that is founded upon human subjugation. In *Don't Ask*, Levine echoes the politics of his anarchist heroes: "I don't believe in the validity of governments, laws, charters, all that hide us from our essential oneness. Anarchism is an extraordinarily generous, beautiful way to look at the universe. It has to do with the end of ownership, the end of competitiveness, the end of a great deal of things that are ugly." Poems such as "Gift for a Believer" and "Francisco, I'll Bring You Red Carnations" suggest the refusal of Levine's heroes to comply with the dictates of the past. Instead, they stubbornly strive to establish the conditions of essential goodness which society negates.

Indeed, at the heart of Durruti's vision—and by extension Levine's other anarchist heroes—is the desire to reverse all historical movements. In prophesying the rise of something altogether new, Durruti goes beyond the fate of the mere individual to declare the salvation of the human community at large. The result is freedom from the dehumanizing strictures of history and time of which present societies are products, and the establishment of a community founded upon cooperation and collective identity, a union of solidarity whose members are all linked "hand to forearm, forearm to hand" in fraternal embrace. In short, with the dismantling of all hierarchical power structures comes the release from the past and the subsequent rise of a dynamic communalism wherein "every man / and every woman gives / and receives the gifts of work / and care."

Yet, in poem after poem, history, the very thing Levine's heroes wish to escape, constantly intrudes to upend any such egalitarian dreams from becoming a reality. Indeed, the underlying irony in all of Levine's work is the pronouncement that the past is both inescapable and uncorrectable. Rather than achieving their new world hopes, his characters continually find themselves ushered back into a reality that subverts all dreams of perfectibility.

In "A New Day," for example, a poem written in 1964 and appearing in *Not This Pig*, Levine renders this notion in dramatic terms. In the poem the speaker finds himself at dawn on the Chicago shores of Lake Michigan. The only other person present is an old boxer who is out jogging and whom the narrator recalls watching fight in a title bout on television. Ironically, he is remembered not so much for his ability as a fighter as he is for the emotions he displayed at the conclusion of his title bout with Ezzard Charles—his weeping with gratitude, his raising two "gloved hands in a slow salute to a God." Levine writes:

> We collect
> Here at the shore, the two of us,
> To make a pact, a people come
> For a new world and a new home
>
> And what we get is what we bring:
> A grey light coming on at dawn,
> No fresh start and no bird song
> And no sea and no shore
> That someone hasn't seen before.

As these concluding lines indicate, Levine strips his unlikely pair of their new world pact and ushers them back into a grim, inescapable reality. And what they get is hardly utopian: a grey lake and a grey dawn, a day flawed even before it starts. Likewise, in "Letters for the Dead," a long poem in ten parts that forms a cornerstone to *1933,* Levine portrays a young man on his first journey across America. Riding a bus over the Ohio River, he believes the other side holds the "dawn of a new world." Yet, upon crossing, his whole vision "greys" and hardens "slowly to stone." Disillusioned and resigned to his imprisonment in reality, he ends his odyssey in Florida, absurdly counting the "slate waves" of the sea and ready to turn toward home.

Dream-seeking and retribution—throughout Levine's poetry one is the natural consequence of the other. The best his heroes can ask for is to have their egalitarian dream remain in the domain of the imagination. When confronted by reality, it is doomed to failure. Like the dark, pin-striped garment in "The Suit," it becomes

> darker and more
> unrecognizeably tattered like all my
> other hopes of a singular life in a rich
> world that would be of a certain design:
> just, proportioned, equal and different
> for each of us and satisfying. . . .

Philip Levine came to prominence in the late 1960s when so many of America's poets looked toward nature as a refuge from the horrors and inequalities of the time. Many failed to listen to the warnings of our past writers that said any utopian search within the confines of nature would be a fruitless one. Remaining predominately in an urban-industrial environment, Levine proclaims the landscape of the city to be just as bankrupt in fulfilling such utopian dreams. At best, his vision is confined to the purely imaginative realm, which in no way should diminish its importance. Within this realm Levine honors people who refuse to resign themselves to the inevitable and who, despite their broken, depraved lives, have a singleness of purpose—a stubborn, virtuous discontent that "goes on in spite of all that mocks it" and that has for its goal something better for a world which for them makes reality unbearable and living tantamount to punishment. In *Don't Ask,* Levine writes: "I don't believe in victory in my lifetime. I'm not sure I believe in victory at all, but I do believe in the struggle and preserving the names and natures of those who fought, for their sake, for my sake, and for those who come after. If what Gabriel Celaya wrote is true, that '*Poesia es un arma cargada de futuro*' (Poetry is a weapon loaded with the future), then perhaps I too fought."

FRED MARCHANT

Cipriano Mera and the Lion:
A Reading of Philip Levine

Not many people in the United States would call themselves
anarchists, but the poet Philip Levine does. In so doing he does
not mean to invoke the image of a terrorist, a bomb in hand.
Instead, he wants to acknowledge his passionate opposition to
any soul-destroying forces in our social relations. His anarchism
means that he does not believe in "the validity of governments,
laws, charters" because they "hide us from our essential one-
ness."[1] Levine has also said that his anarchism is "an extraordi-
narily generous, bountiful way to look at the universe," and that
it has to do with "the end of ownership, the end of competitive-
ness, the end of a great deal of things that are ugly."[2] And while
one can debate the practicality of these ideas, it is clear that they
have been enormously valuable to Philip Levine's poetry. In
eleven books over the past twenty years he has made a rich and
important body of work, all rooted in the generous, radical faith
that human beings are essentially one.

One early benefit of this faith was an intuitive sympathy
with the victims of a predatory, commercial society. Take, for
example, "Animals Are Passing from Our Lives," in *Not This
Pig* (1968). The ostensible speaker of this poem is a pig on its
way to market. Excited, his senses heightened with fear, the pig
smells the blade and block, and can picture the flies and con-
sumers landing on his rearranged parts. Not only does this pig
have a lively imagination, he also has a profound sense of his
own dignity. The pig thinks that the boy driving him along
expects:

Imagine 1 (1984). Reprinted with permission.

that any moment I'll fall
on my side and drum my toes
like a typewriter or squeal
and shit like a new housewife

discovering television,
or that I'll turn like a beast
cleverly to hook his teeth
with my teeth. No. Not this pig.[3]

Levine himself has explained that the poem celebrates the quality of digging in one's heels, and that this fastidious pig has resolved to act with more dignity than the human beings he will feed. But as fine as pigs are, they are not the subject of this poem. This pig represents a type of human being, those who have sacrificed their bodies in the marketplace. In "No. Not this pig," one hears the echo of every person who has ever resolved to be as dignified as possible as he or she marched into an office, factory, mine, or war. In this vein it seems right to recall that this poem was composed in the mid-1960s, when nonviolent resisters as well as dutiful soldiers were passing from our lives.

And if it seems right to recall that era in relation to "Animals," it seems necessary to do so in regard to "They Feed They Lion." Levine has said that this poem is his response to the black "insurrection" in Detroit in 1967,[4] calling it a "celebration of anger."[5] But it is also an explanation of the causes and the legitimacy of a fury that has found its expression:

> From the sweet glues of the trotters
> Come the sweet kinks of the fist, from the full flower
> Of the hams the thorax of caves,
> From "Bow Down" come "Rise Up,"
> Come they Lion from the reeds of shovels,
> The grained arm that pulls the hands,
> They Lion grow.

Given "Animals," it is not surprising that pigs have nourished this lion, or that labor has hardened its muscles. What is surprising is the way that this lion of anger has swept up all before it, black and white alike. The last stanza suggests that the speaker is a white man:

> From my five arms and all my hands,
> From all my white sins forgiven, they feed,
> From my car passing under the stars,
> They Lion, from my children inherit,
> From the oak turned to a wall, they Lion,
> From they sack and they belly opened
> And all that was hidden on the oil-stained earth
> They feed they Lion and he comes.

In fear and exhilaration, the speaker has imaginatively embraced "They," and done it in defiant black English grammatical constructions. And along with its African connotation, the lion suggests a literary antecedent: probably it is descended from Yeats's rough beast slouching toward another city to be born.

One might naturally wonder how a poet whose vision is based on our essential oneness could turn and celebrate the anger of an insurrection. Levine's response to such a question would be to point out that the world of his poetry is not a pastoral setting. Many of his poems are set in the factory world of Detroit, where Levine grew up, and all are grounded in a realist's commitment to depict our actual lives. As such, he is a poet of conflict, whose vision always has a hard edge and whose poems always stand in some degree of opposition to the dominating powers that be. For example, in *One for the Rose* (1981), in a poem he titled "The Fox," Levine says that he thinks he must have been a fox in a prior life. This, he says, would explain a lot: his nose, the hair at the base of his spine, the loathing he feels whenever he sees ladies and gents mounted on horseback. He sees himself standing in the middle of a horsepath in Central Park, rock in hand, shouting and refusing to budge, "feeling the dignity / of the small creature menaced / by the many and larger."

But such anger and defiance have their limitations, and one of the great pleasures of reading Levine's recent *Selected Poems* comes in watching his lyric expressions of anger lead him to new emotional terrain. In 1974 he opened up that new terrain in his sixth book, titled *1933*. The title refers to the year when Levine's father died, when Levine himself was barely six years old. Most of the poems in the book are elegiac, and the book as a whole seems an exploration of sorrow and the poet's memories of the dead. It is not as if either memory or sorrow had been absent prior to *1933*, but now these became at least as important as his anger and defiance.

"Hold Me" is the best example of the new tone and material in *1933*. What follows are the first four stanzas of that seven-stanza poem:

> The table is cleared of my place
> and cannot remember. The bed sags
> where I turned to death, the earth fills
> my first footsteps, the sun drowns my sight.
>
> A woman turns from the basket
> of dried white laundry and sees the room
> flooding with the rays of my eyes,
> the burning of my hair and tongue.
>
> I enter your bedroom, you look up
> in the dark from tying your shoes
> and see nothing, your boney shoulders
> stiffen and hold, your fingers stop.
>
> Was I dust that I should fall?
> Was I silence that the cat heard?
> Was I anger the jay swallowed?
> The black elm choking on leaves?

As with "Animals Are Passing from Our Lives," and with "They Feed They Lion," the first thing one notes about this poem is the disconcerting, ambiguous nature of the persona. Who is this speaker? He may be a dead man, or at the very least a man imagining himself dead. He seems to have come back to haunt a familiar place, possibly a familiar "woman," and what is certainly a familiar "you." Although he can see them, they don't quite register his specific presence, and they are clearly going about the business of their lives without thinking of him. The rhetorical questions of stanza four sound frustrated, annoyed, and maybe angry. We get the sense that he is disappointed that no connections are made. These are about as many inferences as one can reasonably make from the opening stanzas, and the reader, like the speaker, feels frustrated, on the outside of the situation and in need of some connection.

When we turn to the last three stanzas, we become delighted to discover the crystalline imagery of a clearly formulated memory:

> In May, like this May, long ago
> my tiny Russian Grandpa—the bottle king—
> cupped a stained hand under my chin
> and ran his comb through my golden hair.
>
> Sweat, black shag, horse turds on the wind,
> the last wooden cart rattling down
> the alley, the clop of his great gray mare,
> green glass flashing in the December sun . . .
>
> I am the eye filled with salt,
> his child climbing the rain, we are
> all the moon, the one planet, the hand
> of five stars flung on the night river.

The images of stanzas five and six are models of memory and love. As the grandfather held the boy's face in his hands, so too the speaker holds the image of the grandfather in his mind's eye. When the table did not remember the speaker's place, and when the "you" looked up into the darkness and saw nothing, the spirit of the speaker withered into those querulous questions. Now, with the memory of the grandfather and his kinship alive in his mind, the speaker soars into the images of the last stanza. As the tears well up, the hand that had been recalled, that stained hand of the grandfather, now becomes an image which spans the universe. In another age it might have been called the hand of God holding these lights of life as they drift on the dark river. Without the memory of that stained hand, the speaker would have nothing to hold onto, and no one to hold onto him.

Levine had always had an elevated sense of memory, but in and after *1933,* its precious connection with the beloved dead made it a matter of primary importance in his poetry. This did not mean he lulled his vivid, anarchist's conscience to sleep. Instead, memory and its attendant sorrows and joys deepened his poetry. It made his speakers more complex, vulnerable, and in the end, more believable. If in "Animals Are Passing from Our Lives" one hears a voice utterly and justly confident in its moral perspective, one hears a more tentative voice in the first stanzas of "Hold Me." If in "They Feed They Lion," one hears a voice reminiscent of Biblical prophecy, one hears in the last stanzas of "Hold Me" a voice aware of what can be and has been lost. And although there are exceptions, it seems generally true that the speakers of Levine's poetry in and after *1933* seem more vulnerable because they know a great deal more about loss.

A very moving example of this is "To Cipriano, in the Wind," a poem from *One for the Rose* (1981). It begins:

> Where did your words go,
> Cipriano, spoken to me 38 years
> ago in the back of Peerless Cleaners,
> where raised on a little wooden platform
> you bowed to the hissing press
> and under the glaring bulb the scars
> across your shoulders—"a gift
> of my country"—gleamed like old wood.
> "*Dignidad,*" you said into my boy's
> wide eyes, "without is no riches."
> And Ferrente, the dapper Sicilian
> coatmaker, laughed. What could
> a pants presser know of dignity?
> That was the winter of '41, it
> would take my brother off to war,
> where you had come from, it would
> bring great snowfalls, graying
> in the streets, and news of death
> racing through the halls of my school.

The lessons in idealism and death continued on into the spring, when wild phlox leaped in the field, the Germans rolled into Russia, and some cousins died, presumably in battle. The speaker recalls that he

walked alone in the warm spring winds
of evening and said, "Dignity." I said
your words, Cipriano, into the winds.
I said, "Someday this will all be ours."
Come back, Cipriano Mera, step
out of the wind and dressed in the robe
of your pain tell me again that this
world will be ours. Enter my dreams
or my life, Cipriano, come back
out of the wind.

The last lines of this poem are a song of experience. One feels how hard it is to sustain a decent faith in the possibilities of mankind. One hears how hard it is to sustain even the little bit of innocence that this faith implies.

Who was Cipriano Mera? When an interviewer asked Levine about the origins of his anarchism, he recalled that when he was growing up in Detroit there were "two Italians who ran a cleaning and dyeing operation down on my corner who were anarchists, and whom I used to talk to all the time."[6] Naturally one thinks that this must have been Cipriano Mera. But, reading on in the interview, one learns of Levine's boyhood interest in the Spanish Civil War, an interest that has lasted all his life and no doubt introduced him to the tradition of political poetry in Spanish. His fascination with the Spanish Civil War could also have been the source of the name, for there was a Cipriano Mera commanding an anarchist militia in Barcelona in 1936.[7] Probably Levine has merged these people under one name, and such a merger is not so much poetic license as it is an example of that innocent, anarchist faith. The militia commander and the pants presser were but two faces of the same volatile spirit.

As with most of Philip Levine's poetry, "To Cipriano, in the Wind" enacts and embodies the spirit of anarchism's ability to survive in this world. Cipriano Mera does step out of the wind and into the words of the poem. So too in "They Feed They Lion." The white speaker and the black rage merge into a chant that implies a sense of oneness could exist at least in some hearts. The prayer to Cipriano is a more complicated and less confident assertion, but despite the difference in mood and meaning, the spirit of both poems is the same. Cipriano Mera and the Lion are one.

NOTES

1. Philip Levine, *Don't Ask* (Ann Arbor: University of Michigan Press, 1981), p. xi.

2. Levine, *Don't Ask,* p. 91.

3. All poetry references to Philip Levine, *Selected Poems* (New York: Atheneum, 1984).

4. Levine, *Don't Ask,* p. 65.

5. Levine, *Don't Ask,* p. 11.

6. Levine, *Don't Ask,* p. 92.

7. James Joll, *The Anarchists* (Boston: Little, Brown, 1964), pp. 273–74.

GLOVER DAVIS

Silent in America

Several sections of "Silent in America" were first published in the *North American Review*. But this poem was first published in its entirety in a limited edition chapbook I designed and printed on a handpress at the University of Iowa's School of Typography. Harry Duncan, the famous typographer, teacher, and owner of Cummington Press, helped me design this chapbook and endured my clumsiness, my many mistakes. I will never forget the sardonic, despairing look on Harry's face when I spilled a California Job Case full of type.

I set the poem letter by letter and pressed the type into soft, handmade Japanese paper, until I could almost feel those tight syllable lines with my finger tips. I have memorized many of these lines, memorized them because they moved me, and because they deal with the vocation of the poet, what it means to be a poet in America over a hundred years since the death of Whitman. But it is also a key poem in the development of one of our best poets. It not only shows us Philip Levine's formal capabilities, but it also has precursors of what Levine's poetry will be at its best.

"Silent in America" is a poem that has elements of two styles, an earlier formalism with tight syllabic lines, gorgeous off rhymes, and occasional lines of epigrammatic wit. But there are also the relaxed, fluid rhythms of his later, more mature style, a style distinguished by a compassionate identification with the people who enter his poems, people hurt, dispossessed, down on their luck. And he celebrates some of these people with an epigraph from Whitman, "Vivas for those who have failed," and with other dedicatory lines:

Pacific Review (Winter 1990). Reprinted with permission.

> For a black man whose
> name I have forgotten who danced
> all night at Chevy
> Gear & Axle,
> for that great stunned Pole
> who laughed when he called me Jew
> Boy, for the ugly
> who had no chance,
>
> the beautiful in
> body, the used and unused,
> those who had courage
> and those who quit. . . .

The epigraph from "Song of Myself" immediately reminds us of Whitman, and Whitman's unachieved ideal for America is compared to the present-day reality of suburban America in Levine's poem. This contributes to a tone of disenchantment and defiance. For Levine cannot say as Whitman did in "Song of Myself,"

> Walt Whitman, a kosmos, of Manhattan the son,
> Turbulent, fleshy, sensual, eating, drinking and breeding,
> No sentimentalist, no stander above men and women or apart
> from them. . . .

for Levine in "Silent in America" finds that

> My own wife
> and my children reach
> in their sleep for some sure sign,
> but each has his life
> private and sealed.

Levine finds himself painfully separated, and rather than a *kosmos* he is "Fresno's / dumb bard, America's last / hope, sheep in sheep's / clothing."

In his next book, *They Feed They Lion,* and in succeeding books this despairing conception of the self and of the poet will not be so evident. A new power and assurance will enter the poems, and they will have a new depth and a wider frame of reference. The naturalism of his earlier work, work that faces the bitter limitations of the poet in suburban America, is seen in the following lines from "Silent in America":

> I force myself
> to remember
> who I am, what I am, and
> why I am here.

or

> I tell time
> by the sunlight's position
> on the bedroom wall:
> it's 5:30, middle June.
> I rise, dress,
> assume my name
>
> and feel my
> face against a hard towel.
> My mind is empty;
> I see all that's here to see:
> the garden
> and the hard sky. . . .

But in his next book he will be more than a dumb bard. He will speak with prophetic power for the poor, the dispossessed. In the title poem, "They Feed They Lion," he says

> Out of burlap sacks, out of bearing butter,
> Out of black bean and wet slate bread,
> Out of the acids of rage, the candor of tar,
> Out of creosote, gasoline, drive shafts, wooden dollies,
> They Lion grow.
>   Out of the gray hills
> Of industrial barns, out of rain, out of bus ride,
> West Virginia to Kiss My Ass, out of buried aunties,

Mothers hardening like pounded stumps, out of stumps,
Out of bones' need to sharpen and the muscles' to stretch,
They Lion grow.
. . . .
From the oak turned to a wall, they Lion,
From they sack and they belly opened
And all that was hidden burning on the oil-stained earth
They feed they Lion and he comes.

The above is reminiscent of another of Levine's masters, William
Blake in "Songs of Experience," and like Blake, Levine speaks
for others and his voice is changed by this compassion. With a
growing "negative capability" never entirely absent from his
earlier work, especially in poems like "The Horse," "My Poets,"
and "Baby Villon," a more resonant symbolism seems to enter
his poems. There will be angels (though there are angels in the
earlier books) like the angel Christophe in "Angel Butcher" or
"The Dawn Fox" in "Thistles"

> who rode
> the shield of Luca up the impossible
> Etruscan slopes, who turned
> to fight the pig mounted Archers
> of the Moon.
> Tearing his
> yellowed eyes through the screen door
> to get the house cat.

There will be the Spanish stone cutter in "Salami" who works
"ten, twelve hours a day" to rebuild the unvisited church of San
Martin because of his faith, and in the poem, when Levine sees the
stone cutter's belief, he also has a kind of religious experience:

> the Tremontana was tearing
> out of the Holy Mountains
> to meet the sea winds
> in my yard, burning and
> scaring the young pines.
> The single poplar wailed
> in terror. With salt,

with guilt, with the need
to die, the vestments
of my life flared, I
was on fire, a stranger
staggering through my house
butting walls and falling
over furniture . . .

. . . .

I found my smallest son
asleep or dead, floating
on a bed of colorless light.
When I leaned closer
I could smell the small breaths
going and coming, and each
bore its prayer for me,
the true and earthy prayer
of salami.

This is a religious vision in the best sense, a vision that will never
deny the earth or this life for some metaphysical mode of exis-
tence, that will never separate body and soul. Levine instinc-
tively distrusts the kind of life-destroying dualism that Whitman
reacts against when he says

Come, said my Soul
such verses for my body let us write
(for we are one,) . . .

"Silent in America" shows us the beginnings of a movement
from self-consuming despair to a healing, self-integration
achieved through an imagination that is now more frequently
reaching beyond the self to speak with generosity and compassion
for others. There will be poem after poem in which this "negative
capability" shows Levine at his best. There will be "Zaydee":

Where did he go when his autumn came?
He sat before the steering wheel
of the black Packard, he turned the key,
pressed the starter, and he went.

The loss here is so deeply felt that there is no answer to a series of rhetorical questions, some of which are apocalyptic: "Why does the sea burn? Why do the hills cry?" There is no answer for the permanent absence of this person, this grandfather who

> . . . took me up in his arms
> when I couldn't walk and carried me
> into the grove where the bees sang
> and the stream paused forever.

There will be "Starlight," the superb elegy, "Ricky," in *7 Years from Somehwere*. There will be "To Cipriano, in the Wind" in *One for the Rose*. There will be that moment in "The Poem Circling Hamtramck, Michigan All Night in Search of You" in his fourth book, *1933,* where Levine achieves a compassionate union with his two characters, an older woman and a crippled younger man. They have only each other, and their unconventional love would be rejected by most of us, but not Levine, who says:

> If someone would enter now
> and take these lovers—for they
> are lovers—in his arms
> and rock them together
> like a mother with a child
> in each arm, this man
> with so much desire, this woman
> with none, then it would not be
> Hamtramck, it would not be
> this night.

It is this kind of generosity and healing compassion that shows Levine at his best in poem after poem, book after book, and I thought at the time I could see and feel what was coming when I held the chapbook of "Silent in America" and ran my fingers down the black, even rows of print pressed into the soft pages.

MICHAEL PEICH

Philip Levine: The Design of Poetry

There are a number of reasons why most small presses publish a
lot of poetry, but the most obvious one is that the small press is
an alternative form of publishing. Because they are not bound by
the financial constraints of corporate giants like Random House
or Doubleday, and because their publishers are committed to the
power and beauty of language, small presses are more willing to
take chances with the titles they issue. In fact, if it weren't for
small presses, a number of significant texts, particularly poetry,
would not be published.

An interest in the quality of the text also influences the design
of small-press books. Because many publishers are sensitive to
the spirit and nuances of a writer's text, they take great pains to
create physical objects that do justice to that text. Just as the poet
is careful in the choice of words, the designer is careful in the
choice of type, paper, layout, and binding. Most small publish-
ers regard the design of a book as a process that is as important as
the choice of the text. The result is often a happy alliance be-
tween writer and publisher, and the obvious beneficiary is the
reading public.

Small presses have also altered the way poets get into print.
For most poets there is what resembles an apprenticeship: poems
are first published in little magazines, then a chapbook is pub-
lished by a small press, which may lead to a larger book issued
by another small press or a university press, which in turn may
culminate in publication by a commercial house. There are varia-
tions. For example, many poets have never published anything
beyond a small press chapbook or a slim collection with a univer-
sity press. Despite variations, however, this route to publication
is so common that the checklists of a number of contemporary
poets establish the certainty of its existence.

Pacific Review (Winter 1990). Reprinted with permission.

The small-press dedication to publishing poetry in beautifully designed and crafted editions is illustrated in the published work of Philip Levine. His poems appeared in little magazines for about five years before his first inclusion in a book, *New Campus Writings No. 2,* in 1957. Coincidentally, his second appearance in a book was in the collection *Homage to Baudelaire* (1957) published by the Cummington Press, one of the most notable small presses of the era. Levine wanted to place the manuscript of his first book with a commercial house, and, according to him, the University of Chicago Press agreed to publish it, but a difference of opinion between two editors doomed the project and he was never offered a contract.

Kim Merker knew Levine and admired his work. When Merker came to the University of Iowa in 1956 to study in the Writer's Workshop, he took a course in printing with Harry Duncan. As a result of his work with Duncan, he decided to become a publisher and established the Stone Wall Press in Iowa City. Although his press was not then nationally known, Merker published, among other things, *The Collected Poems of Weldon Kees* (1960), and he now wanted to do the Levine book. Once Chicago had rejected the manuscript, Levine agreed to let Merker issue the book in a finely printed edition with the stipulation that Stone Wall also produce a trade edition. The rest, as they say, is history. *On the Edge* (1963) appeared in a letterpress edition of 220 copies from Stone Wall and in a paperback, offset edition of 1,000 copies from the Second Press.

Although he had orginally desired to place his poems with a larger commercial press, Levine could not have chosen a more appropriate publisher for *On the Edge.* The design of the book, the result of a sensitive reading of the text, allows the reader to hear, without distractions, the poems' many voices. The speakers tell a variety of stories, ranging from the poet's tribute to his wife in "For Fran," through the horror of pain in "Gangrene," to the title poem about the outsider Edgar Poe, who sits observing the world while "waiting on the edge of laughter." Whatever the voice or the subject of each poem, the book's design encourages a sense of simple, straightforward expression through the careful imposition of words on the page. The quietly elegant harmony of generous margins, uninhibited white spaces, and Romulus types allows the poems the freedom to speak directly and honestly to the reader. Levine's second small-press book, *Silent in America,* was published under slightly different circumstances. The book, which consists of a single poem in eight sections, was issued in an edition of forty-seven copies by the Shaw Avenue Press in 1965. The publisher was the poet Glover Davis, who printed the book as part of his work in Harry Duncan's typography class at the University of Iowa. The poem, with the epigraph "Vivas for Those Who Have Failed," portrays the lives of those who are outside the mainstream of American life, the "drifters in the drifting crowd," the disaffiliated who float about "beyond the false lights / of Pasadena / where the living are silent / in America." It conveys a powerful sense of the poet's disappointment with America, but the book's design does not do it justice. Unlike the elegantly simple and unified design of *On the Edge, Silent in America* is marred by all the common mistakes of a student effort in the choice of type and layout. Despite these faults, however, it is an admirable little undertaking, since Davis had the foresight to recognize the importance of the text.

Levine's next small-press book, *5 Detroits* (1970), is again remarkable more for the quality of its poetry than for its design. The five poems in this slender volume speak to the frustrations and the inevitable rage of living in Detroit or any other large urban area. This rage is expressed in many of the poems, from "Saturday Sweeping" (Half / the men in this town / are crying in / the snow") to "The Angels of Detroit" ("After the midnight of the final / shift, with all our prayers / unanswered, we gave up"), but the most noteworthy among them is "They Feed They Lion," a testimony to the oppression of inner-city life. Here, Levine collects images of frustrated lives ("Out of the acids of rage, the candor of tar"), which feed "they Lion" until, inevitably, "he comes." The voice in "They Feed They Lion," speaks largely in black dialect, but it conveys the urgency of all oppressed lives to find expression.

The urge to speak in alternative, everyday voices virtually dictated that this volume be issued by a small, alternative publisher, in this case Unicorn Press. Unfortunately, here again, the design of the volume does not measure up to the spirit of the poetry. The publisher attempted to make the book a fine edition by using Joanna types and pleasant machinemade papers, but nice type and good paper do not guarantee that a book's design will succeed. Unhappily, the typography is inconsistent (the pages alternate between too much white space or too little), the quality of the printing is poor, and the rather poorly executed heavy board binding in the edition of fifty almost prevents the text from being read (one is reminded of a coffin into which a body has been placed). In addition, because the publisher has issued three editions, one of which is signed by the author, there is the vague suggestion that creating something of rarity was more important than publishing an important manuscript. The book's physical appearance tends to distract from the pleasure of reading it, a perfect example of the violation of some of the dicta that underlie successful typography: not only should the text dictate the design, but the designer should follow basic conventions in the creation of any book. Nevertheless, although it is flawed in design, we are encouraged to read 5 *Detroits* by the sheer power of the poet's words.

Similar problems exist in *Red Dust,* which was published by Kayak Books in 1971. Beginning with the cover of the book and running throughout the text, there are a number of deficiencies in design and execution. The layout is especially troublesome; for example, there is no consistent top or bottom margin to focus the reader's eyes, and the illustrations by Marcia Maris are not matched with the text to produce a balanced page. In fact, the images are so disproportionate they overwhelm the poems and reduce their visual significance. Although the book suffers in these ways, it again exemplifies small-press publication of a manuscript its publisher feels is important. This is, after all, a solid book of poems, many of which reflect themes Levine is fond of addressing, like the frustrations of urban living ("The Wife of the Foundry Worker"), protests against war ("A War Goes" and "The Helmet"), and a range of other human considerations ("Red Dust," "Sisters," and "A Sleepless Night"). Like the books that precede and follow it, this volume is a good example of the commitment to text so characteristic of the small press.

In 1971, shortly after *Red Dust* appeared, Unicorn Press issued *Pili's Wall*. Like *Silent in America,* it is a single poem in ten sections, precisely the type of work a major publisher would not wish to issue as a separate title. But, as is so characteristic of small presses, Unicorn undertook its publication. Thankfully, the design of *Pili's Wall* shows an improvement over that of *5 Detroits*. There is still a hint of inflated rarity (the book was issued in three states, one of them an edition of fifty signed, hardbound copies), but the design seems more integrated and consistent throughout (although stanza 7 should have dictated the top and bottom margins for the entire book). To its credit, Unicorn created a book that integrates illustration with text, pays closer attention to design, and, on the whole, represents something of the essence of a well-designed book. As if *Pili's Wall* were a harbinger of things to come, the small-press editions of Levine's poetry that followed took a significant step toward more pleasing and typographically sound design.

The poet's affiliation with Scott Walker's Graywolf Press began in 1975 when the chapbook *New Season* was issued. *New Season* is one of a number of father-son poems by Levine, but it also illustrates the poet's penchant for weaving together details from personal life and events from the public domain. In it, he talks about his son Teddy, his mother and her birthday ("My mother is 70 today"), and the race riots that occurred in "my 15th spring" when "the city / was at war for real." This chapbook is simple in its design, and everywhere one turns, the poem is the central focus: The words speak openly and engagingly to the reader, and the title page is unusual in its typographic rendering of the title in the shape of a tree, the plum tree the poet and his son planted together "last fall through three feet / of hard pan." Instead of being a typographic trick that distracts attention from the work, it sparks the readers' curiosity, encouraging them to go to the text and discover the joy of the poet's words. Overall, it is a sensibly conceived volume that reflects the sensitivity of the poet and his relationship to the world around him.

When *The Names of the Lost* was published by Kim Merker in 1976, an interesting crossover from the world of small or fine press publishing to that of commercial publishing occurred. Merker, who disbanded his Stone Wall Press and established the Windhover Press at the University of Iowa in 1971, arranged with Harry Ford at Atheneum Press (Levine's commercial publisher) to issue a limited edition (200 copies) of the book. Reproduction sheets from Merker's design were then reproduced by

Atheneum to create the offset trade edition, which was printed in several thousand copies. The book includes some of Levine's finest, most mature poetry, but it was also an important step for small publishers, who came full circle into the commercial world. Although it was a rare nod in their direction, Atheneum recognized the importance of providing a significant text in a well-designed format.

As the title suggests and the table of contents confirms, these poems speak of individuals who have lost their names: Teddy Holmes, the poets of Chile, Levine's Uncle Joe, David Ber Prishkulnick, and Lt. José del Castillo, to name a few. The poet now wishes to return them to our consciousness and restore them to life. Along the way the poems often paint an angry, graphic picture. There is the violent end of Castillo, shot four times and left to die on a street "he won't walk as a man ever again," or the dark vision of the narrator of "To My God in His Sickness," who proclaims that he sees "the long coast of the continent / writhing in sleep / this America we thought we dreamed / falling away flake by flake / into the sea / and the sea blackening and burning." The poems force us to reevaluate our lives to see if we, too, are guilty. Yet despite the poet's anger, there remains a calm, almost funereal voice that speaks these names in tones of respectful remembrance, of eulogy.

The notion of a tribute or eulogy is conveyed in the design of the book, from the graceful elegance of the Romaneé and Bembo types to the generous margins, which praise the subjects by allowing them the space to come to life once again and reenter our world. Further, each poem begins with a set-in initial printed in red; just as the rubricator's elaborate opening initials in ancient texts called attention to the solemnity and importance of the work at hand, so the design of this book calls the reader's attention to the importance of the lives described. A sensitivity to the text is especially evident in the reproduction of the title on the title page. It is printed in red and over it are blurred names printed in yellow. The effect clearly points to the lost names, the lives that have been erased from time. One cannot escape the fact that, as the poet has lavished attention on these forgotten lives, so, too, does the book's design honor the lost. The elegantly clean, sensitive design allows Levine's words to speak powerfully to readers' sensibilities.

Ashes, which was published in 1979 by Graywolf Press, is similar to *The Names of the Lost,* in that it too was produced first as a limited edition and then issued by Atheneum in a trade edition that used the limited edition's design. It is interesting that this book brought together many of Levine's then uncollected poems with most of the poems from *Red Dust,* as if this volume were conceived to correct the design problems of the earlier one. Once again, the design is distinguished by the simplicity and grace readers have come to appreciate in a well-made small-press book: adequate margins that don't cramp the text, graceful and readable type (in this case Bembo), and a layout that promotes the poems rather than fights with them for attention. It is a fitting structure for the poems it houses.

For some reason, perhaps because in the intervening period Levine has experienced commercial success with his books, there is a ten-year hiatus between *Ashes* and his next small press book, *Blue,* published by the Aralia Press in 1989. This current volume continues the tradition of the three volumes that preceded it by rendering the text in a design that is sensitive to the text and allows the poet's words to speak directly to the reader.

A brief survey of Philip Levine's small-press titles establishes the important place small presses have come to occupy in the creation of America's literary canon, but it also reveals how most poets in the latter half of the century have worked their way into print. If it were not for the willingness of small publishers to print works they believe in, many contemporary poets would not have reached the audiences they enjoy today. Similarly, if it were not for the sensitivity to the text that publishers like Kim Merker and Scott Walker have demonstrated in their book design, we would be deprived of the pleasure of reading a truly well-made book. We should thus salute the efforts of small-press publishers, for without them we would be bereft of some of the more important texts of our era, nor would we know that it is possible to wed text with design to make reading an experience to savor and enjoy.

RICHARD JACKSON

The Long Embrace: Philip Levine's Longer Poems

"I hold that a long poem does not exist. I maintain that the phrase, 'a long poem,' is simply a flat contradiction in terms," wrote Edgar Allan Poe in "The Poetic Principle." For Poe, the essence of poetry is an intense moment that "excites, by elevating the soul," and such moments can only be brief because any intense spiritual or psychological event is always, for Poe, "transient." It is for this reason that he calls *Paradise Lost* "a series of minor poems" and *The Iliad* a collection "intended as a series of lyrics." For Poe the poem is a sort of trance, a dream, something beyond language, and this is a view that has been a major force in modern and contemporary poetry, from the imagists to the deep image poets and beyond. It is a view that helps explain the fragmented construction of poems like *The Cantos, The Bridge,* and *The Waste Land.* However, as the influence of the deep image poems has waned in the last decade or so, there has been a resurgence of the longer poem, and so also a number of strategies for dealing with the problem of maintaining intensity over longer periods of time. By looking at Philip Levine's longer poems, "Letters for the Dead" (*1933,* 1976), "A Poem with no Ending" (*Sweet Will,* 1985), and "A Walk with Tom Jefferson," the title poem from his 1988 volume, we can see an evolving response to the problem of the long poem that also reveals the way Levine's poetry—and it is one of the richest poetries anywhere today—has developed.

If the result of his theory seems a bit strange and naive today, Poe was probably right in suggesting that seeing how a poet deals with the moments that constitute his or her poems is essential in seeing the kind of imagination at work in them. It will be

Kenyon Review, n.s. 11, no. 4 (Fall 1989). Reprinted with permission.

useful, then, to consider what sorts of moments are found in Levine's poems by looking briefly at a few short lyrics before looking at the longer poems themselves. In "Lost and Found," which ends Levine's *Ashes,* he acknowledges that "certain losses seem final," but then as dawn approaches to correct what had seemed like an endless night, he exclaims triumphantly, "for now, the lost are found," they are included in the words of the poem, for as long as the poet can speak. This moment, the "for now" with its colloquial sense of a tentative and temporary holding off of opposing forces, suggests how Levine's moments, his poems, are never fixed and final. Instead, they always imply what will happen after the temporary "now"—they are marked by an integrity and responsibility that means constantly confronting the changing world. This is perhaps something he has learned from Thomas Hardy, a poet whom he admires and who is probably a major influence. In his "Apology" to his *Later Lyrics,* Hardy describes his poems as "chance little shocks" and the whole book as a kind of single poem that is a "juxtaposition of unrelated, even discordant, effusions." For Hardy, as for Levine, any sense of larger unity beyond a moment must accommodate the discordant elements, and the poet has a duty to be honest in dealing with them rather than try to create a false and homogenous unit.

For Levine, this means a moment that embraces as much as possible, a sort of expanding moment, even in the briefer lyrics. It is a moment that embraces other lives, other stories, which radiate from the instant they bisect each other. For instance, "Any Night" (*Ashes*) is a meditation that begins in a moment of pause, where the speaker regrets lost time but then realizes he has to "forget / my name, my childhood, the years / under the cold duration of the clock." The problem is that time becomes cold and static when the focus is just on the self: instead, he will speak of a moment that "could be any night," and the poem turns into a prayer "that life follows death" for some wandering boy who just now passes. Now the moment becomes a shared one, becomes finally the boy's and whatever changing, expanding gestures he will assign to it. This sort of embracing, utterly humane gesture is one of the major sources of power in Levine. The end of "Here and Now" (*7 Years from Somewhere*) works by a similar embrace:

let him take what he can—
the trembling of his hands,
the silence before him, the slow
awakening of his eyes, the windows
of the town opening on first light,
the children starting suddenly
from their twisted sheets with a cry
of neither victory or defeat,
only the surprise of having come back
to what no one promised, here and now.

In these complex lines the poet's voice assumes the consciousness of the young man's, and then as the young man's perspective assumes that of the children, we expect that the process will continue, unendingly. The lyric has the gesture of a much longer poem.

This sort of expansion of the moment through others is the basic principle that generates Levine's first long poem, "Letters for the Dead" (*1933*). The poem, in ten sections separated by asterisks, reads at first like a sequence of lyrics in which the narrator addresses the dead "one by one" in an attempt "to hold your faces" and "to say / something to each of you / of what it is / without you." There are, however, several patterns that link the sections into a more coherent whole. For instance, the poem begins as "the air darkened toward morning" in the first section, and by the end of that section "the winter sun / dipped below the stacks," suggesting in seventeen lines how quickly, almost imperceptibly, time passes. In the last section a similar pattern is expanded upon in the opening lines, when "the porch light takes hold" in late afternoon and in the ending lines after dawn in "warm days." In the eight sections between there are constant reminders of time's passage as, for example, in the references to April (section 5) and March (section 9). There is, then, a general if irregular movement from winter, an image of endings and decay, toward summer, toward a new beginning, a movement that is climaxed in the last lines:

warm days—
the child you never saw
weeds the rhubarb

> white grains collect above the lips
> and flake away in the sudden wind
>
> even the dead are growing old.

The poem ends, then, as we saw the lyrics end, with a reference to the time of another person, a kind of transcending vision that serves to unify the whole, that holds on to the past and promises a future.

There are several other patterns in the poem that are also important. It begins confined in a room with a speaker reading a newspaper and ends outside near a freeway, suggesting travel and freedom. In between, the poem moves through places like Toledo, Covington, Dearborn, Wyandotte, and then even to Spain, to Basque country, Cadiz, Fuengirola, before returning, presumably, to Detroit, but also to a city that could be anyplace. Parallel to this expanding movement from self to larger world is a movement that begins intimately, with references to family members, then shifts outward to more political and social concerns, to memories of people briefly encountered, who as often as not echo this expanding embrace, like the man in Fuengirola (section 9). The man is one the speaker has seen many times, and he now comes carrying

> sea bass
> gaffed and dripping
> down the length of one leg
>
> a small stiff man
> now bowing forward to strike
> his forehead against the earth
> the left hand flung out
> and opened to the sky
> the right hand bunched
> to his breast

The effect of these expansions—and they continue to include the more intimate references as the poem evolves—is to include by implication a whole world of references within the confined space of the poem. This, in turn, is intensified by the poem's gradual move toward the present tense, which becomes a kind of historical present as the boy at the end, as all the dead, continue to exert influences on the present of the speaker.

The overall story, which is a personal odyssey over space and time, is told in terms of fragmented images that, more than any narrative, become the basic unit of progression. They also suggest the limitations of the linked lyric method, of the use of linked moments and images to paste together a whole. Some of the images have more of a deep image or surrealistic feel to them: "the lie is retold in the heart / the old denials burn / down the hallways of the brain." The effect here is to further the gesture of the poem that links inner and outer worlds (brain and hallway), personal and political, specific and generalized, temporal and transcendent. But the more realistic images and straightforward images, as in the description of the old man, like any observations ultimately focus on their own evocative moments, depending upon the larger structural movements and gestures of the poem as a whole for any sense of resonance or staying power. What this method asserts is the basic truth of the poem: no matter how well memory operates, no matter what images are used to unite the possible and the real, to "hold" the present, time still surpasses our efforts after the poem is over, despite the hopeful gestures toward a future. The form of the poem, with its carefully linked sections, its embrace of as much as it is possible to hold, dramatizes the effort here, but in the end the integrity of the poet must admit a failure— "even the dead are growing old." It is this drama, and the refusal to give in to a false hope, the knowledge of what happens beyond the end of the poem, that makes the poem so powerful and so honest, such a success.

It is perhaps this knowledge that seems to motivate "A Poem with No Ending" (*Sweet Will*), a poem in twelve parts marked by asterisks and consisting of over five hundred lines. The dominant image here is not the image but the story, so that, for example, when the speaker mentions a wren it is not to picture a largely unspoken scene but to relate a brief narrative that can contain directly, as it turns out, more time than the single image—

> I began as you did, smaller
> than the wren who circled three times
> and flew back into the darkness
> before sleep.

The desire to embrace moments larger than the present is still a main force, then, but as Levine explains it here, the desire is involved in the stories about it:

> For a moment
> I feel my arms spread wide to enclose
> everyone within these walls whitewashed
> over and over, my own sons, my woman,
> and all the other sons and daughters
> stretched out or curled up in bad beds
> or on bare floors, their heads
> pillowed on their own hard arms,
> their cheeks darkened by cheap newsprint.

The moment moves rapidly to include the stories of several lives as the speaker moves to "recover / each season" serially, as in "Letters to the Dead." However, each section is not limited to one scene or reference, but becomes much more episodic, the episodes progressing by analogous stories rather than by focusing on evocative images as in "Letters." Section 6, for example, refers to a mid-May Monday in New York, 1981, but also draws analogies to a time thirty years earlier when the speaker was delivering groceries. The section also moves from talking about the self to episodes concerning people on the paper route. For instance, there is an old couple who

> sat waiting for weeks
> for a foot locker full of clothes
> and kitchen utensils. They stood back
> when I entered, pretending to be busy,
> and they tried to keep me there,
> but they had nothing to say. They were
> neither young nor old, and I couldn't
> then imagine their days in which little
> or nothing was done, days on which it
> seemed important to smoke before
> dressing and not to go out until
> late afternoon. I couldn't imagine
> who they were and why they'd come
> from all the far-off places
> to be homeless where I was homeless.

The passage balances off their mysterious story against his, their confinement against his leisure to move about, their waiting against his movement along the delivery route, their wanting to hold him against his holding them here in the poem, New York against all the places they have been. This sort of counter-pointing, and it is present throughout the poem, would not be so possible in the more clipped style of "Letters," but here, in the more discursive style of this poem, there is narrative space to make all these connections.

The desire to find a "home" as described in this passage is itself a major controlling ideal in this poem, which deals so much with uprootings. Section 10, for example, describes the speaker's son leaving for Sweden to evade the draft, and the speaker recalls how, after seeing him off, he went back to his own room "and dreamed of finding / my way back to the house where I / was born," a dream where "the rooms / were one and I was home at last." In section 11 he recalls his own leaving home to

>   just keep going,
>   forward or back, until you've
>   found the place or the place
>   doesn't matter.

Now, these lines reveal a complex and subtle form of control, an oscillating rhythm, really, the rhythm of all the oppositions the poem is built on, the leavetakings and homecomings, giv-ings and takings, that are the central themes: the rhythm of how these stories balance each other gives a sense of pacing and timing throughout the poem, and indeed throughout the whole book. In the last section, by the shore, the speaker says, "Now this is home," and then exclaims, "I / see in the ocean of my memory / the shore birds going out and nothing / coming back." But what does approach are the waves, the stories and memories of the poem itself, so that the poem tends to imitate a sort of tidal ebb and flow, balancing losses and gains, forgetting and remembering.

Because this continuous motion is an unending one, with the waves always approaching (in the last lines the speaker sees "each wave taking shape and rising landward," the verbals emphasiz-ing the lack of closure, the sense of always beginning), the poem not only has no ending but, in effect, no clear beginning. It "begins" by deflecting attention immediately to the ending:

> So many poems begin where they
> should end, and never end.
> Mine never end, they run on
> book after book, complaining
> to the moon that heaven is wrong
> or dull, no place at all to be.

As the poem goes on, self-consciously searching for a "place," a home, the poem itself to some extent becomes the speaker's home—"That is the poem I called 'Boyhood' / and placed between the smeared pages / of your morning paper," he says later in the first section after recalling events from that period of his life.

But it is a poem and a home whose walls and boundaries are amorphous; this is its major technical advance over "Letters." In order to understand the poem fully we have to remember that it constitutes the second of the three parts that make up the book. The first poem in part 3 is called "An Ending," linking it to the long poem as a hypothetical end. As it turns out, "An Ending" also deals with "the hope / that someone known and loved / would return out of air and water," with how the speaker "slept alone and dreamed / of the home I never had." The setting and time of the poem is both specific and universal, almost transcendent:

> This little beach at the end
> of the world is anywhere, and I
> stand in a stillness that will last
> forever or until the first light
> breaks beyond these waters.

The scene, of course, recalls the ending of the preceding long poem, but here emphasizing finality not as an event but as a constantly deferred possibility. In fact, the rest of the poems in the third part, culminating in "Jewish Graveyards, Italy," can also be read as endings, and conversely, the poems in part one can be read as hypothetical beginnings. But even those beginnings also contain the rhythm of ebb and flow that defines the long poem, as in "Salt and Oils" where the speaker describes how he's "been going out and coming back / the way a swallow does with unerring grace."

What is happening is that the boundaries of the poem extend beyond its own pages to include other poems, and by implication the poet's entire life's work ("My poem remained long after you'd / gone," he says of "Boyhood"). Instead of a specific beginning and ending, the poem's movement and structure are defined by this ebb and flow, a breathing image, really, that governs the speaker's story of his life in the poem, a story still being told, so always *in medias res,* always ready to include the next memory or desire. This is a very sophisticated structure and constitutes, in effect, a new definition of how the long poem can not only be made up of lyric parts but can, by making use of the essentially unending quality of narrative, appropriate other poems as parts.

In "A Walk with Tom Jefferson," a poem of nearly six hundred lines, Levine abandons the section structure and instead braids three different sorts of narrative into one continuous strand held together as a conversation and meditation during a walk. Here the narrative has a definite, ostensible beginning and end, though the same sorts of expansions and implied narratives extending beyond the borders, as in "Poem with No Ending," are evident. But here, the expansion is achieved by suggesting that the story, besides being very specific, is paradigmatic, the kind of simple story repeated endlessly in the course of human history. The first of the three nearly simultaneous strands consists of accounts, from the narrator's point of view, of Detroit, a place with "only / three seasons, or so we said— / one to get tired, one to get / old, one to die," seasons, then, of the soul. The second strand consists of the narrator's accounts of his own past and reactions to what Tom Jefferson says. The third strand consists of the ideas given by Jefferson himself, either directly when he speaks in quotation or indirectly through the narrator, and includes autobiographical information, comments on the present and historical Detroit, a biblical story, and comments on the garden he keeps. What all three strands confront is the possibility of a wasteland, both spiritual and physical, that the stories attempt to counter. The issue quickly becomes one of belief in this contemporary Georgic of a poem, belief in the possibility that a garden can persevere, that we can

> smell the sticking sap rising
> in the maples, smell it
> even over the wet stink
> of burned house.

Tom Jefferson, a friend of the speaker, plays the role, essentially, of the Wordsworthian leech gatherer, from whom the speaker learns by drawing, in the end, an analogy between Jefferson's work and his own.

In the poem Tom is introduced casually, after a description of the junk yards the city blocks have become, by mentioning his school and its more famous student, Joe Louis. Then Tom's own past and that of his family—they were "lured" from the "cotton fields" by the promise of $5 a day—are counterpointed against his present activity:

> Early afternoon behind
>   his place, Tom's gathering up
> the remnants of this year's
>   garden—the burned
> tomato plants and the hardy
>   runners of summer squash
> that dug into the chalky
>   soil and won't let go.

In this context of the soil, "Alabama is not so far back" in memory, and Tom himself can still see the trees there and believes he can "still feel" the "winter mornings, all of us / getting up from one bed / but for what I don't know." Now, in the context of the catalogue of junk that follows, he says they are "making do." As a character, he seems isolated by his neighbors, who probably associate him with stories of someone running with wild dog packs, a fact that makes his association with the speaker even more intimate by contrast.

The main oppposition in the poem between the narrator and Jefferson, at least early on, is that while the speaker can dream of having the junked landscape "transformed," he does not believe it can happen, "but Tom will. Tom Jefferson / is a believer." As the speaker goes on to say, "You can't plant winter vegetables / if you aren't." Immediately after, the speaker mentions a test of Tom's faith, when his son died in the Korean war. But Tom replies with a phrase at once colloquial (as magical as the "for now" we discussed earlier) and also, in the context of the idea of belief, religious: "That's Biblical." It is a phrase repeated several more times but in increasingly complex emotional contexts. For example, Jefferson talks about his dead wife, knowing her biblically, meaning "so well / you know yourself." But then the narrator talks, and, curiously, in a way that seems to echo Jefferson—there's a sense, though the quotations used for Jefferson drop, that they now speak for each other. What the speaker says reveals the way they will be linked:

> Maybe even
> war is Biblical, maybe
> even the poor white
> fighting the poor black
> in this city for the same
> gray concrete housing,
> the same gray jobs
> they both came
> north for, maybe that's
> Biblical, the way
> the Canaanites and the Philistines
> fought the Israelites,
> and the Israelites killed
> the Amalakites
> always for the same land.

The narrative biblical reference is then picked up by Jefferson to explain why God saved the black man during the "riots of '42."

The poem continues with references to David and Saul and Absalom, with the need, as Jefferson explains it, for the present physical and spiritual cold "season" as part of a natural cycle, referring to gardening, history, to the Indians who were there before them. As it develops, the narrator continues to speak in a

dual voice in addition to quoting Jefferson directly, and then he
seems to absorb some of Jefferson's vocabulary and images:

> It's Biblical, this season
>   of color coming
> to its end, the air swirling
>   in tiny cyclones
> of brown and red, the air
>   swelling in my lungs,
> banging about my ears so that
>   I almost think I hear
> Tom say "Absalom" again, a name
>   owed to autumn
> and the autumn of its hopes.

What happens in the poem, then, is a gradual fusion of points of
view: the braids become one strand, the unity one of political,
social, and personal dimensions, as inseparable as the single
block the poem is written in. In the last two pages of the poem
the speaker describes his own past, working first in a Cadillac
transmission plant and then in a Chevy plant. Of the first he
says, "Whatever it was we / made / we made of earth. Amazing
earth," amazed as he is at all it gave him, a sort of garden.
Ironically, the sense of wonder is compared to watching a train
of military tanks go by, linking this period in the narrator's life
with the period of the 1942 riots Tom described. But more im-
portant, the lines begin to link machine and garden, link solidly
the two men's perspectives, so that by the end of the poem the
poet's earlier denial of belief slips somewhat, so that he can "half-
believe" something from the past, and perhaps from the future,
for it is near the very end that the two men's worlds are fused—

> What were we making out
>   of this poor earth good
> for so much giving and taking?
>   (Beets the size of fists
> by the thousands, cabbages
>   as big as brains
> year after year, whole cribs

335

of peppers, great lakes
of sweet corn tumbling
    by the trailer load,
it gave and gave, and whatever
    we had it took.)
The place was called Chevy
    Gear & Axle—
it's gone now, gone to earth
    like so much here—

"A Walk with Tom Jefferson" is, finally, a poem that faces the unpleasant facts of contemporary life, the horrors of our social, political, and military history, our personal losses, that faces them honestly and clearly, embraces whatever it can, and comes to a conclusion that involves both the desire and the reluctance to believe anything. There is a fidelity to truth here, an integrity that is rare anywhere. This is a poem, we might say, a long time in the making, and its complex fusion of visions could not have been possible in the fragmented and imagistic unity of "Letters to the Dead," nor could its final balance have been possible in separate narratives of "A Poem with No Ending." Here in "A Walk" everything becomes an image of something else, every story becomes part of one story told from a coincidence of points of view; the breath, the give and take we saw earlier, becomes the larger acts of the earth itself, of history, of the players who are both small parts of history and carriers of it. Here is Levine offering his most significant, most encompassing embrace, in a style and structure that seem in the end as seamless as the structures in the shorter poems, that give the lie, as well as any long poem can, to Poe's early complaint about sustaining intensity.

LARRY LEVIS

Philip Levine

I

To attempt to be at all objective about my friend and my first teacher Philip Levine is impossible for me. For to have been a student in Levine's classes from the mid to late 1960s was to have a life, or what has turned out to be my life, *given* to me by another. And certainly then, at the age of seventeen, I *had* no life, or no passionate life animated by a purpose, and I was unaware that one might be possible.

Let me explain: by the age of sixteen I was already a kind of teenage failure, an unathletic, acne-riddled virgin who owned the slowest car in town, a 1959 Plymouth sedan that had fins like irrelevant twin sharks rising above the taillights. Beige, slow as driftwood, the car became interesting only when I cut the engine and lights to coast down a hill in full moonlight outside town as I drove home to the ranch, listening to the wind go over the dead metal and sitting there in the self-pity of adolescence, a self-pity so profound that it made me feel, for a moment anyway, at once posthumous and deliciously alive.

Had I been good at something, had my times in the 400-yard freestyle and 100-yard breaststroke actually not grown *worse* over four years, had I had a girlfriend or a chopped and channeled Merc with a V-8, I would not have read poetry. But I did read it, because a teacher named Moranda showed me Frost's poems, and I couldn't shake them or rid my mind of them.

One night I wrote a poem. I think I actually composed it while listening to music, to some sticky orchestrated sound track from a movie. The poem was awful of course; even I knew that. It was awful except for one thing. It had one good line in it. I was sixteen then, almost seventeen, almost a senior, and about impor-

Pacific Review (Winter 1990). Reprinted with permission.

tant things I did not deceive myself. One good line at the age of sixteen was a lot. I decided then that I would go to sleep, and if the line was still good in the morning, then I would become a poet. I remember thinking that I might qualify the decision by saying that I would *try* to become a poet. The word "try" seemed dead of exhaustion. No, that was no good, I thought immediately. One either did this or did not do it.

When I got up, I looked at the line. It was still good.

Everything crucial in my life had been decided in less than thirty seconds, and in complete silence.

My great good fortune came a few months later disguised as a grade of D in my photography class. That dark mark meant I could not go to Berkeley or to any University of California campus. I tried to persuade my teacher, Mr. Ferguson, that most students thought the course was a kind of joke. This turned out to be the wrong argument. And in fact I deserved the grade, for I had hardly attended the class. I hated the smells of developing fluids and fixers and would hang back with my friend Zamora while the other students filed into the darkroom, then slip out the door and sit smoking cigarettes with him in the empty stadium bleachers. We spoke exclusively of girls, of what wonders must be concealed beneath Colleen Mulligan's cashmeres or within Kathy Powell's white dress. I sat there smoking and earning my D. The D meant I would have to go to Fresno to attend college. Yes, Fresno. Dust and Wind State.

How lucky I was, though my little destiny was completely disguised as failure, for at Fresno State I would spend the next four years in Levine's poetry workshops, although I could not have known that then, smoking with Zamora. No one knew anything then. It was 1964. A few years later Zamora would for some reason wander away from the others on his patrol somewhere in Vietnam and come home in a body bag.

I don't know what happened to Colleen Mulligan, but I saw Kathy Powell years later at a reunion. She had moved to Ketchum, Idaho, and was still beautiful. She had been reading a book of poems by Sharon Olds and asked me about them. At seventeen I would never have imagined that she would ever want to read poetry, for I thought the untroubled life of the beautiful lay before her and that it needed no poems.

At seventeen, I knew so little.

I do know that it was Philip Levine who saved my life. I don't know if anyone could have saved Zamora's. Two years ago, I finally touched the name cut into the black stone of the Vietnam War Memorial along with the other fifty thousand. Zamora was a *chicano* who worked long hours after school at a variety of demeaning jobs, and had, perhaps, outgrown all self-pity by the age of seven. We sat there smoking, me with my invisible great good luck, and Zamora, as it turned out, without any. "All I want for Christmas is to get in her pants," he sang, idly, and flipped his cigarette butt past twenty rows of empty seats.

2

It isn't enough to say that Levine was a brilliant young poet and teacher. Levine was amazing. His classes during those four years at Fresno State College were wonders, and they still suggest how much good someone might do in the world, even a world limited by the penitentiarylike architecture and stultifying sameness of a state college. For in any of those fifty-minute periods, there was more passion, sense, hilarity and feeling filling that classroom than one could have found anywhere in 1964. If the class was difficult, if Levine refused to coddle students or protect the vanities of the lazy and mediocre from the truth about their work, if his criticism was harsh at times, all of this was justified and beautiful: justified because some students thought that an A could be had for repeating the clichés on greeting cards or that everything they did would be judged as mildly as fingerpainting in grade school; and it was beautiful because there poetry was given the respect it deserves and was never compromised to appease the culture surrounding it in the vast sleep of its suburbs, highways, and miles of dark packing sheds (all of which, I might add, if left without the intelligence and beauty of art, is in its mute entirety absolutely worthless).

But beneath the difficulty of the class, of studying and writing in traditional prosody, beneath the harshness of the criticism Levine gave to us, impartially and democratically, there was in the way he taught a humor and a talent for making the most self-conscious young students laugh at themselves and at their mistakes; by doing so, they could suddenly go beyond the uselessly narrow, brittle egos they had carried with them since junior high like a life savings in the wrong currency; that laughter woke them from the sleep of adolescence into something far larger. What was larger was the world of poetry, not only the study of it (passionate rather than impartial in Levine's readings of it), but also the possibility of writing it. If you could forget awhile your whining, hungry, sulking selves, Levine seemed to say to us, you could enter this larger world where the only president was Imagination. Levine made this the necessary world. And doing this made him unforgettable. It was a class like no other if only because it dared all of us in it to be considerably more alive than we wanted to be. In this sense it couldn't be compared to anything else I took there. In French 2B, for example, we recited a paragraph from *Eugenie Grandet* in French, and then once again, translated, in English. Nothing had changed in the format of French 2B since Charlemagne. My French professor was named Wesley Byrd. The one time I stopped in to see him during his office hours he was totally absorbed in plucking his eyebrows before a small hand mirror propped on his desk, and he did not pause in doing this even momentarily as he asked me to come in. "Professor Byrd," I asked, after a short interchange concerning the due date of a term paper, "after Rimbaud, did the alexandrine line disappear from French verse?" "Yes," he replied, snipping away, "gradually, it did." Then I asked, "What do you think of Rimbaud?" "Rimbaud?" he replied, going after another longish and troublesome stray hair, "Rimbaud was a flash in the pan." His pronouncement, his "sentencing," was unhesitating and final, and I never asked him anything else. The difference between Levine and Byrd, both at the same college, is like the difference between the music of John Coltrane and Doc Severinsen. One is amazing and a revelation; the other makes you wonder who hired him.

Levine was the funniest and most unflinchingly honest man I have ever known. In those years, class after class would literally shake with laughter. A kind of rare, almost giddy intelligence constantly surfaced in Levine in comments that were so right and so outrageous that they kept us all howling, for he kept brimming over with the kind of insouciant truths most people suppress in themselves, and none of us in the class were spared from those truths about our work, and, by extension, about ourselves.

"Amazing! You write like the Duke of Windsor on acid!" he said to one passively stoned, yet remarkably pompous student. Or, to another, "For a moment there your imagination made an appearance in this poem and its loveliness astonished us all, but then . . . right . . . *here*—where you say, 'Love is golden, Daddy, and forever,' the grim voice of Puritan duty comes back in and overwhelms you with a sense of obligation even you couldn't possibly believe in. Remember, in poetry you don't owe anyone a thing." Or: "Look at this absolutely gorgeous line crying out to escape from all its dumb brothers snoring beside it there!" Or, to a young woman who had written a wonderfully sophisticated poem about a detested ski instructor: " 'With practiced stance which he has made his own'—notice all of you please, in the deafness of this age, this line. It's amazingly perfect for what it's doing here, lean, scrupulous, and innocent in tone at the outset. And, just now, it's a pentameter that seems to be light-years beyond anything the rest of you can do. Oh, I know you *have* ears, I mean, I can see them right there on the sides of your heads, and yet on some days they strike me as vestigial, like the appendix, and as the age evolves I can see them creeping toward extinction; soon, all that will be left of ears will be their occasional appearance on postage stamps, along with the passenger pigeon, the Great Auk, Adlai Stevenson." Or, to a student full of pretentiously profound yet completely trite statements concerning God, Love, Death, and Time—a two-page endeavor with all the lines italicized in the typescript: "Writing like this suggests that you might need to find something to do with your hands. Tennis is an excellent sport!"

Something animated him. He is the only person I have ever known who seemed to be fully awake to this life, his own and the lives of others. An amazing talker, it surprised me when I noticed how deeply and closely he listened to students. And when someone was really troubled, a special kind of listening seemed to go on, and there was often a generous if sometimes unsettling frankness in his response.

Why in the world did he care so much about what we did? Because we mattered so much to him, we began to matter to ourselves. And to matter in this way, to feel that what one did and how one wrote actually might make a difference, was a crucial gift Levine gave to each of us. All you had to do was open it, and it became quite clear, after awhile, that only cowardice or self-deceit could keep you from doing that.

His care for us seems all the more amazing when I recall that these years were crucially difficult and ultimately triumphant years for him as a poet. For in 1965 he went to Spain for the first time, and what changed him deeply there is apparent everywhere in the poems of *Not This Pig*. Shortly after this, he would begin to write the poems that constitute the vision of *They Feed They Lion*. What still strikes me as amazing, and right, and sane, was his capacity to share all that energy, that fire, with those around him: students and poets and friends. The only discernible principle I gathered from this kind of generosity seems to be this: to try to conserve one's energy for some later use, to try to teach as if one isn't quite there and has more important things to do, is a way to lose that energy completely, a way, quite simply, of betraying oneself. Levine was always totally *there,* in the poems and right there in front of me before the green sea of the blackboard.

3

It is fashionable now to disparage poetry workshops, and why not? Some of them are so bad that they constitute a form of fraud in which mediocre talents accept tuition from those with no talent whatsoever. After a couple of years, these unemployables graduate, and their teachers, in their aspiring emptiness, get promoted. But to categorically condemn all workshops as a destructive force in our poetry is nonsense, a nonsense best said on a cliff overlooking the ocean at, say, Big Sur, where one can pretend, momentarily, to be Jeffers or some other great American Original. And much of Jeffers is just awful. How could a man who looked like that in the photos of him on display at Nepenthe write such dull stuff? Was there no one to tell him how bad it was? In contrast, I think of Pound showing Ford Madox Ford some early work, and of Ford laughing so hard upon reading it (they were not humorous poems) that he actually fell onto the floor and rolled around on it squealing with hilarity at the poems. Pound said that Ford's laughter saved him two years of work in the wrong direction. That was a poetry workshop. That laughter, no matter how painful for Pound, was a useful laughter, even a necessary laughter.

Could I have written poems in isolation? I doubt it. I grew up in a town where, in the high school library, Yeats's *Collected Poems* was removed, censored *in fact,* because two students had been found laughing out loud at "Leda and the Swan." That left Eliot. For two years, largely in secret, I read and reread Eliot, and I told no one of this. But finally one afternoon in journalism class, while the teacher was out of the room, Zamora stretched out, lying over three desk tops, and began yelling at the little, evenly spaced holes in the plyboard ceiling: "O Stars, Oh Stars!" The others around us talked on in a mild roar. Then Zamora turned to me and said: "I saw that book you always got with you. Once again, guy, I see through you like a just wiped windshield." There was this little pause, and then he said, "What is it, you wanna be a poet?" I said, "Yeah. You think that's really stupid?" His smile had disappeared by the time he answered, "No, it isn't stupid. It isn't stupid at all, but I'd get out of town if I were you."

It was true. A town like that could fill a young man with such rage and boredom that the bars of Saigon might twinkle like a brief paradise. You could die in a town like that without lifting a finger.

Whenever I try to imagine the life I might have had if I hadn't met Levine, if he had never been my teacher, if we had not become friends and exchanged poems and hundreds of letters over the past twenty-five years, I can't imagine it. That is, nothing at all appears when I try to do this. No other life of any kind appears. I cannot see myself walking down one of those streets as a lawyer, or the boss of a packing shed, or even as the farmer my father wished I would become. When I try to do this, no one's there; it seems instead that I simply had never *been* at all. All there is on that street, the leaves on the shade trees that line it curled and black and closeted against noon heat, is a space where I am not.

EDWARD HIRSCH

Naming the Lost: The Poetry of Philip Levine

> I force myself
> to remember
> who I am, what I am, and
> why I am here.
>
> ("Silent in America")

In his seminal postmodern meditation, "Thinking against One-self," the philosopher E. M. Cioran argues that "we measure an individual's value by the sum of his disagreements with things, by his incapacity to be indifferent, by his refusal as a subject to tend toward the object." Philip Levine's poetry is characterized by just such a profound disagreement with things as they are, by an incapacity for indifference, and a rage against objectification. Throughout his work his first and most powerful commitment has been to the failed and lost, the marginal, the unloved, the unwanted. His primary impulse has been to memorialize the details and remember the exploitations. The dedicatory seventh section of his poem "Silent in America"—his largest and most summary early poem—is explicit:

> For a black man whose
> name I have forgotten who danced
> all night at Chevy
> Gear & Axle,
> for that great stunned Pole
> who laughed when he called me Jew
> Boy, for the ugly
> who had no chance,

Michigan Quarterly Review 28 (1989). Reprinted with permission.

the beautiful in
body, the used and the unused,
those who had courage
and those who quit—
Rousek and Ficklin
numbed by their own self-praise
who ate their own shit
in their own rage;

for these and myself
whom I loved and hated, I
had presumed to speak
in measure.

Levine is a poet of the night shift, a late ironic Whitman of our
industrial heartland, a Romantic anarchist who repeatedly pro-
claims, "Vivas for those who have failed. . . ." His life's work is
a long assault on isolation, an ongoing struggle against the enclo-
sures of suffering, the private, hermetic, sealed-off nature of our
lives; indeed, he is a poet of radical immanence who has increas-
ingly asserted a Keatsian faith in the boundlessness of human
possibility. One might say that his work begins in rage, ripens
toward elegy, and flourishes in celebration. All three moods—
rage, sorrow, and a kind of wry hopefulness—appear and reap-
pear in his work, sometimes in complex tonal combinations.
One lyric points forward, another backward, and yet the overall
drift and progress of the poems is clear. What starts as anger
slowly deepens into grief and finally rises into joy.

Levine's early work follows a stylistic and thematic arc from
On the Edge (1963) to *They Feed They Lion* (1972). These poems
are written under the sign of the thistle and the fist, what one
poem invokes as the "bud of anger, kinked tendril of my life"
("Fist"). Levine has always written with a special concentrated
fury about the so-called "stupid jobs" of his youth, and his first
books established and developed his working-class loyalties and
themes. They evoke three distinct but related cities: Detroit,
Fresno, and Barcelona, all of which are defined as landscapes of
desolation, rugged cities of the enraged, the exhausted, the ex-
ploited. Levine began as a relentlessly urban writer and one of
the motivating premises of his early work was his determination

to center that work around the city, to create a poetry of the urban landscape. In this regard, the poem which reverberates through all of his work is Wordsworth's sonnet "Composed upon Westminster Bridge, September 3, 1802," which eventually provided the title for his book *Sweet Will*. Wordsworth's last line—"And all that mighty heart is lying still!"—has a special resonance in Levine's case because his work begins in silence and failure: indeed, one of the persistent themes of the early books is voicelessness, the desperate silence of "Silent in America," the failure of poets who don't write in "My Poets." He increasingly insists on the defiant transformation of blankness into speech, and refuses to be quieted. This theme of the necessity of violently breaking silence peaks in the furious incantatory rhythms of "They Feed They Lion," a poem which celebrates the communal insurrection of the Detroit riots of 1967. All that mighty heart is no longer lying still.

Levine's first volume, *On the Edge,* published when he was thirty-five years old, was a book of free-floating despair, hampered by its own formalism, alienated even from itself. Levine himself has said that these were the poems of someone on the verge of despair and breakdown, on the edge of his own culture, even of his own life. One of the formal problems of the poems is that they are too tightly controlled; they are rhyming iambic pentameter lyrics whose underlying subject matter is mostly suppressed and in conflict with the tradition of "pure poetry" out of which they emerge. The sole exception is "The Horse"—a devastating poem about the survivors of Hiroshima—which anticipates the idiomatic and controlled free verse style of Levine's later work. The title poem is a skillful eighteen-line lyric which sounds a brooding note of defiance from the poet's alter ego: "My name is Edgar Poe and I was born / in 1928 in Michigan. / Nobody gave a damn." The poem projects a certain hip bravado but also suggests the depth of the writer's alienation: "I did not write, for I was Edgar Poe, / Edgar the mad one, silly, drunk, unwise. . . ." *On the Edge* was a striking debut stymied by its own pent-up rage: it is about being on the margins, close to breakdown, hedged in by despair.

Levine's second book, *Not This Pig* (1968), exchanged despair for determination, furiously digging in its heels. It is a volume of well-wrought lyrics where the urban furies reign. In this world no one wants to remember who he is, happiness and despair are a "*twi-night* doubleheader," the eight o'clock factory whistle comes "blasting from heaven," and there are no fresh starts. Edgar Poe has been replaced by "Baby Villon," an underdog who is everywhere victimized but continues to fight back, a version of the poet as outlaw. But the book's key figure is a self-conscious pig being driven to market who staunchly refuses to squeal or break down. The pig in "Animals Are Passing from Our Lives," a Bartleby of the animal world, can already smell "the sour, grooved block," the blade "that opens the hole / and the pudgy white fingers / that shake out the intestines / like a hankie," but he refuses to fall down in terror, to turn futilely "like a beast" against the boy who drives him along, resolutely keeping his dignity, proclaiming "No. Not this pig." In a way, the pig is a tough, metaphorical stand-in for his human counterpart, the worker who refuses to give up his dignity or to be objectified.

The bud of anger blossoms into full flower in *They Feed They Lion,* the culminating book of Levine's early work. In his two previous small-press books, *Red Dust* and *Pili's Wall* (both published in 1971), Levine began to abandon his early formalism, developing an increasingly narrative and supple free verse style, a more open and self-questioning approach to the dramatic lyric. He linked a Spanish surrealist imagery to a street-wise American idiom. "Clouds" is representative:

> Morning is exhaustion, tranquilizers, gasoline,
> the screaming of frozen bearings,
> the failures of will, the tv talking to itself.
>
> The clouds go on eating oil, cigars,
> housewives, sighing letters,
> the breath of lies. In their great silent pockets
> they carry off all our dead.

In these poems Levine has turned from a descendant of Poe into a grandson of Whitman. Thereafter his poems seem to have grown directly from the gritty soil of William Carlos Williams. They became larger and more inclusive, representing the rugged, impure, democratic side of our poetry.

They Feed They Lion reaps the fruit of that labor. It is Levine's most eloquent book of industrial Detroit, evoking the world of Dodge Main and Wyandotte Chemical, grease shops and foundries, the city "pouring fire." The poems remember the "unburned" Detroit of 1952 ("Saturday Sweeping") as well as the "charred faces" of Detroit in 1968 ("Coming Home, Detroit, 1968"). Some are set in California ("Renaming the Kings"), some in Spain ("Salami," "To P.L., 1916–1937"), but all record a nightmare of suffering, what "To a Fish Head Found on the Beach near Málaga" calls "the burned essential oil / seeping out of death." Yet their author is also capable of thorny affirmations, of celebrating his own angels of Detroit. The magisterial title poem—with its fierce diction and driving rhythms influenced by biblical language, Dylan Thomas's poetry, and colloquial black speech—is Levine's hymn to communal rage, to acting in unison. The poem has a sweeping musical and rhetorical authority, a burning sense of "the acids of rage, the candors of tar," a psychological understanding of what drives people to move from "Bow Down" to "Rise Up," and it builds to an apocalyptic conclusion:

> From my five arms and all my hands,
> From all my white sins forgiven, they feed,
> From my car passing under the stars,
> They Lion, from my children inherit,
> From the oak turned to a wall, they Lion,
> From they sack and they belly opened
> And all that was hidden burning on the oil-stained earth
> They feed they Lion and he comes.

Both in stylistic and in thematic terms, Levine's next two books, *1933* (1974) and *The Names of the Lost* (1976) are a single unit, a major turning point in his work, the books where he becomes a poet absorbed by memory and preoccupied by the deep past. *1933* is first and foremost a book haunted by the death of the father, ritualizing its suffering, asking the question, "Where did my father go in my fifth autumn?" ("Zaydee"). The fundamental psychological shock at the heart of Levine's work—its first reverberating loss—is the death of the father; indeed, the dead father stands as the authoritative absence at the heart of all his poetry. Thus the year 1933 is not—as so many have assumed—the date of his own birth, but the year of his father's death, his true baptism into the world. The title poem is simultaneously a letter to a man who died long ago ("Father, the world is so different in many places" and "you would not know me now") and a Roethkean elegy to a man who "entered the kingdom of roots / his head still as a stone" when the poet was only a child. The poem typifies much of Levine's most recent work in the way it alternates between the present tense ("I go in afraid of the death you are") and an irretrievable past ("I would be a boy in worn shoes splashing through rain"). As a book, *1933* powerfully evokes what is for the speaker "the blind night of Detroit" in the 1930s. It enlarges the first loss of the father to include a series of family elegies: "Zaydee," "Grandmother in Heaven," "Goodbye," "Uncle," and the centerpiece, "Letters for the Dead." Thereafter Levine will always be a poet who relies heavily on long-term memory. His poems become less protected and defended, more open and exposed, emotionally riskier.

As Levine's work has progressed, a predominant tone of ferocious anger has slowly evolved into a more vulnerable and elegiac tenderness. His poems have developed a softer edge while maintaining their brooding intensity. Almost everything he has written has been characterized by a determination to witness and remember, to memorialize people who would otherwise be forgotten. His middle work begins neither with outrage nor with an Adamic impulse to name the swarming fullness of things; it begins not with *presence* but with *absence,* with a furious determination to remember what is already lost. These are books more concerned with memory than with imagination, defining the poet as someone who names and recovers, who recalls the victimized, the disenfranchised, the fallen. Nowhere is this sense of the writer's task more clearly defined than in his book *The Names of the Lost.* In these poems, Levine explicitly links the people of his childhood whom "no one remembers" with his doomed heroes from the Spanish Civil War. As a lyric like "Gift for a Believer" makes clear, the poems originate with a personal oath to remember ("When old Nathan Pine / gave two hands to a drop-forge / at Chevy, my spit turned to gall / and I swore I'd never forget"), but they also take up the anarchist dream of freedom and justice, the chant of "We shall inherit," the world that Durruti said "is growing here / in my heart this minute." The anarchist struggle for a new world as well as the romantic sense that "the human is boundless" provided Levine with a political as well as a personal way to understand the past.

Levine's next book, *Ashes: Poems New and Old* (1979), is in some ways a transitional volume that looks back toward the two previous books of death as well as forward to the new poems of regeneration. It begins by addressing the dead father, "a black tooth planted in the earth / of Michigan," asking him not to return ("Father"). The whole book is animated by the simple factual recognition that certain losses are final, death and childhood. And yet the book ends on the resolutely optimistic note that "for now / the lost are found" and that father and son, the living and the dead, can enter the world together ("Lost and Found"). Thus what began with the death of the father has been converted into a dream of possibility. The silence and failure of people turning away from each other has been transformed into an idea of communal inheritance. Out of the ashes, the names are given back to the lost.

The motif of regeneration and rebirth resounds through Levine's next three books: there is a plaintiveness in *7 Years from Somewhere* (1979) that turns into a dark optimism and even hopefulness in *One for the Rose* (1981) and a bittersweet acceptance in *Sweet Will* (1985). These books begin with the playful assertion, "I could come to believe / almost anything" ("I Could Believe") and conclude on the image of the late sunlight "promising nothing" and overflowing "the luminous thorns of the roses," catching fire "for a moment on the young leaves" ("Jewish Graveyards, Italy"). In these books Levine becomes a Wordsworthian poet of humanistic naturalism, a poet of joy as well as of suffering.

Many of the poems in *7 Years from Somewhere* have the intimate character of prayers half-addressed to the interior self, half to the darkness. Poems such as "I Could Believe," "Hear Me," "Let Me Begin Again," "Words," and "Let Me Be" have the tone of a man talking—in his own words—either "to no one or myself," disavowing wisdom, asking unanswerable questions. The old angers burn and crackle in "You Can Have It," perhaps the book's single greatest poem, but most of the poems turn away from the hard fury of such a renunciation, in actuality accepting the flawed earth as it is, returning to the here and now, celebrating a world "drowning / in oil, second by second" ("The Life

Ahead"). The speaker in "Francisco, I'll Bring You Red Carnations" returns to the grave of a fallen Spanish Civil War hero not only to remember the dream of a city "where every man and every woman gives / and receives the gift of work / and care," but also to affirm that the dream "goes on in spite of all / that mocks it" and to celebrate "the unbroken / promise of your life that / once was frail and flesh."

This more celebratory mood of acceptance—self-questioning, darkened by doubts—continues to animate many of the more playful and narrative poems of *One for the Rose* and *Sweet Will*. In these books Levine weaves fuller and larger stories, mixing imagination and memory, creating alternative lives for himself, phantasmagorias of the past. He announces with wry irony, "I was born in Lucerne," and "I think I must have lived / once before, not as a man or woman / but as a small, quick fox pursued / through fields of grass and grain / by ladies and gentlemen on horseback" ("The Fox"). We may say that this sly, quick fox is a metonymic cousin not only to the courageous pig of *Not This Pig* and the lion of *They Feed They Lion,* but also a metaphoric relative of the anarchists Francisco Ascaso and Cipriano Mera, the emblematic Spanish immigrant in the poem "To Cipriano, in the Wind." Cipriano worked in the back of Peerless Cleaners and enunciated the word "Dignidad" for the young poet. He told him, "Some day the world / is ours" and "Spring, spring, it always comes after." Levine's politics are utopian and the final hard-won affirmation of his work is a Keatsian faith that the poet's breath can be passed on "to anyone who can / believe that life comes back / again and again without end / and always with the same face . . ." ("Belief"). His vision is humanistic; he concludes by embracing the earth as his own home ("The Voice").

Levine's recent work struggles against the incapacities of the word, the gulfs of language and experience. This is one of the reasons that it has increasingly tended toward rhetorical narrative, toward the healing coherence of a story. His work is neither logocentric nor disjunctive, but asserts a semi-objectivist, semivisionary faith in the radical capacity of language to render up our world. His thirteenth collection to date, *A Walk with Tom Jefferson* (1988), is a book of radiant memories that ramify outward to tell a recurrent story of buying and selling, of how we work (and don't) in America. "I am in my element," he tells us in one poem, "urging the past / out of its pockets of silence," recalling with a certain comic relish his depressing early jobs (in the book's first poem he remembers selling copper kitchenware, Fuller brushes, American encyclopedias), ferociously condemning the brutality of so much of our working lives, speaking out with genuine indignation and moral authority against what is most corrupting and exploitative in American life. He also celebrates the gritty heroism of people who manage to survive against the odds.

The long title poem is the book's narrative centerpiece, the memory of an emblematic walk through Detroit with an unsung black man, a retired factory worker who shares, in Levine's words, "the fierce spirit of independence and originality of his namesake." Tom Jefferson acts as the poet's Virgilian guide—tough, unbowed, faithful, humane—leading him through a neighborhood that had been devastated in the late sixties. In the aftermath of the destruction, amidst the vacant lots and condemned property, the poet discovers that people are leading quasi-rural lives—keeping gardens and animals, mustering their resources, rooting in, making do, cultivating new life. Their triumphs are small but real: they have the courage of survivors. As Levine said in a recent interview in the *Paris Review*, "The poem is a tribute to all these people who survived in the face of so much discouragement. They survived everything America can dish out." Here, as elsewhere in his work, Levine's great subject is the sustaining dream of freedom, the stubborn will of the dispossessed to dig in and endure.

Philip Levine's work is still evolving, still growing and changing. And yet it has already earned a rightful place in an American Romantic lineage that includes Hart Crane's *The Bridge*, William Carlos Williams's "Asphodel, that Greeny Flower," Theodore Roethke's "North American Sequence," Robert Hayden's "Middle Passage," and Galway Kinnell's "The Avenue Bearing the Initial of Christ into the New World." Levine's life's work sounds what Wallace Stevens called "the No that precedes the final Yes," and for all its furious renunciations it ends by being a poetry of praise "for a world that runs on and on at its own sweet will."

Selected Bibliography

Compiled by Chad Oness

Allen, Dick. "Shifts." Rev. of *Pili's Wall*. *Poetry* 120, no. 4 (July 1972): 242.

Anderson, Jack. "Flinty Perceptions." Rev. of *They Feed They Lion*. *Prairie Schooner* 47 (1973): 181–83.

"A Selection of Best Books of 1979: Poetry." *New York Times Book Review*, 25 Nov. 1979, 70.

Atlas, Janet. "New Voices in American Poetry." *New York Times Magazine*, 3 Feb. 1980, 16, 19–20, 24, 51–52.

Barron, John. Rev. of *Selected Poems*. *Monthly Detroit*, Oct. 1984, 143.

———. Rev. of *Sweet Will*. *Monthly Detroit*, Aug. 1985, 118.

Bedient, Calvin. "Four American Poets." Rev. of *1933*. *Sewanee Review* 84 (1976): 351–59.

———. "Horace and Modernism." Rev. of *The Names of the Lost*. *Sewanee Review* 85 (1977): 361–70.

———. "New Confessions." Rev. of *7 Years from Somewhere*. *Sewanee Review* 88 (1980): 474–80.

Bloom, Harold. "The Year's Books: Part I." Rev. of *The Names of the Lost*. *New Republic*, 20 Nov. 1976, 20–26.

Borroff, Marie. "Recent Poetry." Rev. of *They Feed They Lion*. *Yale Review* 62, no. 1 (1972): 87–89.

Boruch, Marianne. "Comment: Blessed Knock." Rev. of *A Walk with Tom Jefferson*. *American Poetry Review*, July/Aug. 1988, 39–41.

"Briefs on the Arts." *New York Times*, 27 Feb. 1973, late ed., 30.

Brown, Laurie. Rev. of *Selected Poems*. *Library Journal*, 15 June 1984, 1243–44.

Buckley, Christopher. " 'Belief': The Expanded Vision of Philip Levine." *Midnight Lamp* 1, no. 2 (1990).

———. "The Extension of Method in Philip Levine's *1933*." *Margins*, 10 Sept. 1975, 62–63, 194.

———. "The Extension of Method and Vision in Philip Levine's *Sweet Will*." *Crazyhorse* 34 (1988): 64–79.

———. Rev. of *Selected Poems*. *Santa Barbara News Press*, 6 Mar. 1987.

Butscher, Edward. Rev. of *7 Years from Somewhere*. *Booklist*, 1 Sept. 1979, 19–20.

Carruth, Hayden. "Making It New." Rev. of *Not This Pig*. *Hudson Review* 21 (1968): 399–412.

———. "Poets on the Fringe." Rev. of *7 Years from Somewhere*. *Harper's Magazine*, Jan. 1980, 77–81.

Cobb, Jeffrey B., ed. "Philip Levine: A Bibliographical Checklist." *American Book Collector* 6, no. 2 (1985): 38–47.

Conarroe, Joe. "Poets of Innocence and Experience." Rev. of *Selected Poems*. *Washington Post Book World*, 5 Aug. 1984, 3, 11.

Costello, B. "Orders of Magnitude." Rev. of *One for the Rose*. *Poetry*, May 1983, 108–10.

Dana, Robert. "Recent Poetry and the Small Press." Rev. of *On the Edge*. *North American Review*, n.s. 1, no. 3 (1964): 76–78.

Davis, Glover. "Silent in America." *Pacific Review*, Winter 1990.

De Maios, Rosaly. Rev. of *Sweet Will*. *Library Journal*, 15 June 1985, 63–64.

De Piero, W. S. "A Poet of Rage." Rev. of *Ashes* and *7 Years from Somewhere*. *Commonweal*, 12 Oct. 1979, 567–68.

Donoghue, Dennis. "That Old Eloquence." Rev. of *Not This Pig*. *New York Review of Books*, 25 Apr. 1968, 16–18.

Drury, John. Rev. of *Ashes*. *Concerning Poetry* 13, no. 2 (1980): 97–99.

Eagleton, T. "New Poetry." Rev. of *The Names of the Lost*. *Stand* (Newcastle upon Tyne, England) 18, no. 3 (1976/77): 75–78.

Epstein, Henrietta. *Monthly Detroit*, Aug. 1979, 25–26.

Etter, Dave. "Current Collections." Rev. of *1933*. *American Libraries*, Nov. 1974, 548.

Fletcher, Connie. Rev. of *The Names of the Lost*. *Booklist*, 15 Oct. 1976, 300.

Fletcher, Janet, et al. "Best Books of 1984." Rev. of *Selected Poems*. *Library Journal*, Jan. 1985, 51.

Fuller, John. "Catching Up—Poetry: The Americans." Rev. of *7 Years from Somewhere*. *Times Literary Supplement*, 18 Jan. 1980, 65.

Gibson, Margaret. Rev. of *Ashes* and *7 Years from Somewhere*. *Library Journal*, Aug. 1979, 1570.

Graham, Desmond. "New Poetry." Rev. of *1933*. *Stand* (Newcastle upon Tyne, England) 16, no. 2 (1975): 75–78.

Gregerson, Linda. "Short Reviews." *Poetry*, Dec. 1989.

Grey, Paul. "Four Poets and Their Songs." Rev. of *7 Years from Somewhere*. *Time*, 25 June 1979, 69, 72.

Grosholz, Emily. "Poetry Chronicle." Rev. of *One for the Rose*. *Hudson Review* 35 (1982): 331–33.

Gunn, Thom. "Modes of Control." Rev. of *On the Edge*. *Yale Review* 53, no. 3 (1964).

Harmon, William. "A Poetry Odyssey." Rev. of *One for the Rose*. *Sewanee Review* 91 (1983): 457–73.

Hedin, Robert. "In Search of a New World: The Anarchist Dream in the Poetry of Philip Levine." *American Poetry* 4 (1986): 64–71.

Helms, Alan. "Over the Edge." Rev. of *They Feed They Lion*. *Partisan Review* 41 (1974): 151–53.

Hirsch, Edward. "Naming the Lost: The Poetry of Philip Levine." *Michigan Quarterly Review* 28, no. 2 (1989): 258–68.

———. "Standing Up for the Fallen." Rev. of *Selected Poems*. *New York Times Book Review*, 5 Aug. 1984, 13.

Hitchcock, George. "A Gathering of Poets." Rev. of *1933*. *Western Humanities Review* 28 (1974): 403–9.

Hoffman, Roy B. "Hand in Hand." Rev. of *Ashes* and *7 Years from Somewhere*. *Village Voice*, 7 Jan. 1980, 31–32.

Hogan, Randolf. "40 to Read Poetry of the City in 10-hour Marathon." *New York Times*, 3 Apr. 1981, late ed., C24.

Howard, Frances Minturn. "Good Thin Books." Rev. of *Not This Pig*. *Michigan Quarterly Review* 8 (1969): 135–37.

Howard, Richard. "Centers of Attention." Rev. of *1933*. *Poetry* 125, no. 6 (Mar. 1975): 354–56.

Hudzick, Robert. Rev. of *A Walk with Tom Jefferson*. *Library Journal*, 15 May 1988, 84–85.

Hugo, Richard. "Philip Levine: Naming the Lost." *American Poetry Review*, May/June 1977, 27–28.

Jackson, Joe. "Levine's *They Feed They Lion*." *Explicator* 41, no. 1 (1983): 56–58.

Jackson, Richard. "For Now; Philip Levine and the Temporality of Nothing." *Poet and Critic* 6, no. 3 (1980): 27–34.

———. "The Long Embrace: Philip Levine's Longer Poems." *Kenyon Review* 11, no. 4 (1989): 160–69.

———. "The Signposts of Words." Rev. of *One for the Rose*. *American Book Review*, Sept. 1982, 20.

Jarman, Mark. "The Eye Filled with Salt." Rev. of *1933*. *Kayak* 38 (1975): 63–66.

———. "The Pragmatic Imagination and the Secrecy of Poetry." Rev. of *A Walk with Tom Jefferson*. *Gettysburg Review* 1 (1988): 647–69.

———. "The Trace of a Story Line." Rev. of *Sweet Will*. *Ohio Review* 37 (1986): 129–47.

Jerome, Judson. "Uncommitted Voices." Rev. of *Not This Pig*. *Saturday Review of Literature*, 1 June 1968, 33.

Jones, Roger. "Sweet Will." *Prairie Schooner* 61 (1987): 110–13.

"Jurors Are Chosen to Select Winners of 1973 Book Awards." *New York Times*, 12 Nov. 1973, late ed., 25.

Kaganoff, Penny. Rev. of *A Walk with Tom Jefferson*. *Publisher's Weekly*, 22 Apr. 1988, 79.

Kakutani, Michiko. "Books of the Times." Rev. of *Sweet Will*. *New York Times*, 29 May 1985, late ed., C21.

Kalstone, David. "The Entranced Procession of the Dead." Rev. of *1933*. *Parnassus: Poetry in Review* 3, no. 1 (1974): 41–50.

Katz, Bill. Rev. of *5 Detroits*. *Library Journal*, July 1970, 1489.

———. "Little Presses." *Library Journal*, 15 Mar. 1972, 1020–21.

———. Rev. of *Not This Pig*. *Library Journal*, 1 Jan. 1968, 86.

Kennedy, X. J. "Underestimations." Rev. of *On the Edge*. *Poetry* 103, no. 5 (Feb. 1964).

Kirby, David. Rev. of *One for the Rose*. *Library Journal*, 1 Dec. 1981, 2319.

Kirkpatrick, Stephen Hale. Rev. of *1933*. *AB Bookman's Weekly*, 4 Nov. 1974, 1934.

Lattimore, Richmond. "Poetry Chronicle." Rev. of *They Feed They Lion. Hudson Review* 25 (1973): 475–77.

Lazer, Hank. "Turning Back on the Road to the Absolute." *Modern Poetry Studies* 11 (1982): 164–88.

Lea, Sydney. "Walkings in Limbo: Robert Pack's *Keeping Watch* and Philip Levine's *The Names of the Lost*." *Chicago Review* 30, no. 1 (1978): 116–24.

Leibowitz, Herbert. "Lost Souls, Lost Cause." Rev. of *Ashes* and *7 Years from Somewhere. New York Times Book Review*, 7 Oct. 1979, 15, 28.

Levis, Larry. "Philip Levine." *Pacific Review*, Winter 1990.

Lodge, Sally A. Rev. of *Don't Ask. Publisher's Weekly*, 6 Feb. 1981, 372.

———. Rev. of *One for the Rose. Publisher's Weekly*, 13 Nov. 1981, 84.

———. Rev. of *Selected Poems. Publisher's Weekly*, 11 May 1984, 267.

———. Rev. of *Sweet Will. Publisher's Weekly*, 19 Apr. 1985, 79.

Marchant, Fred. "A Walk with Tom Jefferson." *Boston Review*, June 1988, 28–29.

———. "Cipriano Mera and the Lion: A Reading of Philip Levine." *Imagine*, 1, no. 2 (1982): 148–54.

Mariani, Paul. "Keeping the Covenant: A Look at Philip Levine's *A Walk with Tom Jefferson*." *Kenyon Review* 11, no. 4 (1989): 170–77.

Marling, William. "Like Dynamite Evaporating." Rev. of *The Names of the Lost. Southwest Review* 62 (1977): 325–28.

———. Rev. of *The Names of the Lost. Arizona Quarterly* 34 (1978): 283–85.

———. Rev. of *The Names of the Lost. Denver Quarterly* 12, no. 4 (1978): 98–100.

Martone, John. "Philip Levine: Selected Poems." *World Literature Today* 59 (1985): 296–97.

Martz, Louis L. "Ammons, Warren, and the Tribe of Walt." Rev. of *One for the Rose. Yale Review* 72 (1982): 63–84.

Matthews, William. "Wagoner, Hugo, and Levine." Rev. of *Ashes* and *7 Years from Somewhere. Ohio Review* 26 (1981): 126–37.

Mazzocco, Robert. "Matters of Life and Death." Rev. of *1933. New York Review of Books*, 3 Apr. 1975, 20–23.

McMichael, James. "Borges and Strand, Weak Henry, Philip Levine." Rev. of *Not This Pig. Southern Review* 8 (1972): 213–24.

McDowell, Robert. "The Mum Generation Was Always Talking." Rev. of *Don't Ask. Hudson Review* 38 (1985): 514.

Meinke, Peter. "Two Poets." Rev. of *1933. New Republic*, 7 Sept. 1974, 24–25.

Mills, Ralph J., Jr. " 'Back to This Life': Philip Levine's New Poems." Rev. of *Ashes* and *7 Years from Somewhere. New England Review* 2 (1979): 327–32.

———. "Critic of the Month: V." Rev. of *Not This Pig. Poetry* 113, no. 1 (Jan. 1969): 278–80.

———. "The True and Earthy Prayer: Philip Levine's Poetry." *American Poetry Review*, Mar./Apr. 1974, 44–47; also in *Cry of the Human*. Urbana: University of Illinois Press, 1975.

Mitgang, Herbert. "Flanagan and Taylor Win Book Prizes." *New York Times*, 8 Jan. 1980, late ed., C9.

Moran, Ronald. "Times of Heterogeneity: A Chronicle of Fifteen." Rev. of *On the Edge. Southern Review*, n.s. 1 (1965): 473–85.

Murray, Michelle. "Five Books Reveal the Men behind the Poems." Rev. of *They Feed They Lion*. *National Observer*, 10 June 1972, 21.

Oates, Joyce Carol. "A Cluster of Feelings: Wakoski and Levine." *American Poetry Review*, May/June 1973, 55.

———. "Books of Change: Recent Collections of Poems." Rev. of *They Feed They Lion*. *Southern Review*, n.s. 9 (1973): 1014–28.

Obery, Arthur. "Against an Iron Time." Rev. of *They Feed They Lion*. *Shenandoah* 23, no. 4 (1972): 95–103.

Olson, Ray. Rev. of *A Walk with Tom Jefferson*. *Booklist*, 1 May 1988, 1473.

Parini, Jay. "Award-Winning Poems." Rev. of *Ashes* and *7 Years from Somewhere*. *Nation*, 2 Feb. 1980, 121–22.

———. "The Roses of Detroit." Rev. of *One for the Rose*. *Times Literary Supplement*, 2 July 1982, 720.

———. "The Simple and the Finite." Rev. of *Selected Poems*. *Times Literary Supplement*, 24 Jan. 1986, 95.

———. "The Small Valleys of Our Living." Rev. of *The Names of the Lost*. *Poetry* 130, no. 5 (Aug. 1977): 198–201.

Parisi, Joseph. Rev. of *One for the Rose*. *Booklist*, 1 Jan. 1982, 582.

———. Rev. of *Selected Poems*. *Booklist*, Aug. 1984, 1592.

———. Rev. of *Sweet Will*. *Booklist*, July 1985, 1506.

Peich, Michael. "Philip Levine: The Design of Poetry." *Pacific Review*, Winter 1990.

Perloff, Marjorie. "Soft Touch." Rev. of *One for the Rose*. *Parnassus: Poetry in Review* 10, no. 1 (1982): 209–31.

Pettingell, Phoebe. "New Songs to the Lord." Rev. of *The Names of the Lost*. *New Leader*, 17 Jan. 1977, 17.

———. "The Politics of Philip Levine." Rev. of *Ashes* and *7 Years from Somewhere*. *New Leader*, 13 Aug. 1979, 16–17.

———. "Voices for the Voiceless." Rev. of *Selected Poems*. *New Leader*, 17 Sept. 1984, 16–17.

———. "Voices of Democracy." Rev. of *A Walk with Tom Jefferson*. *New Leader*, 13 June 1988, 15.

"Philip Levine Wins . . ." *New York Times*, 6 June 1987, late ed., 11.

Pinsky, Robert. "The Names of the Lost." *New York Times Book Review*, 20 Feb. 1977, 6, 14.

Plumly, Stanley. Rev. of *The Names of the Lost*. *Ohio Review* 18, no. 3 (1977): 133–36.

Poss, Stanley. Rev. of *1933*. *Northwest Review* 14, no. 2 (1974): 113–21.

Pratt, W. "Philip Levine: *Sweet Will*." *World Literature Today* 59 (1985): 601–2.

Pritchard, William H. "*They Feed They Lion*." *New York Times Book Review*, 16 July 1972, 4.

Raffel, Burton. Rev. of *Don't Ask*. *Literary Review* 28 (1984): 154–64.

Ratner, Rochelle. "The Two Faces of Philip Levine." Rev. of *Ashes* and *7 Years from Somewhere*. *Soho Weekly News*, 27 Sept. 1979.

Rev. of *A Walk with Tom Jefferson*. *Publisher's Weekly*, 22 Apr. 1988, 79.

Rev. of *A Walk with Tom Jefferson*. *Village Voice*, 19 July 1988, 54.

Rev. of *Ashes*. *Choice*, Oct. 1979, 1022.

Rev. of *The Names of the Lost*. *Kirkus Reviews*, 15 Sept. 1976, 1081.

Rev. of *The Names of the Lost*. *New Yorker*, 13 Dec. 1976, 162.

Rev. of *The Names of the Lost*. *Choice*, Apr. 1977, 201.

Rev. of *1933*. *Booklist*, 1 July 1974, 1176.

Rev. of *1933*. *Choice*, Sept. 1974, 943.

Rev. of *Not This Pig*. *Publisher's Weekly*, 11 Dec. 1967, 43–44.

Rev. of *Not This Pig*. *Kirkus Reviews*, 15 Dec. 1967, 1511.

Rev. of *One for the Rose*. *American Book Review*, Sept. 1982, 20.

Rev. of *One for the Rose*. *Kirkus Reviews*, 1 Dec. 1981, 1515.

Rev. of *One for the Rose*. *Village Voice*, May 1982, 5.

Rev. of *One for the Rose*. *Virginia Quarterly Review* 58 (1982): 92.

Rev. of *Selected Poems*. *Los Angeles Times Book Review*, 21 Oct. 1984, 2.

Rev. of *Selected Poems*. *Virginia Quarterly Review* 61 (1985): 27.

Rev. of *7 Years from Somewhere*. *Choice*, Oct. 1979, 1022.

Rev. of *Sweet Will*. *Kliatt Paperback Book Guide* 19 (1985): 30.

Rev. of *They Feed They Lion*. *Booklist*, 1 June 1972, 844.

Rev. of *They Feed They Lion*. *Virginia Quarterly Review* 48 (1972): 124.

Romer, Stephen. "Song of Myself." Rev. of *Selected Poems*. *New Statesman*, 18 Jan. 1985, 30.

Root, William Pitt. "Songs of the Working Class." Rev. of *Sweet Will*. *St. Petersburg Times*, 3 Nov. 1985.

Sadoff, Ira. "A Chronicle of Recent Poetry." Rev. of *The Names of the Lost*. *Antioch Review* 35 (1977): 241–44.

St. John, David. "Raised Voices in the Choir: A Review of 1981 Poetry Selections." Rev. of *One for the Rose*. *Antioch Review* 40 (1982): 232–33.

———. "Where the Angels Come toward Us: The Poetry of Philip Levine." Rev. of *Sweet Will* and *Selected Poems*. *Antioch Review* 44 (1986): 176–91.

Saner, Reg. "Studying Interior Architecture by Keyhole: Four Poets." *Denver Quarterly* 20, no. 1 (1985): 107–17.

Scammell, William. "Living in the World." Rev. of *Don't Ask*. *Times Literary Supplement*, 11 Sept. 1981, 1043.

Schramm, Richard. "A Gathering of Poets." Rev. of *They Feed They Lion, Pili's Wall*, and *Red Dust*. *Western Humanities Review* 26 (1972): 389–93.

Schultz, Robert. "Passionate Virtuosity." Rev. of *A Walk with Tom Jefferson*. *Hudson Review* 42, no. 1 (1989).

Simon, Greg. Rev. of *The Names of the Lost*. *Porch* 1, no. 2 (1977): 46–50.

Smith, Dave. "The Second Self." Rev. of *Ashes* and *7 Years from Somewhere*. *American Poetry Review*, Nov./Dec. 1979, 33–37.

———. "Short Reviews." Rev. of *Sweet Will* and *Selected Poems*. *Poetry* 147, no. 1 (Oct. 1985): 42–46.

Spender, Stephen. "Can Poetry Be Reviewed?" Rev. of *They Feed They Lion*. *New York Review of Books*, 20 Sept. 1973, 8–14.

Stafford, William. "A Poet with Something to Tell You." Rev. of *The Names of the Lost*. *Inquiry*, 26 June 1978, 25–26.

Stark, Lucien. "Philip Levine." In *Contemporary Poets*, 3d ed., ed. James Vinson. New York: St. Martin's, 1980.

Stauffenberg, Henry J. Rev. of *The Names of the Lost*. *Best Sellers*, Jan. 1977, 341.

Stitt, Peter. " 'My Fingers Clawing the Air': Versions of Paradise in Contemporary American Poetry." Rev. of *Selected Poems. Georgia Review* 39 (1985): 188–98.

———. "Poems in Open Forms." Rev. of *One for the Rose. Georgia Review* 36 (1982): 675–85.

———. "The Sincere, the Mythic, the Playful: Forms of Voice in Current Poetry." Rev. of *Ashes* and *7 Years from Somewhere. Georgia Review* 34 (1980): 202–12.

———. "The Typical Poem." *Kenyon Review* 8, no. 4 (1986): 131–32.

"Synecdoche: Brief Poetry Notes." *North American Review* 261, no. 3 (1976): 90–91; 262, no. 1 (1979): 74; and 264, no. 3 (1979): 62.

Tillinghast, Richard. "Working the Night Shift." Rev. of *One for the Rose. New York Times Book Review,* 12 Sept. 1982, 42.

Vendler, Helen. "All Too Real." Rev. of *One for the Rose. New York Review of Books,* 17 Dec. 1981, 32–36.

Venit, James. Rev. of *The Names of the Lost. Library Journal,* 15 Oct. 1976, 2180.

Wagner, Linda W. "The Most Contemporary of Poetics." Rev. of *The Names of the Lost. Ontario Review* 7 (1977/78): 88–95.

Walker, Cheryl. "Looking Back, Looking Forward." Rev. of *1933. Nation,* 13 Sept. 1975, 215–16.

Walker, David. Rev. of *One for the Rose. Field* 26 (1982): 87–97.

Walsh, Chad. "A Cadence for Our Time." Rev. of *On the Edge. Saturday Review of Literature,* 2 Jan. 1965, 29.

Warner, Jon M. Rev. of *They Feed They Lion. Library Journal,* 1 May 1972, 1721.

Williams, Russ. Rev. of *One for the Rose. Best Sellers,* Mar. 1982, 467–68.

Williamson, A. "Dim Human Arenas." Rev. of *Ashes* and *7 Years from Somewhere. Poetry,* Dec. 1980, 169–71.

Wilson, Robley, Jr. "Five Poets at Hand." Rev. of *Not This Pig. Carleton Miscellany* 9, no. 4 (1968): 117–20.

Yenser, Stephen. "Bringing It Home." Rev. of *The Names of the Lost. Parnassus: Poetry in Review* 6, no. 1 (1977): 101–17.

———. "Recent Poetry: Five Poets." Rev. of *7 Years from Somewhere. Yale Review* 70, no. 1 (1980): 105–28.

Young, Vernon. "No One Said It Would Be Easy." Rev. of *Ashes* and *7 Years from Somewhere. Hudson Review* 32 (1978): 632–34.

———. "Poetry Chronicle: Sappho to Smith." Rev. of *1933. Hudson Review* 27 (1974–75): 597–614.

Zweig, Paul. "1 + 1 + 1 + 1." Rev. of *They Feed They Lion. Parnassus: Poetry in Review* 1, no. 1 (1972): 171–74.

POETS ON POETRY   Donald Hall, General Editor

Poets on Poetry collects critical books by contemporary poets, gathering together the articles, interviews, and book reviews by which they have articulated the poetics of a new generation.